Global Europe

The External Relations of the European Union

Otto Holman

Amsterdam University Press

Also published in Dutch as: *Europa als wereldspeler.* Otto Holman. Amsterdam University Press, 2019

Translation: Gioia Marini, with the cooperation of Jane Pocock

Cover illustration: Boats with refugees arriving to Skala Sykamias Lesvos Greece. Photo: Georgios Giannopoulos.

Cover design: Coördesign, Leiden
Lay-out: Crius Group, Hulshout

ISBN   978 94 6298 537 7
e-ISBN   978 90 4853 646 7
DOI   10.5117/9789462985377
NUR   754

© O. Holman / Amsterdam University Press B.V., Amsterdam 2019

Contents

List of Abbreviations

ACP	Africa, Caribbean, Pacific
BPM	Bureaucratic Politics Model
BRICs	Brazil, Russia, India, China, South Africa
CAG	Competitiveness Advisory Group
CAP	Common Agricultural Policy
CEE	Central and Eastern Europe
CEO	Chief Executive Officer
CFSP	Common Foreign and Security Policy
CI	Commercial Internationalism
COREPER	Comité des Représentants Permanents
CPE	Critical Political Economy
CSDP	Common Security and Defence Policy
DAC	Development Assistance Committee
DCI	Development Cooperation Instrument
DDR	Deutsche Demokratische Republik
EBA	Everything But Arms
ECB	European Central Bank
EDA	European Defence Agency
EDC	European Defence Community
EDF	European Development Fund
EEAS	European External Action Service
EEC	European Economic Community
EMU	Economic and Monetary Union
ENI	European Neighbourhood Instrument
ENP	European Neighbourhood Policy
EP	European Parliament
EPC	European Political Cooperation
ERT	European Round Table of Industrialists
ESDP	European Security and Defence Policy
ESS	European Security Strategy
EU	European Union
EUGS	European Union Global Strategy
EUISS	European Union Institute for Security Studies
EUMC	European Union Military Committee
FAO	Food and Agricultural Organization
FDI	Foreign Direct Investment
FPA	Foreign Policy Analysis
GATT	General Agreement on Tariffs and Trade

GDP	Gross Domestic Product
GNI	Gross National Income
GSP	Generalised System of Preferences
HST	Hegemonic Stability Theory
IA	Impact Assessment
ILO	International Labour Organisation
IMF	International Monetary Fund
IPE	International Political Economy
IR	(The discipline of) International Relations
ISS	International Security Studies
LDCs	Least Developed Countries
LI	Liberal Intergovernmentalism
MFF	Multiannual Financial Framework
MLG	Multilevel Governance
MRA	Mutual Recognition Agreement
NAVO	North Atlantic Treaty Organisation
NF	Neofunctionalism
NGO	Non-Governmental Organisation
NICs	Newly Industrialising Countries
NIEO	New International Economic Order
NPE	Normative Power Europe
ODA	Official Development Assistance
OECD	Organisation for Economic Co-operation and Development
OPEC	Organisation of the Petroleum Exporting Countries
PESCO	Permanent Structured Cooperation
PHARE	Pologne, Hongrie: Assistance à la Restructuration Économique
PSC	Political and Security Committee
RI	Rational-choice Institutionalism
RTD	Research and Technological Development
SAPs	Structural Adjustment Programmes
SI	Sociological Institutionalism
SIPRI	Stockholm International Peace Research Institute
SPG	Spain, Portugal, Greece
TABD	Trans-Atlantic Business Dialogue
TIMBI	Turkey, India, Mexico, Brazil, Indonesia
TPP	Trans-Pacific Partnership
TTIP	Transatlantic Trade and Investment Partnership
UNCTAD	United Nations Conference on Trade and Development
UNHCR	United Nations High Commissioner for Refugees
US	United States
WTO	World Trade Organisation

Preface

I wrote a major part of this book during my stay at the University of Granada in the late summer and autumn of 2017. It was a good place to reflect on Europe as a global player. More than 500 years ago, in 1492 to be precise, this southern Spanish city—the last stronghold of Arab rulers on the Iberian peninsula—was recaptured. With this, the 'Moors' not only lost their 'European capital of Islam', but also ended eight centuries of more or less peaceful co-existence between Muslims, Jews, and Christians. The Catholic King Ferdinand of Aragon and Queen Isabella of Castile celebrated their *reconquista* by rather fanatically giving shape to the restored unity of Spain. Jews and Muslims were presented with a simple choice: they could leave the country or convert to Christianity. Religious intolerance was a fact, and dissenters came into direct contact with the Inquisition instituted by the same *Reyes Católicos*.

1492 was also the year that the Catholic Kings had a historic conversation with Christopher Columbus, in the hamlet of Santa Fe, a few miles from Granada. He was commissioned to discover a faster westward route to Asia, as recorded in the *Capitulaciones* of 17 April. Unhindered by a thorough knowledge of actual distances and packed with an insufficient supply of food, Columbus had fortune on his side and found an unknown continent in the middle. Europe's overseas expansion towards America had begun, as well as the Eurocentric view of world affairs that was to last for centuries. Global Europe was born.

In the course of the 19th century, this situation gradually came to an end and a process was started that was once summarised by the British historian Geoffrey Barraclough as 'the dwarfing of Europe' (Barraclough 1967). World politics was lifted out of its Eurocentric phase by the rise of two superpowers on the flanks of (Western) Europe—the United States and Russia—together with the emancipation and ultimate liberation of non-European peoples from the colonial embrace of modern imperialism. In the 20th century, the 'European world' was replace by a contemporary version of the Treaty of Tordesillas—the 1494 agreement between Spain and Portugal that divided the non-European world between the two kingdoms. No country or people could escape the all-dominating conflict between two systems, capitalism and communism, and the bipolar balance of power between the new superpowers. They were responsible for the division of the world into two almost mutually exclusive spheres of influence.

This short 20th century of bipolarity and Cold War—which began with the Russian revolution of 1917 and abruptly ended with the fall of the Berlin Wall in 1989, the subsequent velvet revolutions in Central and Eastern Europe, and the collapse of the Soviet Union—is now history and has sunk deep into our collective memory. As a young man I experienced the final phase of the Cold War, including the threat of a nuclear confrontation, but as an international relations professor at the University of Amsterdam I have to do my best to convince today's students of the importance of this theme. After all, communism has disappeared as a factor of political power, and new conflicts are emerging, often with a religious element. Mutual deterrence with nuclear arms has given way to a joint effort to prevent the proliferation of nuclear weaponry to so-called rogue states.

The world has indeed changed dramatically in the last three decades. In the following, I will distinguish three major changes. The purpose of this is to outline the context within which recent discussions about the EU's external relations—and more specifically about whether Europe can regain its role as a global player—take place.

The world has become smaller. Even though, according to some, this process began in the early 19th century, there is no doubt that it has been accelerating since the 1980s. It is, after all, only in recent years that everyone seems to be talking about 'globalisation'. Time and space have shrunk due to technological innovations, including in the areas of communication and financial economic services, and due to the removal of barriers to the cross-border flow of goods and capital.

The world has become multipolar. The role of Russia in its former sphere of influence has largely been played out, and that of the US is now subject to serious erosion. At the same time, new powers are emerging. The rise of China appeals most to the imagination, but countries such as India, Brazil, Indonesia, South Africa, and Turkey are also increasingly refusing to be subservient to the former superpowers. For the first time in human history, the decentralisation of power in the international system is coinciding with an unprecedented level of interdependence (mainly economic). Multipolarity and globalisation together make a unique combination.

The world has become more liberal but also more unequal and less democratic. This is the most complicated and perhaps most disputed change, especially regarding the correlations between these trends. The end of the Cold War resulted in all kinds of prophecies about new world orders: the end of history, and the renaissance of liberal, political, and economic values and norms—all well and good, but reality turned out to be considerably more unmanageable. The loss of the discipline that had been maintained within the spheres of influence went hand in hand with an increase in the number of civil wars and subsequent refugee flows. The emergence of new economies, while reducing the gap between these countries and the developed world, increased the differences in prosperity within these economies. This explains in part the political-authoritarian tendencies in these countries. In the US and Europe too, socio-economic differences have widened, and dissatisfaction is on the rise. It would therefore be erroneous to speak of an irresistible (and irreversible) triumph of liberalism after 1989. Resistance is increasing and taking on various shapes, including violent forms of expression.

Where do the member states of the European Union stand in these three processes? To what extent are they instigators, targets, or even victims of these processes? And what effects do the three processes have on the process of European unification? Will they help or hinder Europe to become a global player?

Regarding the first change, the EU member states have made an important contribution, separately and in unison, to what we call economic globalisation. Margaret Thatcher was wrong when she stated in the 1980s that global capitalism left her no choice but to pursue a policy of liberalisation, deregulation, and privatisation ('There is no alternative', was her famous one-liner). In reality, it was Thatcher herself—and later other European governments—who set the invisible hand of free-market capitalism in motion. It was a deliberate strategy to break through so-called rigid patterns and to protect capitalism against the capitalists (and in the case of Thatcher to protect it against the labour movement too). From the moment the crisis of European integration of the 1970s and early 1980s came to a remarkable and sudden end with the relaunch of the integration process—through the completion of the internal market and the establishment of the Economic and Monetary Union— the EU played a pro-active role in globalisation. Instead of being a victim, the EU member states were one of the main drivers behind this process.

With regard to the second change, the role of the EU is different. In the burgeoning multipolar world of state-centric thinking and power politics, 'Europe as a global player' still has little meaning (or so it is generally assumed, not least by the emerging powers). This can be attributed to the nature of the EU itself. The European Union is not a union in a literal sense, and it is certainly not a state. At best, we can speak of a European society, inspired by the famous distinction made by the German sociologist Ferdinand Tönnies (and later further developed by Max Weber) between *Gemeinschaft* and *Gesellschaft*. A *Gesellschaft* (society) is a social organisation based on indirect transactions and impersonal, contractual, and regulated relationships; affection and solidarity between individual members play no role in it. The choice to cooperate is based on rational grounds and on mutual interest. Viewed in this way, the member states of the EU form, at best, a cross-border society. The EU largely lacks a political superstructure and most definitely lacks a common social basis. In its current form, this stunted union is not an actor (or factor, for that matter) in power politics, and it is not a full-fledged player in the multipolar world. And the EU member states on their own are too small to secure a seat at the table themselves.

The third change is the direct consequence of what academics call the neoliberal turn of the 1980s and 1990s. During this period, a shift took place from Keynesian demand steering—which was characteristic of the decades of economic growth following the Second World War—towards a supply-side oriented optimisation of the conditions for profitable and risk-averse business. Governments gradually withdrew from the economy and embraced the neoliberal mantra of liberalisation, deregulation, and privatisation with varying degrees of success and diverse social consequences. There were and still are clear differences between 'old' Europe and the new member states from Central and Eastern Europe. The same applies to the northern member states of the eurozone compared to the southern member states, with Greece as the clearest example of the latter group. If we look at individual citizens within the member states, we see similar differences between groups of people. Neoliberalism has its winners but also its losers. People get a well-paid job or lose a poorly paid job, take advantage of speculation-driven real estate prices or are driven out to the peripheries of big cities by these same speculators, and subsequently come into contact with people from other areas with different cultures... and so on.

The time has come to make the connection between the three major changes in the world and the actual subject of this book: the external relations of the EU. We start with the third change.

The world has become more liberal but also more unequal and less democratic. The overarching theme of 'Global Europe' problematises the role of the EU in a changing world. A central concept we will use here is actorness. We will look for the factors and actors that contribute to strengthening the EU's capacity to act in the global system. At present, the power the EU projects to the outside world is largely determined by the degree of cohesion within the EU. We are not only talking about cohesion and cooperation between the 28 member states but also about social cohesion within member states. We will see later in this book that the precise form and content of the relaunch of European integration in the 1980s and 1990s had an important leverage role in the neoliberal turn. As a result, European citizens who suffered the most from these policy changes—or at least believed that they were among the losers, that they were no longer being heard by the traditional political elites, and therefore that they had been demoted to second-class citizens—began to turn against 'Europe'. However, it was not necessarily Europe and the EU that were selling the myths of free market and positive-sum, but rather the representatives and propagators of neoliberal ideology. Nonetheless, Europe was (and is) the perfect scapegoat. An important component of the populist revolt of recent decades is Euroscepticism, or dissatisfaction with the process of European integration. This has irrevocable consequences for the external actorness of the EU, on the one hand because opposition within member states to the union in general and deeper integration in particular is increasing, and on the other hand because the internal problems of the EU are influencing perceptions and expectations *outside* the EU with regard to Europe as a global player—or 'Global Europe', for short.

called European integration theories, which are partly indebted to the IR theories discussed earlier in the chapter but which sometimes also emphasise the unique nature of the European integration process. An important difference of opinion centres on whether EU countries are willing and/or able to transfer their powers in various policy areas to a higher supranational authority. It goes without saying that we are dealing here with the possibility (or impossibility) of EU actorness in relation to the outside world. To what extent can unity in diversity continue to tip towards national interest-based diversity before we cease referring to Europe as a global player? This question is dealt with in chapter 2, which focuses on the most important insights from the literature on the factors and actors behind the shaping and development of foreign policy. We see that the usual one-liners such as 'the foreign policy of the US' conceal the reality of a constant power struggle between many domestic actors. The outcome in the form of actual foreign policy actions is a reflection of that power struggle. The 'general interest' (as a motto of foreign policy) does not exist if we dissect how that policy came to be. Clearly, this applies to the EU to a much greater extent. Caution is thus required when we speak of 'the EU as a global player'.

The three main policy areas of the EU's external action are dealt with in chapters 3 to 5. Chapter 3 examines the EU's trade policy. The deepening of economic integration in Europe goes hand in hand with an increasingly clear separation between internal and external (or international) markets. This requires that the EU member states have a common trade policy and a supranational negotiator who can interact with third countries on behalf of the member states. But here, too, this negotiator—in the EU's case, the European Commission—is part of a complex power configuration. We will see that the development of the EU's trade policy since the mid-1980s reflects the aforementioned neoliberal turn and the power relations underlying it.

In Chapter 4 we switch the focus onto European development policy. From the very beginning, the EU has played a dominant role in global development cooperation. Here too, it is more accurate to speak of 'the EU and its member states' because a large part of the financial efforts are still generated at the national level. Special attention is given to the relationship between trade and development and the gradual subordination of the latter objective to the enlightened self-interest of the EU in further global trade liberalisation.

The EU's enlargement strategy, which is the third policy area that falls under external action, is examined in Chapter 5. The EU has always been attractive to neighbouring European countries, and every so often some of these countries have applied for membership. But it was only after the end of the Cold War—and in response to the massive interest from Central and Eastern Europe—that the EU formulated a more or less coherent strategy to guide the accession of these new democracies. This strategy is based on transformative power, a reference to the role the EU has played in the double transformation process in Central and Eastern Europe from authoritarian rule to democracy and from state-led to free-market economies.

Chapter 6 brings a number of lines together: economic and monetary policy (internal action and its international dimension) is linked to security policy (internal and external action plus CFSP). The architects of the new Europe failed to complete the constructs of single market and single currency with social and political union. The one-sided emphasis on market integration, austerity measures, and structural reforms had—and still has—implications for the EU's external actorness, as is argued in this chapter, partly because this has increased the socio-economic differences between and within member states and fueled opposition to the EU. Anyone who is against Europe is certainly not concerned with 'Europe as global player'. This existential internal crisis has taken on a multiple international security dimension in the 2010s. Persistent conflicts and civil wars in the Middle East and Sub-Saharan Africa, the explosive combination of population growth and underdevelopment, a sharp increase in migration flows, and the revival of Cold War rhetoric are only the most visible and pressing dilemmas that an unstable EU faces. In the second part of chapter 6, we analyse how the EU has so far dealt with these 'challenges' within the framework of the Common Security and Defence Policy.

In the epilogue we will return to the changes in the international system—and the dilemmas they pose—mentioned at the beginning of this foreword. Here, we will also speculate about the likelihood that Europe will become a global player that not only addresses its own security but also makes an effective contribution to the many global problems facing humanity in the 21st century.

A word of thanks

This book is indebted to many people. They include generations of students whose curiosity and critical academic attitude have forced me to constantly renew and hone my lectures in the discipline of international relations; colleagues who, forced by time constraints, usually did not go beyond the cursory reading of my introductions and conclusions but who always provided meaningful feedback; editors of scholarly journals and anonymous reviewers who taught me that critical commentary, although irksome, is also an essential component of the academic profession; and the support staff, not least the staff at the secretariat of my political science department, whose interest in my work was partly related to the city where the conception and writing of this book all started. I would like to make a few exceptions to this anonymous and collective acknowledgement. First of all, my thanks go to my editors at Amsterdam University Press, Inge van der Bijl and Rixt Runia. Second, I am grateful to Diego Javier Liñán Nogueras and Luis M. Hinojosa

Martínez—both at the *Derecho Internacional Público y Relaciones Internacionales* department—for facilitating my stay at the University of Granada. Third, I would like to thank José Luis Medina and Nuria Oria, friends for life, because they made my time in southern Spain an extremely pleasant one. Finally, my thanks go to my beloved Johanna, whose critical but selfless support has been decisive, and whose writing talent has stopped me from using even more lavish and woolly language.

1. Introduction

Theory formation at the intersection of international relations and European integration studies

It starts on 20 May 2017 in Riyadh, the capital of Saudi Arabia, and not—as is traditionally the case—in Canada or Mexico. The 45th president of the United States, Donald John Trump, is on his first trip abroad since his inauguration on 20 January. He is visiting the rulers of a country with which, in his own words, the US has a partnership based on 'shared interests and values'. When Trump gives a speech on 21 May to Arabian political leaders, the king of Saudi Arabia—a country where religious intolerance, barbaric punishments, and suppression of women and foreign workers are the norm—is listening attentively in the front row. He notes with satisfaction that Trump is targeting one of Saudi Arabia's archenemies, Iran, by accusing it of 'fuelling the fires of sectarian conflict and terror'. The king is also pleased with the 'historic' arms deal worth 110 billion dollars announced at the conclusion of the state visit. Trump is in turn very satisfied with the 'tremendous deals' and 'homerun successes' for companies such as the private equity giant Blackstone and oil company ExxonMobil.[1]

Trump continues his first presidential trip abroad with a visit to Israel, has a conversation with the Palestinian President Mahmoud Abbas, and flies on to Rome on 23 May where he has an audience with the Pope. He then travels on to Brussels where, after ceremonial gatherings with the king and queen and the prime minister of Belgium, he causes irritation at the NATO summit. Trump calls his allies to account for their insufficient financial defence efforts and moreover refuses to voice his support for the obligation to come to each other's assistance embedded in Article 5 of the NATO Treaty. Leaving some NATO leaders in bewilderment, he returns to Italy where he meets some of the same faces again during the 43rd G7 summit in Sicily from 25 to 27 May. At this summit Trump refuses to embrace the climate agreement reached in Paris in 2015. All this leads Chancellor Angela Merkel to conclude that Europe must take its fate into its own hands. Trump is by that time already back in the US.

This trip of just over a week fits into a pattern: Trump seems to want to put an end, as quickly as possible, to the legacy of his predecessor in terms of both foreign and domestic policies. In terms of foreign relations, we highlight the following: the repeated snubbing of neighbouring country Mexico is only the most visible component of a highly restrictive migration policy; in the area of international trade, the US withdraws from the Trans-Pacific Partnership (TPP) free trade agreement, suspends negotiations over a Transatlantic Trade and Investment Partnership with the EU, and takes the first steps towards a global trade war; Trump threatens to withdraw from the Paris climate agreement; the same fate befalls the so-called Iran deal regarding that country's nuclear programme; Trump decides to recognise Jerusalem as the capital of Israel without any consultation with allies in Europe or the Middle East; the confrontation with 'rogue state' North Korea escalates; tensions mount in US relations with China and Russia; and African countries are dismissed as 'shithole countries'.

The reason for beginning this introductory chapter on a book about the EU's external relations with an account of the Trump administration's foreign outbursts has little to do with Trump himself. By the time this book is published, his deeds will have been consigned to oblivion, rendered obsolete, or have turned out to be unrealisable—or perhaps not, but that is not the point here. Trump's comings and goings illustrate the reach and influence of a global player such as the US, the kind of impact that a change of course in a global player's external relations has, and the extent to which a global player's foreign economic and political-military interests are inextricably intertwined. It also shows how a superpower copes with the reality of the rise of competing superpowers.

It is clear that the days when a European country the size of Great Britain could claim global leadership are over. The member states of the EU—the only European countries that alongside Russia and Turkey can lay any claim to a (albeit supporting) role on the world stage—are individually too insignificant to be able to be players on all the international geopolitical and geo-economic chessboards. This raises the question whether, together, the current 28 member states of the EU are capable of developing such a capacity for multitasking—with or without Brexit—and if so, how this 'would-be' role as a global player should be given concrete form. This concerns not only the actorness of the EU—that is, the capacity to act forcefully and effectively in global affairs—but also what aims should be served by such action. This is in essence what this book is about. In this chapter, and the next one, I will give a theoretical answer to these pressing questions. To that end, I first discuss two broad theoretical perspectives on international relations and the role of states: neorealism and neoliberalism. We shall see that the debate between these two isms centres around concepts such as effective state power and economic interdependency. I then analyse the most important theories of European integration. In the last two to three decades, a new debate has emerged between rational choice institutionalism and more reflexive theoretical approaches, which has raised the classical debate within the field of international relations to a higher level. At the end of this chapter I will conclude that while such theoretical contrasts may be useful in assessing the relative importance of various actors and factors, the complicated reality of our world sometimes requires a more eclectic—or, better yet, synthesising—approach.

But I start with a brief history of the EU's external relations. This intends not only to depict the current state of affairs since the Treaty of Lisbon, but also to make clear that, from a historical point of view, it really makes sense to focus on the EU's external relations.

1.1. A brief history of the EU's external relations

It is tempting to insert a caesura in the history of the EU's external relations—as many authors are prone to do—that allows one to compare the periods before and after a decisive treaty amendment or an important event. One popular candidate for just such a point in time is the Treaty of Lisbon, which officially entered into force in 2009. Others emphasise the importance of the 1993 Maastricht Treaty, which announced the beginning of a Common Foreign and Security Policy (CFSP). If we go further back in time, a possible caesura could be the institutional reaction to West Germany's 'Ostpolitik' towards the end of the 1960s when foreign minister Willy Brandt, who was later to become chancellor of West Germany, tried to find a diplomatic opening with the *Deutsche Demokratische Republik* (DDR). Such tentative first steps were enough for France to fear a German *Alleingang*. Unlike in the past, this French Pavlovian reaction was successfully managed through the integration process. Germany's ambitions with respect to Eastern Europe were embedded within a new mechanism called European Political Coopera-tion (EPC)—according to some, the rudimentary beginning of the EU's foreign policy—the first step of which was taken during the European summit in The Hague in 1969. Others go back even further to mark the beginning of external relations in the 1950s with the Treaty of Rome, or the earlier treaty that established the European Defence Community (EDC), even though this treaty was never ratified.

All of these possible turning points depend heavily on one's definition of external relations. If we favour a broad definition, as I do in this book—that is, if we include in our analysis what is officially called external action, the external dimensions of internal policy, the CFSP, the Common Security and Defence Policy (CSDP), and, although not prominently, the external relations of individual EU member states—then we would have to conclude that instead of sudden changes brought on by specific events or treaties, what we really have is continuous movement. The EU's external relations change continuously in reaction to internal and external developments and almost always in the direction of deeper integration. If we briefly consider the period from the 1950s until now, we can conclude that there has been a shift in emphasis in almost all areas, away from national sovereignty and intergovernmental cooperation and towards supranationality. Thus, even in its external relations, the EU has become a hybrid, polycentric entity.

Nonetheless, this book does make use of a caesura: the period from the mid-1980s to the beginning of the 1990s. In 1985, after a long period of Eurosclerosis (from the early 1970s to the beginning of the 1980s, which is often designated as the first phase of crisis and disintegration), it was decided that the EU needed to be given new impetus. The newly established European Commission, under the presidency of the Frenchman Jacques Delors, presented a plan to complete the single market. In general terms, this meant that economic integration would be facilitated at a significantly higher level, namely towards a market in which not only the free movement of goods but also the free movement of people, services, and capital would be guaranteed. This big step forwards was made legally, institutionally, and politically feasible by the jurisprudence of the European Court of Justice, by more supranational decision-making, and by the development of adjoining policy areas.

The decision to complete the single market enjoyed broad support from both the political left and right—admittedly for different reasons—and heralded a period I have described elsewhere as one of *extended relaunch*, since the relaunch of European integration (following the phase of Eurosclerosis) lasted all the way up to the historic summit bringing the European government leaders and the French head of state together in Maastricht in December 1991. It was there that the process of *economic* integration reached a provisional culmination through the plan to set up the Economic and Monetary Union (EMU) and to introduce a single currency. The EU would henceforth not only be distinguished by one market but also by a single currency, at least for those countries that fulfilled the conditions for accession to the EMU. The result of this summit, which become known as the Maastricht Treaty, encountered some hitches in the ratification process, notably in Denmark but also in Great Britain; it eventually came into force on 1 November 1993. It was from that moment that the European Union came to be referred to as such.

The period between 1985 and 1993—the period of extended relaunch—created a situation that can justifiably be considered a break with the past, also in the light of the EU's external relations. Firstly, the decision to complete the internal market had repercussions for relations between the EU (and EU member states) and third countries, if only because these third countries feared that it would all lead to what was referred to as Fortress Europe. Secondly, the EU decided in Maastricht that it was time to really work on making something of the Common Foreign and Security Policy. This step cannot be seen in isolation from the political revolutions taking place in Central and Eastern Europe and the subsequent collapse of the Soviet Union and the reunification of the two

Germanies. In this sense, the Treaty of Maastricht can be considered the first European treaty after the fall of the Berlin Wall and consequently as the first post-Cold War EU treaty.

After Maastricht, there were several treaty amendments of varying importance, but the next drastic change in the area of external relations came about by means of the European Constitution, which ultimately took effect in 2009 as the Treaty of Lisbon. This created the new permanent post of president of the European Council, which brought an end to the practice of a rotating presidency. On the one hand, this was meant to bring more continuity to the operations of the European Council. On the other hand, it resulted in the addition of a new person (with corresponding ego) to the EU's executive structure, alongside the president of the European Commission and the High Representative of the Union for Foreign Affairs and Security Policy, whose position had been strengthened by the Treaty of Lisbon. The latter is not only responsible for the secretariat of the Council of Ministers (hereinafter referred to as the Council) but is also vice president of the European Commission and head of the newly established European External Action Service (EEAS), the diplomatic service of the EU. The EEAS is made up of civil servants of the secretariat and the Commission as well as civil servants on a secondment basis from the member states. This makeup was meant to optimise the coordination between member states' external policy and that of European institutions. Finally, the need for an integrated and more consistent approach to external relations was recognised. This meant that the EU had to cooperate across horizontal and vertical domains: horizontal meaning the various internal and external policy areas of the EU, and vertical referring to the EU's external relations and those of the member states. And at the institutional level as well, there needed to be horizontal and vertical cooperation—between the European Commission's directorates-general, and between European institutions, national ministries and the diplomatic services respectively.

Despite these meaningful changes institutionalised in the Treaty of Lisbon, we must conclude that in quantitative terms—that is, as a share of the EU's total budget—the EU's role in the world is disproportionate in comparison with expenditures that fall under internal policy areas such as structural policy and agricultural policy. Table 1.1 shows what are known as commitment appropriations from the multiannual financial framework for the period 2014-2020. The amount reserved for 'Global Europe' represents only 6.1% of the EU's total expenditure. By comparison, the percentage of the 2018 US federal budget reserved for defence, diplomacy, and foreign aid is three times as large, and we must also bear in mind that the US federal budget as a percentage of its Gross Domestic Product (GDP) is far larger than the EU budget, with the latter representing only 1% of the EU's total GDP.

Table 1.1. Multiannual Financial Framework EU, 2014-2020 (EUR million – current prices)

Commitment appropriations	Total 2014-2020	Percentage of total
1. Smart and inclusive growth	513,563	47.2%
1a. Competitiveness for growth and jobs	142,130	
1b. Economic, social, and territorial cohesion	371,433	
2. Sustainable growth: Natural resources	420,034	38.6%
3. Security and citizenship	17,725	1.6%
4. Global Europe	66,262	6.1%
5. Administration	69,584	6.4%
6. Compensations	29	–
Total commitment appropriations	1,087,197	100%
(as % of total GNI of the EU)	(1.03%)	–

Source: http://ec.europa.eu/budget/mff/index_en.cfm and author's own calculations.

Although the EU's budget for external relations is comparatively small, we can conclude (and substantiate in the coming chapters) that some 60 years of European integration has led to a substantial deepening in the area of 'Global Europe'. There has clearly been a dynamic process at work here, and this calls for an explanation. In the remainder of this chapter I will try to comprehend this dynamic in an abstract way using a selection of the most relevant theoretical approaches. I start with the classical theories in international relations as an academic subject.

1.2. Approaches within the field of international relations

In an article from the beginning of this century, Mark Pollack contends that theorisation within the fields of international relations (IR) and European integration studies have moved towards each other, and he identifies the above-mentioned *extended relaunch* as the tipping point. Previously, practitioners of IR—most of them American—did focus on integration in Europe, Pollack argues, but they remained imprisoned within that European reality without trying to make more generally applicable and theoretically informed statements that could be of use to the broader field of IR. It was only with the relaunch of European integration in the 1980s and 1990s that this situation changed. The EU was no longer primarily studied as a sui generis phenomenon, that is, as a more or less unique process with specific regional causes and characteristics. Generally applicable IR theories were brought to bear on the EU with the intention of contributing to the broader discipline of IR through deduction and induction (Pollack 2001). Although Pollack's interpretation is not one hundred per cent conclusive, as we shall see further on, his thesis of the fusing of IR and European integration theories is useful for the argument I will make in this book. Let us first examine how traditional IR theories view the opportunities for integration and the risks of fragmentation in the international system and—by implication, at least for the time being—what conclusion we can draw from this regarding the prospects for deeper European integration.

I begin this section with the standard textbook classification of traditional IR approaches: neorealism, neoliberalism, and social constructivism. In section 1.3 I will move on to look more specifically at integration theories focused on Europe and point out how these are derived from or are indebted to theorisation within IR but partly deviate from it in the way they are applied to the EU. The leading principle in this theoretical discussion is the following overarching question: how can we interpret and better understand the creation, the current state of affairs, and the future development of the EU's external relations from more abstract, theoretical reflections? Subsequently, in the following chapter I will consult a traditional IR domain: the study of the foreign policies of more or less sovereign states. Although the EU does not qualify as a sovereign state, these insights will give us a better understanding of the possibilities and limits of the EU as an effective global player.

Neorealism
Realism and neorealism emerged as IR theories in the course of the 20th century and have since been further developed. Realism originated as a reaction to the idealistic belief in sustainable peace that enjoyed a runaway period of success in the 1920s and 1930s. Realism is part of a long tradition that includes thinkers such as Thucydides, Machiavelli, and Hobbes. The 'neo' in neorealism refers primarily to the scientification of what was originally a political-philosophical current under the influence of behaviourism in political science. Here I use the terms realism/ neorealism as constituent parts of *modern* IR as defined by Buzan and Lawson, i.e. a field of study that emerged as part of the so-called *global transformation* at the beginning of the 19th century (Buzan and Lawson 2015).

Realism and neorealism are inextricably tied to the state-centric thinking within IR. Advocates of this current within IR regard the state as a transhistorical reality in the international system, certainly since the Peace of Westphalia (1648), which they see as coinciding with the emergence of the modern state system. From that moment onwards, states have been the only relevant actors in the international system, a conclusion that is also fostered by the assumption that states exercise monopoly over formal violence and thus have the exclusive right to wage war. States operate in an international system that is characterised by anarchy, which means that there is no overarching authority (or, put more simply, no world government). States are the ultimate bearers of sovereignty; within democratically organised states, national parliaments represent this sovereignty on behalf of the population. Some of the most important tasks of a state—if not the most important—are to guarantee national security, to protect its citizens, and to defend its territorial integrity.

In performing these tasks, a problem arises that is known in the literature as the security dilemma. To protect its citizens and its own territory, a state must develop capabilities that deter other states to a sufficient degree. An example is military means built up purely for purposes of self-defence. These could and most likely would be seen as a threat by other countries (especially neighbouring countries). These other countries would then increase their own capabilities purely out of self-defence, which in turn would provoke new reactions elsewhere, and so on. Without a supranational authority, this pattern of action and reaction can spiral out of control. The realists came up with a mechanism to ensure that this dilemma—which can occur with multiple configurations of states—does not lead to a permanent state of conflict or warfare: balance of power. This means that states in an international state system will forge coalitions to prevent a third state (or states) from believing it can act as *primus inter pares*—first among equals—and from operating as if it stands out from other states, with all the attendant consequences.

In political terms, therefore, there is a permanent competition between states, which is ultimately a struggle for power and for the distribution of that power. What we are talking about here is political-military power; that is, the capacity to prevent —with military means if necessary—other states from attacking your territory and population. In accordance with the practice within economic systems, this competition gives rise to copycat behaviour. States that are successful in maximising their power are likely to be followed by other states. A good illustration of this is the level and strength of military technology. States not only react in quantitative terms to other states' armaments programmes but also view with suspicion the technological development of their rivals' weaponry and if necessary attempt to copy or improve upon it. This is in fact a strategy of best practices, where if a state neglects the successful paths to power, it will irrevocably be set back and be in a losing position. As a result, any surplus of power is only temporary in nature. This kind of reasoning assumes a zero-sum game where the gain of some states in the international system implies the loss of others.

A central concept within the neorealist view of foreign policy is the concept of *national* interest. States are unitary actors that operate rationally. In their behaviour abroad they will act in the general interest, either offensively by pursuing this interest in an aggressive manner, or defensively as protection against or prevention of an attack from the outside. Offensive and defensive behaviour are difficult to distinguish here. Was the military pre-emptive intervention by the US in Saddam Hussein's Iraq purely offensive? And is there an exclusively defensive purpose behind North Korea's nuclear tests and rocket launches, announced as a rational security strategy to deter other countries?

In this view of power politics and realism, cooperation between states is only an option when states experience a common external threat, such as during the Cold War, or when states can be kept in line by a hegemon, as the cooperation within the Bretton Woods system led by the US demonstrated (see chapter 6).[2] A type of cooperation that neorealists do not consider to be possible is sustainable and stable integration between states based on consensus, where the participants are willing to hand over their sovereignty (or at least a part of it) to supranational organisations or institutions. Mutual mistrust and diverging interests will surface time and again, and fragmentation and conflict constitute a permanent danger.

Neoliberalism
Realists are, of course, not blind to the ever-growing degree of economic interdependence between countries. They nonetheless assume that this increasing interdependence—nowadays referred to as globalisation—is subordinate to the overriding power politics of states. Even when countries are heavily oriented towards each other, if national interests are at stake—for example in times of economic crisis—these same countries will not hesitate to fall back on protectionism and economic nationalism.

Neoliberal scholars view things quite differently—and, one could add, more optimistically. Without denying the existence of different approaches and nuances within neoliberalism (and the same holds for neorealism), we can postulate that adherents of this IR theory stress cooperation rather than conflict. We live in a world of complex interdependence: states as well as actors within states are increasingly dependent on each other as a result of transnational trade and investment flows. This economic interdependence implies that business transactions between states should be deregulated, which almost by definition means that supranational re-regulation must take place. And this is where international organisations such as the International Monetary Fund (IMF) and the World Trade Organization (WTO) come into play. In the absence of a global authority, international organisations take the form of quasi-state structures. It is in states' mutual interest to cooperate; there is, in short, a loftier general interest conceivable than that of national states. And that loftier interest can be understood as a positive sum: by working together, the participating states all benefit in absolute terms, and a zero-sum effect can be avoided. Economic integration, for example via trade liberalisation, results in growth for all participating states.

A variation on this neoliberal theme is the assumption that a correlation exists between democratisation and economic development and modernisation (read: Westernisation). Economic development makes democratisation possible and democratisation facilitates international cooperation. Without going into the plausibility of this correlation (let alone the causality), we can say that in postwar Western Europe, economic development, democratic consolidation, and international integration coincided in time. (Sceptics, including neorealists, would emphasise that this was until recently indeed the case but that the current era shows that also the opposite may be true.) Another point that neoliberals would make about Western Europe is that the security-threatening component of the relationship between two traditional archenemies—France and Germany—was effectively neutralised.

This points to another difference between neoliberalism and neorealism: whereas the more hard-core realists and neorealists have a view of history that rests on repetition, on recurrent conflicts, and on patterns of action and reaction that belong to the very essence of the international system, adherents of neoliberalism put much more faith in processes of progress, in cooperation between states, in transnational contacts between non-state actors, and in integration. Individuals and collectivities can learn from history and rectify their mistakes. The postwar integration process in Europe is a good example of this. The current EU looks very different compared with the European Economic Community (EEC) created sixty years ago. Movement led to change and often to a deepening of integration, as a result of which European institutions not only evolved but gradually began to have a greater influence on the process of change itself. The result is not an EU characterised by balance of power at best and state anarchy at worst but rather a hybrid, polycentric entity that has both supranational and intergovernmental traits, one where multiple decision-making centres function alongside and with each other. The EU's external relations are a good example of this. Over the decades, the EU's relations with the rest of the world have not only expanded into new areas of interest and policy domains, but these policy domains have also gone through a drastic process of deepening.

Despite the significant differences between neorealism and neoliberalism, both approaches have one important aspect in common: they both assume that states act rationally and make rational decisions. Both theories presuppose the existence of selfish motives based on self-interest. Schematically, neorealists are focused on political-military security and territorial integrity (i.e. power), and neoliberals more on economic gain via cooperation (i.e. prosperity). The one theory focuses on national sovereignty and stateness, and the other on interdependence and market integration. Regarding this last notion, I should emphasise for the sake of clarity that we are talking here about market integration *without state-building*. Neoliberals resolve the permanent state of anarchy in the international system—an essential feature they share with the neorealists—by giving international organisations a role in the regulation of interdependence and market integration; a role that according to the neorealists has no parallels in the political-military domain.

In the next section we shall see that in the most recent discussions within the European integration literature, an important attempt has been made to bring about a synthesis between the two IR approaches described above. We will, however, also see that in the wake of this synthesis—which is referred to by Pollack as *rational-choice institutionalism* (RI, see Pollack 2001)—a new dividing line has emerged between adherents of a rationalist research programme on the one hand and proponents of a more reflexive, post-positivist approach on the other.

1.3. European integration theories

In the previous section, we were able to stipulate that realism justifiably deserves the qualification of being a 'theory of non-integration' and has over the years failed to offer a plausible theoretical analysis of European integration (Waever 1995; Collard-Wexler 2006). Neoliberal scholars generally limit themselves to an analysis of economic cooperation and integration, excluding foreign and security policy (or, more generally, political-military conflict) from their analysis. With the relaunch of the European integration process in the 1980s, it was time for a more eclectic approach, particularly when a big step in the direction of further economic and monetary integration was taken with the Treaty of Maastricht and a new integration pillar was introduced in the form of the CFSP.

Liberal intergovernmentalism

From the moment the American political scientist Andrew Moravcsik wrote his first groundbreaking articles at the beginning of the 1990s, which eventually led to the publication of his important book *The Choice for Europe* in 1998, his theory of liberal intergovernmentalism (LI) was, for a long time, the first thing that fellow European integration theorists insisted on criticising before moving on to the main issue (i.e., their own arguments). LI came to be seen as a scientific reference point that could not be ignored. This was primarily due to the fact that Moravcsik had presented one of the most consistent and coherent theoretical approaches to European integration studies yet, particularly in *The Choice for Europe*, which moreover boasted an impressive empirical foundation (Moravcsik 1998; and for comparison 1993).

LI is an elegant theory built on three steps. Each step studies a phase in the process of European integration: the phase of the establishment of national preferences, the phase of interstate negotiations, and the final phase of making credible agreements and promises to which present and future governments should be subject (known as *credible commitments*).

National preferences (let us call them the general or national interest, for the sake of convenience) are not fixed givens that are set in stone. They are formed as a result of input from society—or from civil society, to be precise. All sorts of groups try to make their particularistic interests known at the state level. The aim is to be included in the national preferences, which are determined by the national government on the basis of a rational selection from among the issues raised by interest groups. The playing field is pluralistic; that is, various groups can lobby for issue-specific interests. It is crucial to add that Moravcsik is referring here to economic issues and economic interests. His goal, after all, is to explain the dynamic of European integration, which in his opinion primarily involves market integration and monetary cooperation. And this is why his starting point is the primacy of the economy. Due to economic interconnectedness (mainly through trade and investments), national economies begin to look more like each other. To put it in more academic terms, economic structures and economic cycles increasingly converge. When this is the case, national interests naturally begin to converge as well. This makes it possible to realise a certain form of integration on the basis of lowest-common-denominator agreements.

Before this 'certain form' of integration takes on a treaty-based, institutional shape, it is self-evident that interstate negotiations must take place in the second phase. In demarcating this second phase from the establishment of national preferences and negotiating positions, Moravcsik owes much to the two-level game analysis of Robert Putnam. According to this model, domestic negotiations as well as negotiations with other countries take place. While these two levels of negotiations are formally separate, they are inextricably linked and can even take place concurrently. Domestic negotiations in fact correspond to the first phase described above. The negotiator operating on behalf of a state does so on the basis of a national coalition of relevant stakeholders. The success of interstate negotiations thus depends on the success with which the ultimate result can be submitted for approval to this domestic coalition. An agreement between states is reached when all participating states manage to win domestic approval for such an agreement (see Putnam 1988).

The consequence of this two-level game analysis is that the state (referred to here as 'the negotiator') is the connecting factor. In other words, this is a state-centric view of international relations and European integration. The state is and remains the most important actor within IR, similar to the state as a transhistorical reality within realism/neorealism (see above). This is not to say that states are presumed to be equal. In his analysis of the postwar European reality of recurrent treaty amendments, Moravcsik takes as his premise an asymmetrical interdependence between states. To paraphrase George Orwell, all states are equal but some states are more equal than others. There are member states that are large in terms of territory, population, and military presence, and there are small (or smaller) member states. But what is even more important in a world where economic integration reigns supreme is the difference between prosperous, wealthy, and highly developed states and states operating at a lower level of development.[3] This is why the notion of side payments plays an important role in interstate negotiations. Economic integration between unequal entities can be advantageous for countries with a high degree of competitiveness due to the market openings that integration offers. To convince other, less vigorous countries to go along with such a project, it must be the case that not taking part in the project is a worse option than going along with it. Second, the relative advantages enjoyed by the exporting countries must be offset by financial means, the official aim of which is to take the importing countries to a structurally higher level.[4]

If all states participating in the negotiations see the end result in terms of a win-win situation and a positive-sum game (and can present it as such to their domestic constituencies), it is essential in the third phase to turn these agreements into credible commitments. This means they must be adhered to, not only by the negotiating governments but also by future governments. To this end, an institutional structure must be set up that primarily has the role of a watchdog. And this is the concrete significance of the development of a European structure of institutions such as the European Commission and the European Court of Justice. The sole goal of these institutions is safeguarding the system of credible commitments. Moravcsik somewhat jokingly calls these institutions supranational political entrepreneurs and believes that these entrepreneurs have no further significance apart from their monitoring role. He even qualifies them as 'futile, redundant, and sometimes even counterproductive' when discussing their role in decisive steps in the process of European integration (Moravscik 1998: 270). In doing so, he explicitly criticises neoliberalism which, as we saw above, envisages international organisations in general and European institutions in particular as fulfilling a pro-active and initiating role.

Neofunctionalism
For the perceptive reader, the theory of LI resembles a combination of neorealist and neoliberal elements. Its very name already makes this clear: the noun 'intergovernmentalism' is diametrically opposed to supranationalism and implies that the EU is an interstate confederation of sovereign entities with no place for any higher authorities. The adjective 'liberal' refers to the primacy of economic interests and to the interdependence within the EU. The combination of these two words implies that there is also an opposite direction possible: as soon as divergence emerges and interdependence diminishes, diverging interests will increase the likelihood of disintegration.

The most important counterpart to intergovernmentalism has traditionally been neofunctionalism, a theoretical current that does assign an added value to European institutions in their role as initiators. The notion of spillover plays a crucial role in this theory.[5] The concept can be broken down into different subcategories. The first such subcategory—and the starting point for the theoretical explanation of the incremental process of European integration—is functional spillover, with the word 'functional' here best understood as pertaining to a particular policy domain or to a part of a policy domain. This means that an initially restricted, sector-by-sector step in the direction of integration almost automatically leads to the need to decide on integrative steps in other policy areas. There are many examples of just such a dynamic, and a politically relevant example of functional spillover is one that occurred upstream in the integration process. The decision in the mid-1980s to embark on the completion of the single market was meant primarily to create a level playing field for all economic actors within the EU. Despite what may have become of such aims as 'equal and fair competition' and 'full competition', they did form the ultimate legitimation of what is called the Europe '92 project. But the conclusion was quickly reached that a level playing field could not become a reality as long as national governments could artificially (and hence 'unfairly') improve the competitiveness of their businesses via the exchange-rate mechanism (that is, by devaluing their national currency). The conclusion was that if we really wanted to make something of this Europe '92 ambition, the logical consequence would be to take the next step and introduce a single currency. As Europe's organised business community aptly put it on the eve of the Maastricht summit: one market, one currency!

As we will see later (in chapters 3 and 6), the reference to 'Europe's organised business community' is an implicit pointer for a second mechanism within neo-functionalism: political spillover. This concept is based on the previously mentioned reality that European integration has evolved considerably in the last 60 years and that European institutions have played an increasingly important role in that process. As the mechanism of functional spillover materialised, and as more and more competences and policy domains spilled over at least partially to Brussels, the European Commission's role as initiator enshrined in the treaties of the EU became increasingly important in terms of regulation and legislation. And as European decision-making came under increasing democratic control from the mid-1980s, the significance of the European Parliament in the decision-making merry-go-round substantially increased.

As these supranational institutions assumed greater importance and began to play a decisive role in various phases of the decision-making process, interest groups became motivated to move their lobbying activities from their national capitals to Brussels. It is no coincidence that with the relaunch of the integration process in the 1980s (as a result of which the EP was granted legislative power under the codecision procedure), the number of lobbying agencies and lobbyists stationed in Brussels increased exponentially (see Van Schendelen 2013).

The importance of this form of spillover cannot be underestimated. It means that national political systems are prised open and that non-state actors venture across borders where they reorganise their activities, consider entering into coalitions with similar actors in other member states, and for that reason alone are subject to a process of European socialisation. In a famous phrase, Ernst Haas, the founder of neofunctionalism, defined integration as a process 'whereby political actors in several distinct national settings are persuaded to shift their loyalties, expectations and political activities toward a new centre, whose institutions possess or demand jurisdiction over the pre-existing national states' (Haas 1958: 16). Before looking in more detail at the consequences of this shift of loyalties, I must mention a third form of spillover: geographic spillover.

Geographic spillover refers to the allure of a successful integration project between two or more countries on geographically adjacent countries that at first see little point in participating, or do not (yet) meet the requirements for joining, but after a while want to (or are able to) take part. Historical examples abound: the United Kingdom which initially didn't want to take part and later did; a neutral country such as Sweden which after the end of the Cold War felt less hampered to join; and the *big bang* enlargement towards Central and Eastern Europe. Widening and deepening (different terms for the three spillovers) were the engines behind this ever-closer union. Later in this book we will see that this geographic movement can change course and go in the opposite direction, a kind of spillback. This is not only the case with the United Kingdom (once again) and Brexit but also with the EU's diminishing appeal in candidate countries such as Turkey (see, for example, chapter 5 and the epilogue).

Institutionalism

Neofunctionalism (NF) ascribes much value to the role of transnational or supranational institutions. While Moravcsik banteringly refers to European institutions as watchdogs, NF postulates that these institutions are gaining increasing importance in the course of the integration process and are appropriating competences that they shouldn't be allowed to have according to the intentions behind the treaties. Moreover, they are important drivers of integration, not least because they can benefit from such a process. The study of institutions under the umbrella term new institutionalism has become a key part of the political sciences (see Hall and Taylor 1996). Hall and Taylor distinguish three approaches within new institutionalism. I will briefly introduce them below, focusing on the elements that will be useful to us later as building blocks of a synthesis.

Hall and Taylor first explain historical institutionalism, which within European integration studies is chiefly associated with Paul Pierson. What is important here is the notion of unintended consequences. Certain decisions taken in the past might have consequences in a later period that were not foreseen at the time of decision-making. This could be due to the functional spillover mechanism; that is, that decisions made in one policy domain irrevocably (or logically) make it necessary or advisable to make decisions in adjacent areas. But it can also mean that institutions inadvertently begin to take on a powerful role simply because they have a longer time horizon than most national policymakers. This mechanism is reinforced by the fact that the costs of an exit (the ultimate consequence if one is against the unintentional effects) increase the more the integration process deepens (Pierson 1998). This approach thus confers the same initial value to institutions as LI does but gives a more dynamic analysis of what can happen afterwards.

Second, Hall and Taylor—and in their wake a series of other authors including Pollack, as we have seen—distinguish a second approach called rational choice institutionalism, which I will describe here briefly. Actors have a fixed, exogenously determined set of preferences that they try to realise instrumentally. A key element here is strategic calculation, which includes estimating the calculations of other actors. In line with these characteristics, the analysis of institutions has a heavily instrumental character: institutions are established in order to get the most benefit out of cooperation at the lowest possible transaction costs.

Finally, Hall and Taylor identify sociological institutionalism (SI) as the third approach. This approach takes a much broader perspective on institutions: material interests and preferences are less crucial and are in any case not exogenously determined. Moreover, SI understands institutions and institutes not only in the formal sense—as tangible people working in concrete buildings and acting in accordance with written legal regulations—but also as informal (and implicit) values and norms. Institutions are established not purely on the basis of efficiency considerations, in order to maximise national interests, but they also serve to transmit and perpetuate cultural practices. The question is not only why institutions are set up; what is also important is what form and substance they have (what values and norms they disseminate—in short, what identity they represent) and what influence they can exercise on decision-makers. In this process, symbols, cognitive scripts and frames play roles that are not always clear or easy to operationalise.

Social constructivism
Sociological institutionalism can be put on a par with a relatively recent IR theory that has acquired an important place within the study of the process of European integration: social constructivism. Concepts such as history, ideas, norms and values, and identity are key to this approach. Adherents of this theoretical approach believe that international politics—and therefore also European politics—must be interpreted in more than just material terms. Much of what occurs around us takes place at the level of ideas. And ideas are made up in the mind or, to put it

another way, they are (at some point) constructed. The famous statement of one of the leading constructivists within IR, Alexander Wendt, renders this beautifully: 'Anarchy is what states make of it' (Wendt 1992). Elsewhere, Wendt stated with a certain degree of prescience that the few rockets owned by North Korea are a greater threat to the US than the much more extensive and deadlier weapons arsenal of Great Britain (Wendt 1995: 73), for the US has what is famously called a 'special relationship' with the latter (a relationship that incidentally is largely constructed).

A constructivist focuses on social interaction, for example between states. Through interaction on the basis of shared norms and values, states can readjust their national preferences because interests and identities are not fixed (exogenous) variables but rather constructed and therefore susceptible to change (deconstruction being a real option). Thus, European integration could emerge by virtue of a shared understanding among national elites and populations about the role of Europe in the world, and by virtue of common norms and values, a shared history, and—indeed—identity. Regarding this last point, an attentive reader might note that in recent years the social interaction between national elites and the greater population has not exactly been moving towards common ground. While this may be true in terms of the political rhetoric and even outside of the political arena, at the same time a constant *European* socialisation of actors is taking place on a day-to-day basis. This can be illustrated in both abstract and concrete terms.

In abstract terms, it is useful to recall the elegant theory of LI. This three-step theory is strictly linear, with the shaping of national preferences leading to credible agreements via interstate negotiations. A constructivist, however, would contend that the credible commitments obtained through social interaction will subsequently trickle down and lead to some form of socialisation at the national level; national elites, civil societies, and citizens will focus more and more on the new (European) reality and will accordingly adjust their (individual and national) preferences. In other words, state and non-state actors 'construct' each other through their cross-border relations and thus contribute to the further construction of the EU. This comes close to the above-mentioned political spillover mechanism within neofunctionalism. The shift of political loyalties towards a higher decision-making level is paradoxically another way to indicate that top-down socialisation emanates from European institutions and European integration. It is no coincidence that Ernst Haas, in the new introduction to the reissue of his classic study *The Uniting of Europe* written just before his death, emphasised the affinity between neofunctionalism and constructivism (Haas 2004).

More concrete reference should be made to just how far-reaching the process of market integration was. Who can still remember the days of national monopolies (often state-owned) in telecommunications, for example? And who would want to return to that time? We could also point to the establishment of the euro.

Notwithstanding the potential for conflict between and within member states during the euro crisis, businesses and citizens within the eurozone continued to enjoy the ease of cross-border payments. The euro has become part of our daily reality, and it is only in the outer reaches of Euroscepticism that pleas can be heard for a return to the mark, the franc, or the peseta. But also in areas where there is seemingly no possibility for supranational integration, such as some policy areas within the EU's external relations (primarily foreign policy and defence policy), a practice has developed in which interstate cooperation and coordination are almost considered to be standard operating procedures.[6]

International Political Economy / Critical approaches
The concrete examples given above with regard to the euro do not detract from the fact that—as a result of the euro crisis—groups of people have seen their living conditions worsen (in some cases significantly), while other groups have remained more or less unscathed or have done well from the crisis. Both types can be found in all member states to a greater or lesser degree, even in member states that are not part of the eurozone. Most practitioners of social constructivism, however, hardly ever address the consequences of formal or informal institutional processes on social realities such as socio-economic inequality and the related power relations. *Social* interaction remains primarily a metatheoretical game of ontological and epistemological principles.

Although recent critical studies on the political economy of European integration owe much to constructivism (of which more later), the approaches that are seen as relevant here have another view on deconstruction and also in particular on reconstruction. To shed light on this, we must first go back to the above-mentioned IR theories. Proponents of critical political economy (CPE) disagree with the positive-sum assumption of neoliberalism. Economic cooperation or integration does not necessarily benefit all participating parties; in fact, it is more likely that trade liberalisation, for example, will lead to both winners and losers. At the same time, CPE is critical about the rigid zero-sum approach of neorealism with regard to international politics, which is based on realists' inclination to give states a central role in their analysis. What is considered by realists to be the general or national interest does not exist in reality. Behind the facade of the nation-state, there are special interests that are represented by societal forces whose relationships with each other are in turn hierarchical. This assumption does correspond to the shaping of national preferences within LI but subsequently deviates from it by emphasising the inequality between non-state groups and their lobbying representatives.

This has consequences for the assumption that states are rational actors, an assumption that is shared by both neorealists and neoliberals (and incidentally by many neofunctionalists and institutionalists). In fact, when we talk about rationality we actually refer to a kind of modified or *soft rationalism*. That is, *the* national or general interest does not exist and, as a consequence, *the* rational choice does not exist either; there are always particular interests involved that, in order to be successfully represented, must be formulated as the general interest. To paraphrase a famous statement by the Canadian political scientist Robert Cox: '(Rational choice) is always for someone and some purpose' (in the original, the word 'theory' is used instead of rational choice; see Cox 1981: 128). This refutes the idea that 'the state' (read: governments or government representatives, decision-makers) stands above national parties as a neutral entity and, after careful and rational consideration and on the basis of all available information, takes a position that is 'best for the country'.

Who or what, then, determines the societal hierarchy—and hence the unequal access to the process of national preference formation? There is no clear-cut answer to this question except if one were to engage in all sorts of metatheoretical reflections. What is important here is simply to note that both power and welfare are unequally distributed both within countries and between countries; this is, as it were, a transhistorical reality. Moreover, the unequal distribution of power is often correlated with the unequal distribution of welfare, which indicates an essential difference between CPE and many other approaches. Instead of separating economics and politics and studying them in isolation, as neoliberals and neorealists do, within CPE they are considered to be inextricably linked as constitutive parts of a single totality.

CPE gives institutions an important autonomous role but always in conjunction with aspects of power and welfare distribution. One example from a recent school of thought within the European integration literature illustrates the difference between CPE and other approaches. This school of thought analyses the EU *not* as a superstate and *not* as an instance of pure intergovernmental cooperation between sovereign states but rather as a hybrid organisation characterised by a multi-level governance (MLG) system. Just as with all the other schools of thought and theories we have dealt with so far, the emphasis here is heavily on the institutional side of European integration. As the name suggests, decision-making takes places at various levels, with institutions (at the subnational, national, or supranational level) functioning as independent variables (as explanatory factors) for integration. The institutions themselves are not problematised, i.e., they are not implicated in the analysis as *dependent* (to be explained) variables. Why is this worrying? In a later chapter I will deal with this question more extensively (see chapter 6), but for now I will simply refer to the practice of multi-level governance: we can conclude that some policy areas have been effectively transferred to the European level (for example, monetary policy for the eurozone is largely determined by the European Central Bank), while other areas are considered to be the exclusive competence of national governments (such as most social policies). This raises the question of why this is so. Does this rest on coincidence or an oversight, or did the architects of today's EU have a particular aim in mind with this 'division of labour'? If the latter is true, does the architecture reflect the unequal division of power and welfare within member states (and the convergence of these inequalities and thus of the resulting national preferences)?

We can bring the argument to an even more complex level. An important component of CPE as an approach is its emphasis on transnational processes. Particularly within the EU, we are seeing the formation of more and more cross-border partnerships between what were formerly national civil society organisations, and the emergence of transnational social networks. There are plenty of examples: non-governmental organisations (NGOs) in the field of development cooperation have been combining forces for years, and the same holds true for environmental activists, trade unions, and indeed also companies. These examples are part and parcel of a process that I referred to above as political spillover.

Here another problem pops up: various lobby groups have different means at their disposal to organise (or reorganise) themselves at the European level. This leads to asymmetric political spillover, for some actors are more capable of acting at the European level than others and thus have a better chance of taking part in a *European* process of preference formation. Also within the EU, therefore, it may be assumed that power and welfare are unequally distributed. And this unequal distribution within the EU has taken on a transnational dimension; that is, it connects and separates groups of people across national borders—a reality that has developed alongside the previously existing national dimensions.

If we assume, still reasoning from the standpoint of CPE, that inequality exists and at some moments in history even significantly increases, the question arises as to how all of this is legitimised. How do we convince the losers of globalisation—the losers of the redistribution of wealth and welfare at either the European or national level—that it is all ultimately also in *their* interests, that there are no alternatives, and that, after all, we all live in the best of all possible worlds? It is at this point that it becomes clear that CPE is indeed indebted to constructivism and essentially takes a middle position in Pollack's dichotomy, mentioned above, between rational choice institutionalism and constructivism (although presumably considered as irrelevant by him, and disregarded accordingly). In the metatheoretical 'struggle' between material forces and ideas, CPE contends that they are both important and part of a larger whole (similar to the interplay between politics and economy). Ideas play an important role in the production and reproduction of social inequality.

This finally brings us to the following question: what exactly is critical about critical political economy? Unlike the more established schools of thought within IR and within European integration studies, CPE tries to unpack and dissect the process of integration in social terms. We could call this the deconstruction of 'reality as it appears to us at first glance'. For this, unmasking is too big a word and is moreover not quite the right phrasing, because it suggests a permanent conspiracy that is hidden from view. The critical thus supersedes the methodological self-criticism of many positivists (the primacy of falsification). Critical here means a search for the social processes underlying integration. But critical also means something else: reconstruction. The aim is not solely to come to a better understanding of integration but also to reflect on the possibilities of other forms of integration. There is much talk now, for example, about what is labelled the democratic deficit of the current EU. Often an institutional analysis is given about the role of the European Parliament and/or national parliaments, about negotiations between government representatives behind closed doors, and so on. The why question is seldom put forward: why is there a democratic deficit within the EU? And what exactly does that democratic deficit mean? Is there perhaps another, social reality that lies deeper than the purely institutional problems? And ultimately also: how can we remedy this deficit, and what are the alternatives that we can bring forward for a more democratic EU? Of course, only modest claims are appropriate here; and in any case, it is not the aim of this book to present a blueprint for a different Europe. But as we slowly enter into the terrain of the EU's external relations (from the next chapter) and consider such issues as disparities in development at the global level, migration flows, or the EU's relationship with countries situated at its immediate periphery, then the following question inevitably comes up: what can the relatively prosperous EU contribute to a better, i.e. more equitable, world, and why is the practice of EU external relations all too often unruly?

1.4. Conclusion

Traditional IR theories—which have been discussed here in the generic forms of neorealism and neoliberalism—have different visions of interstate cooperation and the possibility of supra-state integration. In the case of neorealism, much emphasis is put on national interest and sovereignty. Cooperation between sovereign states—assuming it were possible—is born out of necessity, is limited to a minimum, and is of a temporary nature. Especially with regard to policy areas that symbolise the distinction between domestic and foreign, namely diplomacy and defence, states will not easily relinquish their powers. After all, interstate relations are driven by power and power maximisation. Neoliberalism—which should not be confused with the policy turnaround in the 1980s targeted at market liberalisation and privatisation (see foreword and chapter 6)—is a theoretical approach that perceives another reality than state power in the international system: an increasingly complex form of economic interdependency that brings states and non-state actors closer together and pushes them in the direction of peaceful cooperation. The cross-border movement of goods, capital, and services should be regulated by international organisations. States must therefore take into account other states in their foreign policy, with the importance of defence decreasing as that of international economic relations increases.

A brief look at more than sixty years of European integration has shown that cooperation is indeed possible (even between former enemies), that it can be very sustainable, and that it has been up to the challenge of internal and external crises (for the time being). European integration theories have dealt with the question of how this was achieved, what the engine behind the process of European integration is, and what dynamic must exist for sovereign states to be willing to hand over a part of their sovereign competences to supranational institutions. A central theme was the discrepancy between theories that primarily base the role of European institutions on rational considerations ('choices') and theories in which a steering and integrative role—either materially or ideologically—is attributed to these institutions. Many of the discrepancies covered above leave one with an intuitive sense that the truth is 'somewhere in the middle'; that we are not always dealing with irreconcilable entities. The political-economic vision of European integration outlined here in the final part of this chapter allows for a more synthesising approach. The unequal distribution of power and wealth at the national and European levels may very well be correlated, just as politics and economics are, more generally, not separate realms but constituent parts of a social totality. The material reality of European integration, as an explanatory factor, is not at odds with analyses that emphasise the level of ideas. Moreover, the praxis of European integration has shown that a rigid, state-centric view is an outdated one, at least in this part of the world. The notion of multi-level governance is pointing at this fact of European life; it also means that state and non-state actors will increasingly operate at both the national and transnational European levels. All of this has consequences for national and European policies and for the external relations of the EU, as we will see in the coming chapters.

Suggestions for further reading

Books about the history of Europe are useful as background literature for the themes that are addressed in this and later chapters. An excellent introduction to early modern and modern Europe is (Palmer et al. 2014). Readers primarily interested in postwar Europe can indulge themselves in (Judt 2005) and (Kershaw 2018). The website https://www.cvce.eu/en, currently administered by the University of

Luxemburg, contains much information about the history of European integration and offers access to a series of original documents.

There is an exceptionally extensive selection of books and articles on the three main areas of this chapter. I limit myself to a selection of books that have been of added value to me and my students in recent years. With regard to the history of the EU in conjunction with the institutional structure and the most important policy domains, I recommend the fourth edition of (Dinan 2010) in combination with the seventh edition of (McCormick 2017). Both books are written in an accessible way. Theories on IR and International Policy Economy are introduced in a first-rate manner in (Jackson and Sørensen 2017). For the more seasoned reader, I would recommend (Burchill and Linklater 2013) and (Heywood 2014). The advantage of all three books is that the authors present a broader perspective and a more comprehensive view of IR/IPE than the average American textbook writer. The best introduction to European integration theories are (Rosamond 2000) and (Wiener and Diez 2009). The latter book in particular does justice to the breadth of the field and to the diversity of theoretical perspectives. At the time of writing, the authors were working on a new edition (expected in 2019).

Finally, I should mention two book series: *The New European Union Series* by Oxford University Press and *The European Union Series* by Palgrave Macmillan. Both cover a large quantity of themes, often with very recent editions.

2.   Foreign policy theories and the external relations of the European Union

Factors and actors

In the previous chapter I discussed the different theoretical approaches within two (sub-)disciplines of political science: international relations and European integration studies. Within IR, the role of the state in the international system was examined as well as the different views on the possibility of—and the limits to—cooperation between states. In the case of the EU's external relations, the main issue is the theoretical possibility that states transfer part of their self-determination with regard to their foreign relations to a supranational entity. This touches on the sensitive matter of national sovereignty. With respect to the various schools of thought within European integration studies, we first and foremost looked at the various explanations given for the dynamic of European integration and the role of state and non-state actors at different levels of analysis. In this chapter we take a closer look at another area within IR, which is the study of the foreign policy of states. The central question will be what lessons can be learned from this literature for the study of the EU's external relations.

The reason for taking this further step into the world of theory formation can easily be explained. If we want to determine the extent to which the EU can operate as a stand-alone actor in the international system, we are in fact posing the question about the degree of statehood of the EU. The literature on foreign policy analysis takes this statehood as a given and tries to unravel the factors and actors behind the realisation of national foreign policy. In the most 'enlightened' analyses, foreign policy is understood in the broad sense that we assign to EU external relations in this book, which includes not only the traditional elements of diplomacy and defence but also economic relations, cooperation (ranging from trade agreements to policy integration within international organisations or supranational institutions), and all the intended and unintended consequences of 'domestic' policy for other countries. A glance at this literature increases our understanding of the possibilities of—but also limits to—the EU's actorness as a global player.

Another reason for separately examining the literature on foreign policy analysis is that the integration theories discussed in the previous chapter tend to only implicitly pay attention to so-called high politics and (the how and why of) the gradual and partial transfer of those policy areas that fall under this heading of high politics to the supranational European level. The fact that the respective theoretical insights have not been applied to the EU's external relations can be attributed to a somewhat artificial division between internal and external politics—and in the case of one of these theories, liberal intergovernmentalism (LI), to scepticism about the feasibility of integration in the area of foreign policies. Referring to the persistently wide public support for a common defence policy at the European level, as evidenced by opinion polls such as Eurobarometer, Andrew Moravcsik speaks in clear terms about the probability of such high-politics integration at the European level:

> Little has come of schemes for a powerful European military, however—and little will. A common European force with the capacity to wage high-intensity, low-casualty war around the globe remains a pipe dream. Whatever they may tell pollsters, European publics will not tolerate the massive increases in military spending required to come anywhere near the American level, and more efficient use of current European resources, although desirable will achieve only modest gains (Moravcsik 2003: 83).

Clearly, this interpretation of political-military ambitions as a pipe dream is not exactly conducive to an extensive study of this field. And indeed, there are very few studies of the CFSP by adherents of LI other than those that are primarily critical and negative. As we saw in the previous chapter, this is largely due to their viewpoint on European integration as – first and foremost – economic integration. They believe that while a certain degree of convergence of economic structures and interests can lead to cooperation based on the lowest common denominator, such a process does not occur in the more sovereignty-sensitive domains of foreign, and in particular defence, policy.

In the case of other integration theories, the situation is more nuanced. Analyses that break away from the somewhat linear and state-centric LI model do delve into specific external policy areas. For example, there are several theoretical analyses that examine the development of European trade policy, the relationship between the EU and developing countries, the EU's policy on enlargement, or indeed the development of the CFSP with an emphasis on diplomacy and security policy. These analyses tend to either explicitly or implicitly part company with the rigid distinction between high and low politics, and they also abandon the inflexible two-level game (see previous chapter). But a recurring problem is that the various policy areas are rarely interpreted collectively and that the objective of the Treaty of Lisbon—namely the adoption of an integrated and comprehensive approach to external relations (including the external consequences of its internal policies)—has yet to be handled from a theoretical point of view.

It may come as a surprise that neofunctionalism is also guilty of this 'omission'—a fact that was explicitly confirmed in a recent article by authors sympathetic to a contemporary version of this integration theory (Bergmann and Niemann 2018: 422). This is all the more curious given that the most important assumptions and key concepts of neofunctionalism would seem to invite us to deepen and extend our analysis of the EU's external relations. Firstly, the mechanism of functional spillover is not necessarily limited to the internal policies of the EU. It is perfectly conceivable that, in the long term, economic and monetary unification will also bring the need to defend common interests. This can be done in all sorts of ways, and the development of a political-military capability is one of them. Moreover, internal policies may have all kinds of consequences for the relationship between the EU and the outside world and, as a result, encourage new policies. The EU's Common Agricultural Policy is a good example of such a vertical or upwards spillover. Furthermore, inconsistencies in the external elaboration of various European policy areas may lead to lateral or horizontal spillover.

Secondly, neofunctionalism—but also the theoretical contributions that were discussed under the heading of 'new institutionalism'—can provide insight into the proactive actions of what are called supranational political entrepreneurs, such as the European Commission, the various directorates-general of the Commission, or various actors such as the European Defence Agency and the High Representative of the CFSP. The involvement of the European Parliament and even the European Court of Justice should also be mentioned in this context.

Thirdly, the fact that all of this does not always happen without a hitch but rather is the outcome of a political struggle in which non-state actors also play an essential role can also be deduced from neofunctionalism, and particularly from the mechanism of political spillover. We will see in later chapters how this form of Europeanisation, including the pull factor of European policies on previously national interest groups, manifests itself both in economic external relations and in foreign and security matters. Even in the area of defence policy—surely a cornerstone of national sovereignty and a playing field of national interests—a form of political spillover can be found.

Fourthly, and finally, the mechanism of geographic spillover should also be mentioned, i.e. the attraction that a successful integration process can exert on third countries. In this context, the aforementioned authors speak of external spillover; they also include the external consequences of internal policy as well as the impetus that external events can give to the dynamics of integration in the field of the CFSP (ibid.: 429-30).

All in all, there are plenty of reasons for us to continue looking for the building blocks of a more integral—and perhaps also somewhat eclectic—theoretical approach. In this chapter it is expressly not the intention to design a new theory 'that makes all other theories redundant'. The objective is much more modest: to create a theoretical framework that will allow us to better understand substantive choices, focus areas, priorities, and partly also the conclusions reached in later chapters. In this chapter I will further elaborate on the statements made in the previous chapter on (international) political economy in the belief that such a perspective holds the potential to unite and synthesise the best elements from various theories. Before going into this more specifically, we should first take a look at the literature on foreign policy analysis.

2.1.   The study of foreign policy

A common denominator in the literature on the foreign policy of states is the study of decision-making processes and/or the role and behaviour of decision-makers in the field of foreign policy. Below I will identify a number of relevant approaches within foreign policy analysis (FPA) and specifically address the significance these different analyses could have for the study of *European* external relations. I start with a perspective on foreign policy that is still influential, also outside academia, in order to indicate how much the EU deviates from persistent assumptions such as the unitary capacity to act and the rational balancing up of interests.

Rational choice theory
As we saw in the previous chapter, neorealism and neoliberalism start from the primacy of the national interest and take a state-centric perspective on international relations. States are rational, unitary actors, and whether they are fighting for power or for prosperity, they do so deliberately and out of enlightened self-interest.

All possible criticisms of rational choice approaches in general and of the study of the foreign policy of states in particular apply to the EU, to the same extent or even more. The national state cannot be regarded as a unitary actor, and certainly the EU cannot be regarded as such, with its various national interests, traditions, and foreign-policy stereotypes. Secondly, the assumption of rational behaviour among decision-makers is based on the optimal acquisition of knowledge, which is difficult to realise even in more or less coherent national decision-making centres, let alone in a polycentric unit such as the EU. Thirdly, psychological factors and cognitive limitations that can influence the actions of decision-makers—an insufficiently explored theme within rational choice theories—are also naturally at work at the European level (and are perhaps even more pressing due to the complexity of the EU's multi-level governance system). Finally, crises represent another challenge for approaches based on rationality: the unannounced and unexpected nature of crises makes it difficult to make the right assessments and choices in a relatively short period of time. The EU encounters a much more richly varied number of crises—both within and between states—as well as crises that affect the different member states in an uneven manner. For this reason alone, any analysis that considers the Europeanisation of rationality posible is premature, to say the least.

The Bureaucratic Politics approach

An important step beyond the view of sovereign states as unitary actors was taken by academics who focused on the existence of particular interests within the state apparatus and concluded from this that the state was an arena of conflicting visions (see in particular the pioneering work of Allison 1971). Many ministries and government bodies deal directly or indirectly with issues that generally fall under the heading of foreign policy. In the United States, for example, this would be the president and their staff, often the vice president and their staff, the National Security Council, the Department of State but also the Department of Defence, and so on. In addition, various actors such as the Chief of Staff of the US army, security agencies, and Congress play a role in what we could call 'the US public sector'. The idea that all these actors within the state apparatus work in unison is an illusion. Rather, there is fighting and competition whereby people or institutions will not hesitate to withhold information as a means to achieve their aims. This was something Secretary of State Colin Powell came to realise in 2003, after he had accused dictator Saddam Hussein of possessing weapons of mass destruction on the grounds of wrong information provided to him by the CIA. His allegation, made in the UN Security Council, was to become an important legitimation of the US military intervention in Iraq.

It is clear that the situation within the EU is far more complicated. Not only do we have to deal with numerous self-respecting European institutions and a European bureaucracy consisting of various directorates-general relevant to the EU's external relations, but the 28 national bureaucracies in the member states also play an essential role in the predominantly intergovernmental setting of the CFSP. The result is a genuine cacophony of voices, opinions, and interests. The 1970s quip 'Who do I call if I want to speak to Europe?'—attributed to Henry Kissinger and repeated ad nauseum—is still relevant, despite demonstrable and explicit attempts to streamline and clarify external policies. It must be added though that, in line with the Bureaucratic Politics Model (BPM), a telephone call to the American president does not always guarantee that we are talking to the right (i.e. the most relevant) person either.

Countless examples can be given of turf wars and rivalries between the different European institutions and committees that are formally involved with the CFSP. A random selection might include the following: the Council Secretariat is not always acting along the same lines as the bureaucratic apparatus of the European Commission (Dijkstra 2009); in the area of government procurement on defence, the Commission—a supranational institution—must deal with the intergovernmental

European Defence Agency (EDA) (see Fiott 2015); the Committee of the Permanent Representatives of the Governments of the Member States to the European Union (COREPER) must tolerate the interference of the Polical and Security Committee (PSC), founded in 2009, in preparations for the Council's meetings (Delreux 2015: 154); the establishment of the European External Action Service (EEAS), which resides under the High Representative of CFSP, coincided with the removal of the Directorate-General for External Relations which had been part of the European Commission; and so on. Finally, there is an almost natural rivalry between the various directorates-general engaged in the EU's external action and those in charge of the external dimensions of internal action, for example between the directorates in charge of trade and agriculture (see chapter 3 for the substantive side of this rivalry). Treaty amendments can be both the cause and the effect of shifting accents and changing power relations within European bureaucracy. But despite repeated attempts at streamlining and integration, intra-bureaucratic forms of fighting and turf wars continue to be part of the almost daily practice of European external relations.

An essential element in this analysis of BPM is the assumption that foreign policy in the preparatory, decision-making, and implementation phases is partly determined by non-elected civil servants or public and semi-public officials. It is plausible to assume that this occurs on the basis of particular interests that are linked to the specific position of the persons in question within the state apparatus. Consequently, and contrary to what rational choice theory wants us to believe, the end result is not necessarily optimal, the most efficient, or in the general interest. This is due to what is called 'group thinking': instead of choosing the best possible option from various alternatives, the members of a certain subgroup are trapped in the strategic straitjacket and the associated stringency and (self-)discipline. This can ultimately result in an suboptimal and thus irrational outcome, with even policy failure as a consequence (see Janis 1982). Within the framework of the EU, this could occur if national bureaucracies hold on to certain traditions, priorities, or prejudices and hence oppose European cooperation that would demonstrably lead to better results. Even an important European institution such as the Commission cannot avoid this kind of group thinking. For example, it has been concluded that so-called Impact Assessments (IAs)—formally introduced in 2003 to assess all major policy initiatives on their environmental, social, and political-economic consequences and to compare alternative policy options in the light of this—have all too often served to confirm the Commission's own position and to legitimise preconceived notions. In the words of a group of researchers: '[The European Commission] engages with IAs to provide a presentation of self, to establish EU norms and values, and to create consensus around policy proposals by using causal plots, doomsday scenarios, and narrative dramatization' (Radaelli et al. 2013: 500). It also does not seem to be an exaggeration to state that the recent Global Strategy—drawn up under the leadership of Federica Mogherini, the High Representative of the CFSP and head of the General Secretariat of the Council—partly suffers from the same problem (see also chapter 6). Finally, the rigid adherence to strict austerity measures at the time of the euro crisis could be interpreted as group thinking—and the internal discipline ('cohesion') that goes along with it—within the European Commission, the European Central Bank, and the finance ministries of the euro zone (the same incidentally applies to the International Monetary Fund's involvement in 'resolving' the Greek debt crisis).

Cognitive and constructivist approaches
The examples above demonstrate that the shaping of (foreign) policies is not always the result of rational considerations and does not always lead to the best of all possible worlds. Group thinking and group discipline are examples of what constructivists would call social interaction within parts of the state apparatus. The influence of ideas and identities as well as psychological factors play a key role in this. This becomes even clearer when we zoom in on the individual decision-maker. One of the criticisms of BPM is that the bureaucracy—i.e. the parts of the state apparatus and their representatives who aren't democratically accountable—is assigned too important a role and that the agency of chosen politicians is correspondingly underexposed. The perception and character of a prime minister or a president (of the European Council, the Commission, or an individual member state such as France) may, according to certain cognitive approaches, indeed have an influence on foreign policy formation. Within the EU, personalities at the helm were able to make a difference in part because of their vision, such as the former president of the European Commission, Jacques Delors (1985-95), or because of their mutual understanding (also referred to as 'chemistry'). The collaboration between Helmut Kohl and François Mitterrand in the 1980s and early 1990s is an example of the latter. It is obvious that a more individual view of decision-making also takes into account the cognitive limitations of the decision-maker, their incomplete access to or grasp of all relevant information, and their ability to act adequately in times of acute international political crises. Moreover, an individual decision-maker's values and norms, rigid convictions, and (psychological) characteristics can be an obstacle to necessary changes of foreign policy directions.

If we turn our attention back to collectivities, an important focus area within FPA is the impact of ideas on the formulation of foreign policy priorities. 'Strategic culture' is a widely used term referring to a country's particular traditions and deep-rooted ideas. This concept is often used to denote the hard reality of military power in the foreign policy of states, and then leads to the assertion that there is little or no likelihood of defence cooperation within the EU because the strategic cultures of the 28 member states (supposedly) differ too much from each other. I prefer a broader interpretation and choose to speak of a culture that encompasses several elements of a country's external relations. Within the EU, we can distinguish between countries that focus more or less on international trade or have very different geographic orientations that often pertain to their colonial past. In the field of development aid, too, clear differences between the EU member states can be discerned—the difference between the Scandinavian member states and the new members from Central and Eastern Europe being a salient case in point (see chapter 4). Another example is the different geopolitical opinions that several EU member states held after the end of the Cold War regarding which countries in Central and Eastern Europe could or should join the EU first. Finally, Britain's so-called special relationship with the US is not necessarily desired by all member states in the same way—if such a relationship were even possible, of course. There is no doubt that in many of these examples, material interests play (and have always played) a major role, but it would be wrong to suppose that the aforementioned traditions—or the ideas and beliefs that have established themselves in external relations—do not have a life of their own or, indeed, make the promotion of material interests more difficult.

Social constructivists have studied the EU's external relations in at least three areas (see Aydin-Düzgit 2015). First, the enlargement strategy since the fall of the Berlin Wall can serve as an example of the relative importance of ideas, in the sense that the partly rational considerations for not rushing to enlarge the EU in the direction of Central and Eastern Europe were summarily brushed aside. A historical obligation to guide the 'other Europe' back into the family of freedom-loving and prosperous countries outweighed a sober calculation of the political and economic risks. In addition, by setting the conditions for membership in terms of democratisation and free market integration, the EU initiated an important change in mentality in the former communist countries next to, of course, very concrete material economic and legal reforms. The point is, still reasoning from a constructivist perspective, that the transformation of material reality would not have been possible without the compelling persuasiveness of the ideas, values, and norms that symbolise the successful European integration process. Those same values and norms were also responsible for the fact that the EU pursued a different strategy towards Turkey than, for example, towards Poland, long before the autocratic tendencies of Recep Tayyip Erdogan came to the fore. In chapter 5 I will discuss the EU's enlargement strategy and its so-called transformative power. We shall see that the normative power of the EU recedes the more the prospects of accession diminish. Something more must therefore be going on here.

A second area of interest within the social constructivist literature on integration concerns the more general image of the EU in international politics and its influence in terms of power politics on other countries and people. A brief introduction to this theme is in order here. Shortly after the European government leaders and the French head of state had decided in Maastricht on a major deepening of the economic integration process, Christopher Hill published an influential article entitled *The Capability-Expectations Gap* (of the EU, see Hill 1993). In it, he argued that there was a certain tension between, on the one hand, the expectations that were aroused outside the EU (which were only to grow further) as a result of the successful internal integration process, and the capability of the EU to fulfill these expectations on the other. The more the EU acted as one economic unity, through the single market and (soon) also the single currency, the more the focus would come to lie on the EU as a would-be effective international actor. For various reasons, the EU could not (yet) meet these expectations in 1993. It simply lacked the capacity to act, not only due to the continued existence of national foreign policy and corresponding interests but also because of, for example, the absence of any joint military potential. The EU was, so to speak, an economic giant in the making but a political dwarf (and, according to some, a military worm). Sooner or later, Hill argued, the EU would face international political dilemmas as a result of this gap between capability and expectations. This gap could only be closed in two ways: through an increase in political-military capabilities or through a reduction in existing expectations. Hill's implicit assumption was that ultimately (and in due course) the first solution would be chosen; that external 'expectations' would give rise to an internal dynamic of integration in the area of the CFSP.[1] From the perspective of this book, Hill's analysis is somewhat problematic for two reasons. In the first place, he took the necessary capabilities primarily in a material sense and thus remained largely trapped in the jargon of 'low' and 'high' politics. And secondly, he did not sufficiently broaden his analysis to include more general external relations.[2]

A decade after the publication of Hill's article, a new concept was embraced that directly touched upon the EU's alleged lack of international actorness, but which now paid particular attention to the non-material capabilities of the EU. Instead of emphasising expectations elsewhere in the world, the focus was on the EU's image as a community of values and on its influence on processes of change and transformation abroad. At the beginning of chapter 3, I will discuss the genesis and later applications of this concept, which has come to be known as Normative Power Europe (NPE) following the publication of Ian Manners' article of the same name. The EU does indeed have soft power in the sense that it can serve as an example for other countries or people—or, as Manners put it, has 'the ability to define what passes for "normal" in world politics' (Manners 2002: 236). The example (or case study) that he cites in his article—the abolition of the death penalty—is perhaps not the happiest choice, but the idea that the values and norms expressed – and partly realised – by and through the European project find their resonance elsewhere has been taken up by a number of other academics. And rightly so, even if we might not always agree with some of those values and norms (such as a free market ideology that has been taken too far). In fact, Europe serves as a source of inspiration for integration projects elsewhere as well as for groups of people striving for greater freedom. Europe has also played a major role in the globalisation of economic ideas such as liberalisation, deregulation, and privatisation. Neoliberalism as a body of thought and ideology has many founders, of whom a large number come from Europe.

A third area of focus is the tension between national (foreign) policy on the one hand and *European* external relations on the other (as conceptually indicated in the preface of this book). The common term used for this part of the literature on integration is 'Europeanisation' (although this term is also used in other policy areas and/or parts of the integration process). There is a multiple dynamic at work here: upwards, downwards, and outwards. Upward Europeanisation, known as uploading, refers to European policy that is based primarily on national policy. In other words, European policy is nothing more than what national states have added to it. The Common Agricultural Policy stems from the way in which national policies were previously conducted. This does not necessarily mean that all member states have the same influence on the final European outcome (for example, France had a decisive role in the realisation of the Common Agricultural Policy); the same holds for the CFSP and more generally for external relations. The larger member states obviously have a greater impact on external relations than the smaller or medium-sized member states. But even a small member state such as Portugal can attach considerable importance to uploading one of its traditional foreign policy priorities: relations with its old colonies in Africa or with Brazil. Europeanisation of this policy may be more effective in promoting national interests for the simple reason that an Angolan or Brazilian government is more likely to listen to the EU than to Portugal. What applies to Portugal applies to all member states to a greater or lesser extent, and it is important to add that this concerns not only national material interests but also different traditions and ideas about one's own position in the world, about free trade, about the relationship with less developed countries, about the use of military means, and so on.

The influence of constructivists becomes even more apparent when we look at the opposite trajectory: downward Europeanisation. National policy is increasingly embedded and sometimes even determined by European policy. Trade agreements between the EU and third countries have a direct effect at the national level. But even in the more sensitive areas such as foreign and defence policy, there is downward Europeanisation and especially socialisation. National foreign policy elites—including all those who swarm around them (such as commentators, employees in what are labelled think tanks, and yes, even academics)—are, in their thinking and in the way they operate, increasingly determined and inspired by the European reality and EU frameworks. This also holds for the 'big three' (Germany, France, and Great Britain; see Wong and Hill 2011; and Hadfield et al. 2017). The third variant, outward (or horizontal) Europeanisation, is related to the aforementioned normative and transformative role of the EU with regard to third countries, for example with the candidate countries. I will frequently come back to this in the following chapters (e.g. in chapter 5).

Comparative Political Economy
A distinct approach that compares the foreign policy and external relations of nation-states—thereby assessing the likelihood of international cooperation and/ or integration—is comparative political economy. At the heart of the matter, we are dealing here with a pre-theory that attempts to identify relevant independent variables for explaining foreign policy without making statements about the relative weight of the individual variables. Nonetheless, this approach is interesting enough to mention here separately because it offers a much broader perspective than the somewhat limited political-institutional perspective of mainstream FPA.

Factors that can influence foreign policy and the external relations of a country (or in the case of the EU, a group of countries) include: 1) the geographic location of a country, for example being in the vicinity of important trade routes or near unstable countries or regions; 2) the degree of socio-economic development of a country, with the assumption that a higher level of development correlates with a more active, internationally oriented, and perhaps (in a military sense) more peaceful foreign policy in which economic relations play a relatively important role; 3) the political regime type of a country, with the assumption that a democratically governed country will conduct a more international, more peaceful, and more cooperative foreign policy that is also more predictable than that of autocratically governed countries; 4) the character traits of the political leaders (or foreign policy decision-makers), especially in autocratically governed countries, with this factor gaining in importance when there is a crisis situation in the international relations of the country concerned (incidentally, this also applies to democratic leaders—the democratic checks and balances can temporarily function less optimally in times of crisis); and 5) the national identity or foreign policy tradition of a country, which translates into a series of priorities with a certain element of continuity. For example, the issue of neutrality is so important for countries such as Ireland and Sweden—and has been part of their national identity for so long—that other priorities are subordinated if necessary.

As said before, this approach offers a much broader perspective involving political and economic factors as well as historical development processes and identities.

Towards a synthesis: power and prosperity, institutional configurations and identity

In general terms, we can conclude that the EU's external relations are the result of two factors and a large number of actors. The EU as a global player is the result of the interaction between a historical and a global context. On the one hand, the development of internal political, economic, and social structures and their associated values and norms are of considerable importance in the EU's external relations. On the other hand, we know that things do not work in isolation and that changing environmental factors have great significance, if only because the EU is forced to anticipate or respond to these external changes. It is useful to analyse these changing factors, as they entail a historical and/or external necessity, but it is ultimately the actors who have to do the job. After all, necessity does not imply any capacity to act. I will briefly discuss these three dimensions—the historical context, environmental factors, and actors—in succession.

Bringing together the different elements from the aforementioned theoretical approaches, the first remark that should be made is that the historical context is an important factor in the realisation and possible development of the EU's external relations. This is true on two levels. The first is the level of the nation-state, which is an essential level, if only because states still have a monopoly on formal violence. Well, states change, and they do so in an uneven and asynchronous way compared to other states. Even a comparison of the same state at different times in history yields interesting insights. What currently belongs (or should belong) to the values and norms of every member state of the EU was anything but self-evident not so long ago, say a hundred years ago. In other words, a certain historical relativism is useful here whenever we measure third countries against the yardstick of our current system of values and norms. In addition, current success in areas such as democracy and human rights (or free trade) is absolutely no guarantee of success in the future. This raises a pertinent question: to what extent is this system resistant to unexpected changes at home and abroad?

On the second level, that of the international system in which the EU and its member states operate, we also encounter constant historical change. Here, too, we can state a self-evident fact: a foreign policy that is relatively effective at some point in history can, as a result of a changed international context, work out completely differently at a later time. The age of nuclear weapons and long-range missiles has fundamentally changed international relations. Economic globalisation is another obvious challenge that requires different answers today than in the nineteenth century.

If we then apply this to the current EU, we immediately see the importance of the international context. What started out as an economic integration project, partly on the initiative of and at least for a long time under the political-military wing of the US, was able to grow relatively undisturbed—both in terms of trade and of prosperity—in the shadow of the Cold War. The international economic crisis of the 1970s and early 1980s marked the first dent in confidence in 'an ever-closer union', as described in the preambule of the Treaty of Rome. But with the collapse of communism and of the Soviet Union, and with it the end of the Cold War, much has changed for the once so tight Western countries, both in relation to non-Western countries and among themselves. There have been increasing calls to give the EU a more efficient and decisive capacity to act because Europe can no longer rely on NATO and the US; and, once again, not on Russia. Apart from alleged external threats and changing environmental factors, the EU itself is not a stationary entity. If we were to take a picture right now of the current capacity of the EU to act, then there is perhaps much to criticise, and the critics are to some extent correct when they speak of a lack of capabilities. But we have to zoom out and watch the film of sixty years of integration and take note of what has taken place over that period. Even in the area of external relations, there is a world of difference between the cooperation that took place at the end of the 1950s and that of today. It is much more impressive when we examine Europe in movement than when we see it in a snapshot (see also chapter 6).

However, we must not forget that the EU is not a machine in perpetual motion and that there is no inherent obviousness to the aforementioned movement—something that seems to be assumed in many of the analyses and predictions within the literature on Europeanisation and, in part, in those about the EU as a normative power. In the latter case, this is not only due to an overly positive interpretation of so-called common European values and norms, but also to the implicit assumptions of immortality and universality. Commonality and movement (to be understood here as progress) are interrelated, but neither are irreversible. It is very easy to fall into the trap of overconfidence, and thereby disregard counterforces, also within the EU itself. In addition, quite a few academics assume that the disappearance of the EU would mean that Europe and the wider world would relapse into a state of atavism and anarchy, and that political life on earth—conceived in terms of peaceful cooperation and individual liberties—would vanish. Some even consider such a scenario to be unthinkable simply because it is normatively undesirable. Nonetheless, a large proportion of the world's population will not be agonised by the disappearance of the EU (if they notice anything at all). And there is reason to suspect that this is also the case for a not insignificant (and perhaps increasing) number of Europeans.

The historical and global contexts are therefore key to understanding the behaviour of collectivities. But inertia is always lurking in the shadows; we can assume that collectivities (or individuals) respond adequately to changing internal or external factors, but it is justified to question whether they will actually do so (and moreover, what does 'adequate' mean?). In other words, so much can change in the environment of the multi-level decision-making process, but if there are no actors taking action in the entire process of decision-making (including agenda-setting, preparatory steps and negotiations, actual decision-making, and finally the implementation of the decisions taken), then nothing will happen.[3] This brings us to the question of who the relevant actors are with regard to the EU's external relations.

Thus far, a number of actors have been casually or more extensively reviewed as part of the different theoretical approaches within IR, European integration studies, and FPA. As attention is focused on the policy areas that have been uploaded to the European level in recent decades, the literature shows a greater interest in European bureaucratic structures, institutions, and characteristics. The insights from BPM discussed above, applied here to the EU, are an excellent example of this. The emphasis here is almost exclusively on the European administrative apparatus and on bureaucratic substructures and institutions operating within that apparatus. This means no attention is given to non-bureaucratic influences, to actors who are operating outside the bureaucracy but who can play a role in the decision-making process. In other words, this concerns the forces in society that reside outside the multi-level management system but that are part of existing (and changing) power structures. In the course of this book, we will come across various examples of such direct or indirect influencing but here, for the time being, a somewhat abstract argument will suffice.

Every political community in the past and in the present is characterised by an unequal distribution of power and welfare. We should not beat around the bush about this, nor should we attach any a priori value judgement to it. It is part of the ontological facts that make the work of a social scientist a little more orderly. A completely different story concerns the *degree of inequality* within and between communities, which can fluctuate historically and give rise to some of the most violent conflicts. Here we are confronted with an important problem: what level of inequality can a community sustain before it disintegrates into conflicting parties? In the jargon of the EU, what we are talking about here is the problem of cohesion. David Mayes defines social cohesion as 'the political tolerability of the levels of economic and social disparity that exist and are expected in the European Union and of the measures that are in place to deal with them' (Mayes 1995:1). For the sake of completeness, I should add, alongside economic and social inequality, political inequality. The advantages of this definition is that it has a dynamic component (it may improve or worsen in the future, or do neither), it takes into account how inequality is perceived and therefore offers scope for subjectivity, and it allows policy measures to be a part of the political acceptance of inequality.

Socio-economic and political inequality (or the unequal distribution of welfare and power) is not an anonymous fact but rather something that can ultimately be traced back to concrete individuals or groups of individuals. Anyone can understand that a combination of political power and socio-economic prosperity, i.e. a pooling of individuals who stand to gain in both areas, can potentially be a most explosive one. Each community is dependent on the forming of coalitions for its survival (or for realising at least a minimal required degree of cohesion). Even the most selfish dictator will at least need the support of (parts of) the army in order to remain in power. This support can be obtained in a tangible, material way or through the power of ideas, i.e. on the basis of concepts that reflect the commonality or (partial) overlap of interests. Without prejudice to inequality, which is after all structural, we can assume that the more democratically governed a community is, the more likely it is that the power of persuasion will prevail and instances of pay-offs and nepotism will be reduced, although some remarkably large and persistent grey areas would remain. But what does the above have to do with the EU's external relations?

If the outside world and thus the external relations of a community become more important for the production and reproduction of that community's power and welfare, including their unequal distribution among the individual members of that community, then it is plausible to assume that the social strata that benefit the most from existing socio-political configurations will become more and more involved in these relations, either directly by going into politics, making donations to like-minded political parties, or lobbying effectively, or indirectly by seeking common ground in one single strategy or ideology. In short, when it comes to studying the foreign policy of a country, it seems obvious to look not only at the institutional structure and institutional actors within the public sector, but also to involve broader societal relations in the analysis. A country's foreign policy is, in any case, partly a reflection of the unequal distribution of welfare and power (and the interplay between the two). For example, how can the long-term foreign policy orientation of the Netherlands towards the Anglo-Saxon world be fully explained without involving the complex financial interweaving of the Dutch economy with the Atlantic heartland? Once again I would point out that behind the abstraction known as the 'Dutch economy' are ultimately real individuals or groups of individuals, all of whom benefit from ensuring that the US and the Netherlands remain on good diplomatic terms.[4] And there begins the short march through the EU institutions.

This political-economic analysis does not alter the fact that 'institutions' do matter. In that sense, what I wrote earlier about constantly changing historical contexts applies to state-society configurations as well. State-society configurations form the context in which institutional balances between a large number of actors at different levels of decision-making are shaped. And this is certainly the case for a hybrid and polycentric entity such as the EU. Institutions are extremely relevant but form part of a broader range of actors that matter in the creation, continuation, and altering of external relations. What is important here is which variables are independent and which are dependent. Neoliberalism (the IR variant rather than the free-market ideology) does, for example, provide an explanation for supra-state integration in the field of external relations but does a much less convincing job of explaining how trade flows and investments, and transnational networks underlying these external relations (the system of complex interdependence), were able to develop. Ultimately, this is about which actors have played a decisive role in the integration process but are not part of the formal state apparatus.

Table 2.1.   Actors playing a role in the development of the EU's external relations

	State actors	**Non-state actors**
Subnational	Cities Regions / Provinces	Civil society actors (local/ regional) Political parties (idem)
National	Member states	Civil society actors (national) Political parties (idem)
Intergovernmental	European Council Council of Ministers High Representative of CFSP	–
Supranational	European Commission European Parliament High Representative / Vice-president European External Action Service European Court of Justice	–
Transnational	Public sector bodies Committees (national and European civil servants)	Businesses Trade unions NGOs European political parties (EP) Lobby groups

Table 2.1 gives an overview of the most relevant state and non-state actors at four different levels (a distinction is made between national and intergovernmental, but in fact this amounts to one and the same decision-making level). This overview is, of course, not exhaustive. For example, under the various European institutions there are scores of directorates-general, committees, and the like. Where relevant, these 'subordinate actors' will be touched upon in the rest of this book (such as the European External Action Service in chapter 6).[5]

For now it is important to make three additional remarks with the above table in mind. First, the table gives an overview of actors without putting them in a hierarchy, which while schematically understandable is factually incorrect. No matter how often and justifiably we speak of the EU as a system of multi-level governance, the fact remains that the field of external relations, and in particular that of the CFSP, is still mainly a matter of and between sovereign states. As we shall repeatedly see, this has consequences above all for member states' relationships with the supranational European institutions, in particular the European Commission and to a lesser extent the European Parliament. And these member states each have their own history, their own state-society configuration, their own structures of socio-economic and political inequality, their own resultant national preferences, and finally their own traditions and foreign-policy culture. Each state can then be identified on the basis of the following checklist (which is not necessarily comprehensive):

- its level of development and its international economic orientation towards trade and investment (and labour);
- its political-institutional structure including its party system, its form of government and its system of checks and balances in foreign policy decision-making;
- its national identity in the areas of security and territorial integrity including views on migration and the use of military means;
- the importance it attaches to international development cooperation as part of its external relations;
- its prevailing views on European cooperation and integration;
- its prevailing views on transatlantic cooperation;
- its emphasis on bilateral or multilateral cooperation;
- its specific geopolitical and economic priorities (whether or not arising from a colonial past);
- other nation-specific characteristics in foreign policy and external relations belonging to its national identity.

Although there has been a convergence of economic structures and foreign policy identities since the first steps were taken in European integration—for example between old and new member states—there are still large and almost irreconcilable differences. To bring some nuance to the image of 28 different member states all clinging to their national identities and priorities (and therefore to their national sovereignty), the compilers of a recently published collection of essays divided the member states into five groups (see Hadfield et al. 2017). In creating this classification, the emphasis was on what the compilers call 'regional value sets'. Hadfield et al. distinguish a first group of northern member states consisting of Sweden, Denmark, and Finland and the three Baltic states of Estonia, Latvia, and

Lithuania. However, a closer look at the similarities and differences within this group reveals that a community of values and norms barely exists—at most, there is a potential commonality—and that developments after the end of the Cold War point to a divergence rather than a convergence of foreign policy interests and conceptions. This conclusion is probably justified if we focus (as the authors do) on foreign and security policy. But if we look at the broader external relations of Sweden, Denmark, and Finland in particular—which the authors do not do, entirely in the tradition described at the beginning of this chapter (i.e. traditional FPA approaches)—then we discover strong similarities in these countries' preference for multilateral frameworks of international policy (in particular economic policy) and development cooperation (see chapter 4).

A second group, the so-called Western EU member states, includes Great Britain, Ireland, the Netherlands, Belgium, and Luxembourg. The authors of this particular chapter admit that this cluster is not very common. Geographic proximity seems to be their main criterion; there is little in this chapter referring to any common ground between these countries, even less than in the case of the first group. An important issue, of course, is the difference between Great Britain—which is normally counted among the Big Three in the CFSP, together with France and Germany—and the other smaller states. Then there is the neutrality policy of Ireland that is not shared by the other four countries. Although the three continental countries are supposed to be aligned in the Benelux politico-economic union, this does not manifest itself in any clear commonality in foreign policy areas. With the possibility of a Brexit, little remains of this group, and some countries—especially the Netherlands and Ireland—are likely to reorient themselves and possibly enter into new external alliances.

The third group of no less than eight eastern EU member states, namely Austria and seven countries from the former Eastern bloc (Poland, Czech Republic, Slovakia, Hungary, Bulgaria, Romania, and Slovenia), also yields little in terms of common values and principles in foreign policy, despite an initial hint of solidarity based on geographic and historical factors. The group includes Poland, a large member state that initially had ambitions of playing a prominent role within the EU; Austria, which did not belong to the Eastern bloc, but benefited disproportionately in economic terms from market liberalisation in Central and Eastern Europe after 1989; and Slovenia, which separated itself from the former Yugoslavia at an early stage and hence managed to avoid the 1990s civil war, in the process enjoying special protection from Germany. Even the strong presence of Russia in the region does not give us enough reason to speak of substantial sub-regional convergence.

A fourth group consists mainly of the southern member states of Italy, Greece, Spain, and Portugal. Here as well, there is little commonality in values and foreign policy principles. Nonetheless, this group of countries does confirm the abovementioned mechanism of Europeanisation through uploading, or rather the attempt to do so. Instead of gradually introducing European conceptions of foreign policy, these countries try to get their own concerns and priorities on the European agenda and make them part of a common EU policy. Recent examples include Greece on the Cyprus issue, Spain with regard to Morocco, and Italy together with Greece in connection with the refugee crisis. This last example also shows how an attempt at EU commonality can be frustrated by a structural lack of solidarity and the absence of a shared sense of urgency.

Finally, France and Germany are treated together as 'central' Europe. The author of the chapter in question clearly had difficulty with the geographic design set up by the editors and decided to give a different meaning to the word 'central'. Instead of looking for common traditions and values—which in the case of these two countries largely stem from their bloody confrontations in the past—he states that the true meaning of 'central' must lie in the role played by Paris and Bonn/Berlin as the engines of the European integration process, including its external relations. This central role reached a peak under the Kohl-Mitterrand tandem and was partially impaired by the big bang enlargement of 2004-2007. As a result of the expansion towards Central and Eastern Europe, the position of Germany was strengthened at the expense of France. France has tried to compensate for this by presenting itself as more Atlantic and by strengthening its ties with the southern member states (Simón 2017). I will return to this issue in the final chapters, to question whether this trend will ultimately turn out to be a short-lived ripple in bilateral relations.

Despite the criticisms that can be made about an edited volume like that of Hadfield et al., the problems that the book deals with indicate irrefutably that member states still occupy a central position in the architecture of the EU's external relations—and that that architecture is vulnerable and sensitive to external and internal shocks, drastic enlargements, and nationalist and populist reflexes. What we can also glean from this collection is that detailed research (at the member-state level) and comparative research (between countries and between certain periods) into Europeanisation is still largely in its infancy. Finally, the study also shows that European foreign policy is all too often reduced to the domain of the CFSP and that premature conclusions about the lack of sub-regional convergence of national policy largely ignore broader external relations.

Returning to the above table 2.1, the second remark I would like to make is that, at a deeper level, there is an inequality that is necessarily obscured in the table. Earlier I spoke of limited or soft rationality to indicate that states in many cases do indeed make rational considerations and choices. But I added that rational choices are always in the interest of a certain group and serve a specific particularistic cause, even if it is subsequently presented as the national interest. This is due to the reality of socio-economic and political inequality in a country. In reality, there is little question of pluralism. To put it differently, access to decision-makers is unevenly distributed, and this undoubtedly has to do with social positions, for example in relevant social networks, and with prestige derived from power and prosperity. The CEO of a large transnational corporation probably has the private telephone number of the country's prime minister, while it is doubtful whether the same holds true for the director of a national NGO in the field of environmental issues. Shared networks are often a reflection of similar or overlapping conceptions of social reality and of the way in which social antagonisms must be neutralised. As we will repeatedly see in subsequent chapters, this form of influencing based on shared interests and/or conceptions is crucial, especially in the early stages of the decision-making process.

Third, the table identifies a fourth level of analysis that will appear frequently in the following chapters: the transnational level. This is essentially related to the political spillover mechanism. As the supranational level of government gains weight, more and more non-state actors will take the leap and move to Brussels to make their voices heard.[6] But here as well, there is an uneven playing field. Not all non-state actors have the means to make such a move effectively, and not all non-state actors who do take the leap are equally successful in establishing contacts with representatives of European institutions. The image of the EU as a political arena characterised by a pluralistic coming and going of civil society actors with equal opportunities to penetrate into the centres of agenda-setting and decision-making is largely based on an illusion. Then again, an arena of *state* actors has arisen, a process that we could interpret as the transnationalisation of the public sector. By that I mean that parts of the government apparatus at the individual level—ministers, civil servants of all sorts, senior officers—are included in cross-border networks that play an important but often hidden role in the broad process of decision-making. It is clear that this cross-border cooperation makes a significant contribution to the aforementioned socialisation of national political elites and bureaucrats. The fact that this will make an almost unnoticed contribution to the strengthening of the EU's actorness—of Global Europe—will be emphasised in the following, final section of this chapter.

2.2. The EU as an actor in the world: internal power and external power

The book by Hadfield et al. on continuity and change of EU member states' foreign policy through Europeanisation touched upon an important research question, but it did not sufficiently elaborate upon it. The geographic division into five groups proved to be, on closer inspection, fairly arbitrary and unable to determine much about possible commonalities; and the empirical substantiation remained stuck in generalities. But even more important was the implicit analysis of states as 'black boxes', the strong emphasis on foreign and security policy and not on wider external relations, and the predominantly institutional view of the relationship between member states and the EU. This is symptomatic of much of the literature on the CFSP, as we saw earlier. It is also reflected in the studies that explicitly focus on EU actorness, on the question of whether and to what extent the EU can operate as an autonomous and effective actor in the world and whether it is regarded and accepted as such by third countries. Thus both internal and external factors together determine the role of the EU as an actor in international relations. Figure 2.1 (below) shows schematically which factors and indicators are important. I decided to deviate from the more institutional definitions of actorness and to place more emphasis on social and ideational factors.

As can be seen on the left side of the figure, the EU's internal power is mainly determined by two factors: cohesion and capacity/means. In the current literature on actorness, cohesion is often referred to as the presence of shared national preferences, their translation into common policies, and subsequently the implementation of those policies by both member states and European institutions. This is a fairly institutional and procedural, and thus somewhat static, definition. In Figure 2.1., cohesion is linked to power, which points at a much broader interpretation of the concept of cohesion: declining social inequality within and between member states is an important source of cohesion and ultimately also of actorness. A lack of cohesion at the member-state level may lead to the renationalisation of policies; a lack of cohesion at the EU level can seriously curtail the capacity of EU institutions to act and, moreover, affect the perception of the EU as an efficient actor abroad. The refugee crisis is a good example of this dynamic, which far exceeds the procedural and decision-making dimension. This does not mean that this 'institutional' side of the matter can be dismissed as irrelevant. But even if the European Commission succeeds in formulating a common policy to regulate the flow of refugees, if the social pressure on national governments is then large enough, little will come of the implementation of that policy. Ultimately, institutional cohesion is a derivative of social cohesion. This was not always the case. In the first decades of European integration, there was passive support for this process among broad strata of the population (the masses) but little knowledge and moreover limited interest in it. This gave national and European political leaders (the elites) the leeway to deepen the process without too much opposition (Slater 1982). This so-called *permissive consensus* came to an end with the acceleration of both the deepening and widening of the integration process in the course of the 1990s, and the subsequent debates at the national level about the benefits and drawbacks thereof. This has led some to speak of today's *constraining dissensus* (Hooghe and Marks 2009).

Figure 2.1. **The actorness of the EU: internal and external factors/indicators**

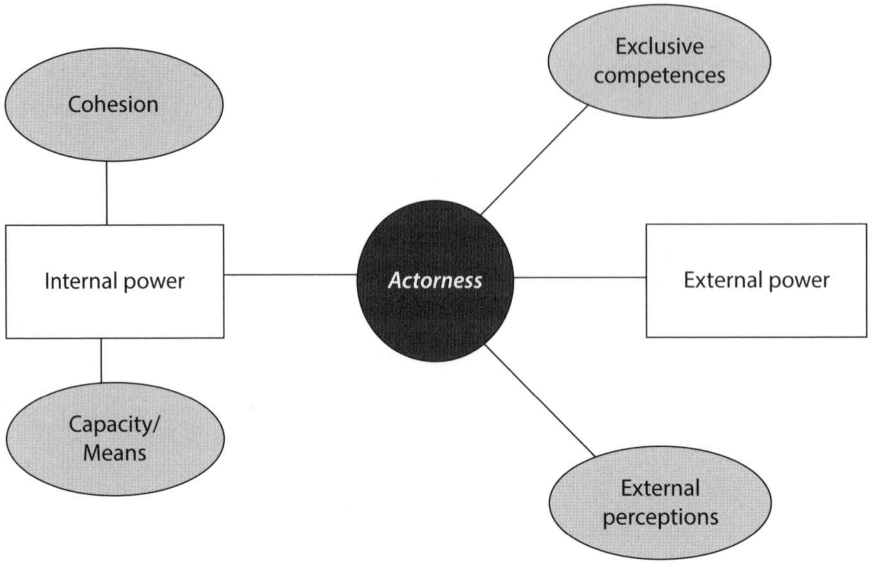

Source: Author

The second internal factor (or indicator) is the capacity of the EU to unite the large variety of actors—both state and non-state—behind a common project or strategy, as well as the means (financial, military, legal, etc.) to speed up or enforce this unity internally and to promote it externally. An example is the structural funds that are also used to increase support among (parts of) the different populations for the European project. In the absence of a supranational military or police capacity, the availability and capacity of policy instruments in the field of international trade agreements, as well as the financial and legal powers conferred on the European institutions through the treaties, are other examples. This is, however, only part of the story. EU capacity also includes the competitive, financial, and technological strength of European businesses. The so-called Lisbon objective, set in 2000, to make Europe the most competitive and dynamic knowledge-based economy in the world by 2010 was as absurd as it was illustrative of what this is about: 'the' European economy is an abstraction behind which concrete industrial enterprises and financial institutions stand—behind which, incidentally, there are also concrete employees and shareholders—that together determine the competitiveness of the EU, thereby contributing to and forming an integral part of the EU's external strength and power.

A decisive factor in the transition from internal power to external power is the presence or absence of European (i.e. supranational) competences in policy areas that have a direct or indirect external impact. We will see in the following chapters that this varies considerably per issue area, but we can conclude here that as EU institutions, and in particular the European Commission, have exclusive competences, they accordingly generate more internal and external actorness. This is first of all related to what is mentioned in most of the literature on EU actorness as an external indicator: the recognition of the EU as an actor by third countries. There are two sides to this: the legal recognition of the EU as a '(quasi-)state' and delegated negotiator, and the de facto acceptance of the EU as an international actor (for example, at international forums such as the G7, the president of the European Council and the president of the European Commission join the seven world leaders). Second, the correlation between exclusive competences and actorness is evident because the EU acts as a representative of the 28 member states. The role of the European Commission as a point of contact in development cooperation with the so-called ACP countries can serve as an example here (see chapter 4).

Finally, the factor of 'external perceptions' plays an important role. We have already seen above that the notorious capability-expectations gap is also largely about the perception that exists outside the EU. On the one hand, this is a function of the capacities and means that have just been discussed; these generate (either high or low) expectations outside the EU. On the other hand, this depends on the extent to which the EU can maintain its internal cohesion. The way in which both the euro crisis and the refugee crisis have been divisive has not gone unnoticed outside Europe. The more the EU 28 come into conflict with each other—the more that constraining dissensus gets the upper hand—the less the EU will be able to function as a role model for other (groups of) countries. This is above all a matter of perceptions and ideas (i.e. as integral parts of our conceptualisation of external actorness), which can change quite dramatically as a result of all kinds of developments. One such development is the emergence of new powers in the international system, something I mentioned earlier. As these new players become an alternative—for example, for developing countries—this will doubtlessly have consequences for existing external perceptions of the EU. A pattern of diminishing expectations and less favourable perceptions—not to mention anti-Western resentment—will have a negative impact on what we might call the EU's external power.

2.3.   Conclusion

In this chapter, some of the most important insights from the literature on FPA were discussed, as a supplement to the theories of international relations and European integration studies in chapter 1. It is clear that we cannot interpret the EU in traditional, foreign-policy terms as a political actor comparable to sovereign states, with its own interpretation of what is still mistakenly called high politics. The EU can hardly be called a security community, and EU institutions have no powers whatsoever in the traditional fields of diplomacy and defence.

Nonetheless, the EU does possess actorness, and increasingly so. If we compare the current EU with its predecessor some thirty years ago, we see that substantial progress has been made in terms of the convergence and integration of national policy. If we subsequently look at the changing external context of the EU, we can conclude that the end of the Cold War has given a new sense of urgency to cooperation at the European level with regard to external relations. And finally, if we consider that most of the more sceptical approaches to EU actorness highlight the traditional CFSP side instead of using a broader, integrated view of external relations, we can conclude that this scepticism is understandable but misconceived as an ultimate evaluation of how the EU as a global player can contribute to solving pressing global problems.

All of this is heavily dependent on the unfolding and further development of the balance of power between the large number of more or less relevant actors at the sub-national, national, transnational, and European levels. On the one hand, these power relations are issue-specific—that is to say, different per policy area—but on the other hand they must also exhibit a certain degree of convergence if the objective of an integrated approach to the EU's external relations as expressed in the Treaty of Lisbon is to be realised.

Suggestions for further reading

(Alden and Aran 2017) offer a nice introduction to the analysis of foreign policy in general (i.e. not specifically about the EU) that pays special attention to the most recent approaches. A more extensive treatise with more than twenty chapters on very different themes, written by a series of authors, is (Smith et al. 2016).

There are many studies on the EU's foreign policy, but the most comprehensive overview is offered by the two volumes of the *Sage Handbook* (Jørgensen et al. 2015) and the second edition of (Keukeleire and Delreux 2014). Keukeleire maintains a nice website with lots of additional information (see http://www.eufp.eu). A slightly older but very accessible introduction is the second edition of (Cameron 2012). Another option is the comprehensive third edition of (Hill et al. 2017), specifically written from the perspective of international relations. (Hadfield et al. 2017), cited in this chapter, analyses various groups of EU member states and their foreign policy.

Finally, those who are interested in the legal aspects of the EU's external relations can indulge themselves in (Kuijper et al. 2015)

It goes without saying that the professional journals that focus on the EU such as the *Journal of Common Market Studies*, *Journal of European Public Policy*, and *European Integration* regularly contain articles covering the broad domain of the EU's external relations. The first journal publishes an annual review that includes an account of the most important developments in the EU's foreign policy over that past year. The *European Foreign Affairs Review* is also an important source of information.

3.   The European Union's trade policy

At the end of the previous chapter, I provided a short definition of what could or should be understood by the term actorness. In Figure 2.1, the concept of power appeared in two forms: internal and external power. Making use of Steven Lukes' famous definition, I will begin this chapter with a brief description of how the EU's internal and external power can be analysed. I will then take a look at the literature which, from the end of the 1990s until the beginning of the euro crisis, started to qualify the EU, seemingly out of the blue, as a superpower (or in words to that effect); indeed, as a power with a high degree of external actorness—even if most authors contributing to the discussion did not use this notion explicitly. An important self-declared reason for this upgrading was the alleged economic and normative status of the EU in the international system. This is why I reproduce this discussion – in conjunction with the debate on Normative Power Europe (NPE) – in this chapter on the EU's trade policy: for if the EU is anything, it is a *trading state* with a large, integrated internal market; a single currency (for a majority of its member states); and a common trade policy towards non-EU countries.

Following this conceptual exposé, I will turn to the emergence, development, and current status of the EU's trade policy. The emphasis will be on the unique supranational character of the decision-making process, the most important institutional and power-political frameworks within which policy priorities are set, and the most significant dilemmas associated with European trade policy. I will end the chapter with two case studies. The first focuses on the hitherto unsuccessful trade agreement between the EU and the US, known as the Transatlantic Trade and Investment Partnership (TTIP). This case study proves that an analysis of external relations should not be limited to a strict institutional enquiry but should also include power relations within society. In the second case study, I will consider the European Common Agricultural Policy (CAP), partly because of its highly disruptive effects on free trade but also because of the importance, yet again, of underlying power relations and the growing pressure, both internal and external, to modify this policy. Both examples—the TTIP and CAP—are battlegrounds in which state and non-state actors face each other in changing configurations. As with the other chapters, I will end this one with a short conclusion and some suggestions for further reading.

3.1.   The EU as a power factor (and actor) in international relations

According to the well-known definition that Steven Lukes takes as his starting point in his acclaimed book *Power. A Radical View*, A exercises power over B if A influences B in a way that goes against the interests of B—in other words, if A can get B to do something that B otherwise would not do. This was Lukes' definition in the first edition published in 1974—a definition he radically changed on two points in the 2005 second edition. In this second edition, he firstly stated that power does not refer to the exercise of power as such but, much more broadly, to the *ability* to exercise power. The threat of power can often be enough and, furthermore, power is often implicit. Secondly, and closely linked to this, Lukes asserted that the influence that A exercises over B does not necessarily have to go against the interests of B; that B does not necessarily have to be forced to do something that he/she would definitely not do without A's power. A can be very powerful by ensuring that B's interests are protected and promoted. Power is, in short, much more than direct domination (Lukes 2005). A good example of this latter revision is the post-war hegemonic configuration within Pax Americana. The so-called Bretton Woods system—named after the small American village where the decision to set it up was made—was the financial and economic framework within the American sphere of influence that was established in 1944. This framework had the clear aim of representing American interests but became such a success due to the fact that Western European countries in particular were happy to accept the American rules of engagement; for various reasons they stood to gain from participating in Bretton Woods institutions such as the International Monetary Fund and the World Bank (see chapter 6).

Lukes identifies three dimensions of power. The first dimension is the means of power and the concrete application of power. In this dimension, power can, in a manner of speaking, be measured. A country's military capability, the ability to decide whether or not to deploy this military power, and the effectiveness of the intervention are examples of this dimension. What is true of military power is also true, for example, of financial means.

The second dimension refers to the power to determine the decision-making agenda, so-called agenda-setting. This is primarily the power to include, or exclude, points on the agenda. Earlier I referred to this as the art of non-decision-making. Not adding a specific topic to the agenda—for example air pollution caused by a prestigious company that generates not only emissions but also jobs—can seriously harm the interests of local residents but would probably prevent measures from being taken against the company. In a later chapter I will look more closely at this dimension in the context of the concept of asymmetrical regulation. For example, during the discussions that took place in the wake of the completion of the internal market on which policy areas should be transferred to European decision-making, member states' social policies were deliberately and explicitly kept off the European agenda (see chapter 6).

The third dimension is power as 'false consciousness'. This is the most invisible expression of power and power relations and, one could add, also the most nebulous (and often criticised as an extremely elitist view of power). In essence, this dimension suggests that opinions, including public opinion, can be manipulated in such a way that ideas take hold that do not correspond to the holders' material interests—or at any rate ideas they would not have held had they not been manipulated. No one would spontaneously declare at breakfast: 'I want peanut butter on my toast!' if this product had never been before produced and was therefore unknown. No one would identify themselves as a Eurosceptic if this concept had not already been formulated and propagated. This somewhat blunt comparison between peanut butter and Euroscepticism shows, on the one hand, that the material world and the imagined world are closely linked (reality and the representation of reality are inseparable and can, furthermore, lead to unusual—or at least unexpected—alliances). On the other hand, it shows that every reality has to be 'sold' as such (peanut butter must be seen as tasty or healthy; Euroscepticism must be seen as acceptable and as protecting one's self-interest). That a thing does not have to be 'true' in order to be 'believed' is clear from the alternative facts propagated by Donald Trump's regime. I will return to this singularly constructivist dimension of power again and again in the course of this book.

3.1.1. The remarkable renaissance of the superpower thesis

It is important to link Lukes' multidimensional definition of power to the EU and its external relations. The best way to introduce this topic is probably to briefly discuss the short period of time during which a surprising number of publications appeared with 'Europe as a superpower' as their theme. These publications appeared within a period of no more than four years prior to the 2008 euro crisis. As a first example, we can take the publication by the well-known futures theorist Jeremy Rifkin. He called his book *The European Dream* as a way of indicating that the European way of life could increasingly serve as an example to the rest of the world. Whereas the American dream emphasises unrestrained economic growth, individual wealth, and the pursuit of self-interest, Europe focuses on sustainable development and the quality of life, the nurturing of community ties, cultural diversity and universal human rights, and global cooperation rather than the unilateral use of force. This idealistic ode to Europe, this 'giant laboratory for the reassessment of the future of humanity', is sustained over no less than 400 pages (Rifkin 2004). It should come as no surprise that Rifkin has been an important influence as a thinker and political advisor in circles connected with the European Parliament and the European Commission: such a forecaster needs to be kept close to hand.

A year later, Mark Leonard, another well-known name in the quasi-academic sector and political consultancy, went so far as to predict the dominance of Europe in the 21st century (Leonard 2005). Here again, we see references to the passing of the American century and the approaching European century. Although countries such as China and India are engaged in an impressive economic catch-up, they are, just like the US, too big, too nationalistic, and too hierarchical to find the necessary means to soften the harsher aspects of globalisation. Europe is in a much better position to do that because Europe's population will put a halt to any federalist moves. The old Europe dragged itself out of the swamp of war and destruction to develop a new form of power based on 'a network of power' that connects states and people within those states through the market, European institutions, and, most notably, international law. Whereas Rifkin emphasises European values and norms, for Leonard it is the non-hierarchical, political and legal setup of the European system that is paramount. And this system is much more effective than the rigid, hard-power-based model of the US. In a time of globalisation, the so-called transformative power of the EU reaches its full potential (as we will see later, Leonard is not the only one to use the term 'transformative', see chapter 5).

A third example is the book by John McCormick, an American professor of political science, with the somewhat bombastic title *The European Superpower*. He too argues that the EU personifies a new type of power that is not coercive but is based on power by example. The extent to which Europe should be included in the world of economic superpowers is inversely proportional to the diminishing importance of military power. What is important here is not so much Lukes' first dimension of power—the dimension related to the means of power such as weapons, territory, and population—but rather control over elements such as trade and investments, technological knowledge and information; and it is here that the EU is particularly well-equipped. Referring to Lukes' dimensions of power, McCormick comes to the conclusion that the successful way in which the EU achieves this should serve as an example to other countries (which incidentally is not totally in line with what Lukes meant). The emphasis here is on Europe's economic and technological power and the unique way in which democracy and capitalism are connected (McCormick 2007).

This latter argument is taken even further in a book published in 2010 entitled *Europe's Promise*. This argues that Europe combines the best of all possible worlds: the social market model that has managed to blunt capitalism's sharpest edges; a democratic pluralism aimed at consensus; superior health care; and sustainable economic development. And here too, under the precept of Global Europe, the main argument is that in a world that is moving towards multipolarity, 'Europe is transforming our very notions of "effective power"' (Hill 2010: 5).

We can all read what we want into these reflections and predictions, and we may reasonably doubt whether these authors would have made the same statements if they had been writing during or after the 2008-2013 euro crisis, but the question remains why the European century was proclaimed with such fanfare during this short period. A positive explanation can be found in the context of the period spanning from 2000 to 2005 in which these books were written, when the EU was going through a complex process of deepening and enlargement. On the one hand, there was the 2003 agreement on the so-called Constitutional Treaty, the purpose of which was to prepare the EU politically and institutionally for the biggest enlargement since its inception. On the other hand, this big bang enlargement was already in its final phase or had just been completed. The 2005 French and Dutch referenda on the constitution—which had the effect of silencing the euphoria, and plunging the EU into a long period of institutional crisis—and the 2008 euro crisis came too late for most of these publications to include them in their analysis.[1] It is therefore highly likely that the optimism of the period had repercussions on the enthusiastic projections of Global Europe. A union of states that, in a relatively short period of time, had managed to oversee the transformation in former Communist countries and was subsequently able to absorb these countries while maintaining its own cohesion could surely not but serve as a shining example to the rest of the world, especially when this success story was compared to the US military interventions that were taking place in the Middle East during the same period.

Later in this book I will introduce some nuance to this optimistic explanation for the sudden flood of studies very keen to raise EU actorness to the level of possible superpower status. I will elaborate on the willingness of European institutions, especially the European Commission, to embrace such predictions, and conclude that the political interest in this quasi-academic literature was (and still is) partly motivated by internal considerations that initially had more to do with the dynamics of the European integration process and less with a concrete and honest assessment of the reality of the global position of the EU as a political, economic, and/or normative power. But first we will take a closer look at an important area in the literature on external relations, namely the question: what sort of power?. Despite the many differences between the studies mentioned above and the ones I look at next, there is one important similarity between them: none of the studies about the EU as a possible international power sees it as a hard or military power. Despite recent attempts to militarise the European integration process, all authors agree with the earlier-cited Moravcsik that such a scenario belongs to the realm of pipe dreams, at least for the time being.

3.1.2.   The proliferation of adjectives: power as a grab bag

In a short overview article that also serves as an introduction to a special edition on the effectiveness of the EU as an actor in the international system, Bretherton and Niemann correctly argue that the emphasis on the question of what kind of power the EU is should be subordinated to and preceded by an analysis of power itself, specifically the effectiveness of such power (Niemann and Bretherton 2013: 262-63). Nevertheless, the flow of adjectives linked to the concept of power as applied to the EU is breathtaking and still growing (see, for example, Wagner 2017). It seems that coming up with a new and original adjective is an attempt to rise just a little bit higher in the Google citation index (see Google Scholar).

Be that as it may be, many of the new contributions to the power debate begin their analysis with a reference to the early characterisation of the EU as a civilian power. It was François Duchêne who, as early as 1972, described the then still very young integrated Europe in those terms. European integration was never intended to make the move into high politics. In the post-war geopolitical configuration, protection was sought and found within Pax Americana. Foreign policy was formed at the national level in consultation with the American foreign policy establishment, and defence policy was collectively organised through the Atlantic Alliance. Within the context of the Cold War, EU member states were able to concentrate on market integration. Foreign policy and defence were a non-issue at the European level for a long time, with the exception perhaps of repeated attempts by France to subject the alleged resurgence of an aggressive German foreign policy—a possible German *Alleingang*—to greater European control. Duchêne formulated this fundamental, non-military integration project as follows:

> Europe would be the first major area of the Old World where the age-old process of war and indirect violence could be translated into something more in tune with the 20th-century citizen's notion of civilised politics. In such a context, Western Europe could in a sense be the first of the world's civilian centres of power. (Duchêne 1972:43)

It is interesting to note that a number of the studies featured in the previous sub-section (3.1.1), written more than thirty years later, are either consciously or unconsciously indebted to this original way of characterising the EU. In particular, the idea that military power will play a less prominent role and will be replaced by economic and financial power is a recurring one in the literature on the international role of the EU. Even Ian Manners, the originator of the aforementioned Normative Power Europe thesis, stated this in so many words, but he also put emphasis on the different focus of his approach (Manners 2002). Although Duchêne did indeed mention Western Europe's specific values and norms, he highlighted civilian means such as trade, investments, and finances, i.e. 'direct physical power in the form of actual empirical capabilities'. In contrast, Manners was more concerned with the role of the EU as a promotor of international norms and 'the power of ideas and norms rather than the power of empirical force—in other words the role of normative power' (Manners 2002: 238). He felt it necessary to go beyond the discussion of state-like elements in external relations, particularly the one-sided focus on European institutions and policy, and concentrate on the EU's international identity.

Manners is particularly concerned with the power to influence opinion, in other words ideological power: the power to determine what is or should be 'normal'. Where does the EU get this power from? Its shared history plays a role, as does its quasi-constitutional political-legal framework. But it is primarily because of the hybrid and polycentric character of the EU—that is, the absence of an overarching, supranational authority—that the emphasis has come to rest on the principles and norms that are shared by all actors in the multilevel governance (MLG) system.[2] Following a summary of these shared norms, Manners correctly concludes that this basis does not mean that the EU is indeed an external normative power. That would require a complicated process of norm diffusion that he claims takes place in six different ways. Without going into too much detail, a study of these diffusion mechanisms makes immediately clear that at least some of them depend on concrete material means to persuade third countries to accept EU norms. For example, under the heading of transference, Manners considers the norms that are tied to financial transactions to less developed countries: the political conditionality (democracy, the rule of law, good governance) linked to EU development assistance is one such more or less forced transfer of norms, which incidentally has not been particularly successful (as we will see in the next chapter).

This last point underlines a problem mentioned earlier in relation to the 'what kind of power' literature: the emphasis is primarily on the adjective and on an ontologically biased polemic over material versus ideational, hard versus soft, or military versus civilian or normative designations in which the noun power—in other words, the effect of such power—is assigned a less central role and/or is not sufficiently substantiated empirically. As a result, a true proliferation of alternative concepts has emerged over the years. A small selection would include Military Power Europe, Normal Power Europe, Market Power Europe, Liberal Power Europe, and any number of variations of power such as soft, smart, negative, military, global, world, small, would-be, great, super, and trading. And it is only very rarely the case that the actual impact of the definition in question is explicitly commented on. A good example here, again returning to NPE, is the case study described by Manners in his 2002 article. As briefly mentioned in the previous chapter, he takes the abolition of the death penalty as an example. This is ostensibly a strong illustration of normative power, as few would argue that there are hard material interests behind the EU's call for its abolition. But if we look at the effects of such a call, the results are downright disappointing. The US, a close ally of the EU, takes little notice of European norms in this area. But even closer to home, candidate member state Turkey has hinted that it will reintroduce the death penalty. A recent study shows that, in the case of Turkey, the EU's normative power produces a sharp split between the government and the opposition, one in which the government seems to be less and less influenced by NPE and the opposition more and more so (Aydin-Düzgit 2018).

This points to an important distinction that can be articulated in two ways. First, receptiveness to EU norms and values seems to depend, at least in part, on specific interests that are in turn related to concrete material positions, in this case within Turkish society. We are, therefore, not necessarily talking about universal, or universally accepted, norms here. Second, the problem of socio-economic and political inequality discussed in chapter 2 may also be relevant here. 'Might gives right', and that does not necessarily have to be European normative 'might'. This brings us to a crucial observation. It is easy but incorrect to criticise the NPE literature by simply stressing the overriding importance of material power. It is even easier to then conclude that it is all about a combination of material and normative power. Rational considerations are central to both the EU and the recipient party. But rational considerations are always particularly rational for some groups and usually serve a specific self-interest. By presenting this self-interest as 'the general interest' and thereby legitimising it, it can become part of a national, regional, or international power configuration.

This brings us to a second much-cited author who, like Duchêne, felt the need at the beginning of the 1970s to shed light on the EU's external power.[3] The author in question is the famous Norwegian sociologist and peace researcher, Johan Galtung. In his 1973 book, *The European Community: A Superpower in the Making*, he criticised the lack of interest within the EU for the, at the time, imminent deepening and widening of the union. The book also included a warning of the consequences of this lack of interest for the world proletariat and the world community, to put it in the jargon of the 1970s. In this, he was one of the first, and also one of the few, researchers who not only raised the question of the EU's superpower status but also commented on the undesirability of such a role in the world. Whereas the NPE almost exclusively highlighted the positive aspects of this form of power, and while many of its adherents speak at best in neutral terms about EU power, Galtung's book was clearly rooted in social criticism.[4]

He saw the EU as a bastion of capitalism that maintained or created internal and external inequality. He believed that the European integration project was explicitly intended to re-establish European power in the world and that its primary aim was thus the resurgence of a Eurocentric worldview. Galtung emphasised two concepts here: structural violence and structural power. The first, developed by Galtung in the 1960s, boils down to the idea that the prevention of physical violence (military repression, war) should only form one aspect of the international peace agenda. Peace did indeed include the absence of violence, but violence could also be structural in the form of withholding basic needs from a large proportion of the population, resulting in child mortality, famine, disease, and so on. A successful peace strategy should focus not only on the absence of physical violence (negative peace) but also on a reduction in global wealth disparities (positive peace), on poverty alleviation and, more generally, on all structural causes of inequality (Galtung 1969). One of these causes was the structural power of the EU which was expressed via three mechanisms: exploitation, fragmentation, and penetration.

Without going very deeply into these three mechanisms, Galtung's message is crystal clear: it is not enough to merely analyse and understand the reality of international power relations—it is just as important to change it. In this context, he saw a danger in the further unification of Europe, as this would entail the maintenance of structural violence through the mechanisms of structural power. But the superpower in the making that Galtung feared was unavoidable. In his final analysis of the possible counterforces (an approach that was customary at the time), he showed little optimism about the possibility for people within the EU to come to this realisation and to rise up in opposition. Counterforces were primarily to be found in the less developed and socialist countries, respectively the third and second worlds (how ironic this now sounds in hindsight, nearly 50 years later). For Galtung believed that workers in the first world, the capitalist West, were too much a part of the system of oppression—influenced as they were by the ideological power of capitalism (Lukes' 'false consciousness')—to be moved to action (Galtung 1973).

If we set aside for a moment the fashionable but rather facile aversion to anything that smacks of (neo-)Marxism, then Galtung's ideas, if adapted to the future, provide at the very least an alternative to the rather self-conscious and positive-optimistic reflections on the current development of the EU's external power. Unlike Manners' NPE example of the abolition of the death penalty, we can identify enough aspects of broad external relations that stem from material interests and can thus be traced back to concrete actors. Given that we have already accepted (in chapter 2) that inequality is a hallmark of societies, then it would be strange if we could not also apply this phenomenon to global society. The key question is whether the EU uses its external power to maintain or increase this global inequality, or to reduce it. This is a question that, more often than not, is answered in ideological terms, and it is a discussion within the social sciences that is largely conducted from the theoretical trenches. One of this book's important underlying objectives is to make this question and the corresponding discussion explicit, and thereby to go beyond most of the general treatises about the EU's external relations—without claiming to give a final twist to either the problem or the debate. Perhaps that should be the book's overarching conclusion: that such a definitive verdict is impossible, precisely because of the ontological reality of the political and socio-economic inequalities that exist within and among the still dominant organisational forms that states are. This is the downside of, and inherent to, the definition of power used in this book.

It is from this perspective that I will review the EU's trade policy in the remainder of this chapter. This is probably, for the time being at least, the area that comes closest to the theoretical reflections on the EU's external relations that are based on assumptions of rational choice and material power. The next section looks at the development and realisation of EU trade policy. This is followed by two sections that consider the various issues from two separate perspectives: internal European power relations and the subsequent conflicts of interest surrounding the TTIP; and power relations and the subsequent conflicts between the EU and the rest of the world with respect to the trade in agricultural products.

3.2.   EU trade policy

Taking a purely quantitative look at the EU's economic presence in the world, there is no doubt that it can be ranked as one of the most important global players. The European Commission itself leaves no doubt about this. The website of the Directorate-General for Trade clearly states how preeminent the EU is in terms of trade and investment.[5] With 500 million consumers, the EU's internal market is essential for exporters from outside the EU and for non-EU companies that move at least a part of their production to Europe. Furthermore, the regulation of this internal market is transparent, with a trustworthy *acquis communautaire* (the cumulative body of all EU laws and regulations) and stable institutions. In 2017, the EU was the second largest importer of goods in the global economy (after the US) and the most important export market for many countries outside the EU (in 2013 more than 80). It was second only to China as the largest exporter of goods. The EU was also the largest exporter and importer of services in the global economy in 2017 (Eurostat 2017). A similar point can be made about the robust position the EU holds in the world economy in terms of incoming and outgoing investments.[6]

Summarised in this manner, national and international trade appears to be a simple matter that can easily be captured in numbers of containers and in euros. In reality, this is an extremely complex, technically demanding subject over which many thousands of lawyers and other specialists chew daily. This chapter will not go into details about this (Meunier 2005 gives a primarily non-technical overview of the

EU's trade policy and the complexity of the associated international negotiations). My primary intention here is to situate the EU's trade policy within the context of the political economy of its external relations (see chapter 2). The challenge here is multi-dimensional, as is often the case. First, the EU has to continually adapt to changing external circumstances and to changing international power configurations. The emergence of new economies, particularly China, means that relatively more growth will take place outside of Europe. This illustrates the importance of international trade for the EU, now and especially in the future. Second, as a single voice in international free trade negotiations, the EU is in actual fact the channel through which a large number and large variety of public and private as well as subnational, transnational, and supranational interests must be negotiated. Third, in terms of bargaining power, the EU also has substantial leverage in the form of a large and valuable market as well as a population with significant purchasing power. And finally, by concluding bilateral trade agreements, the EU tries not only to gain access to new markets but also to influence internal socio-economic and political changes abroad.

That has not always been the case. The power of the EU's supranational trade policy is a function of the depth of its internal integration process. The relatively simple idea of a free trade zone in which two or more countries decide to allow the free movement of goods across their borders does not of itself include a common approach towards third countries. This changes with the next step towards a customs union, which not only gives rise to the free movement of goods but also to an external common trade policy. Obviously, such a common policy cannot be implemented by a single member state. The risk that national considerations would play too large a role is simply too great. In other words, what is required is a supranational negotiator and watchdog to allow the customs union to function appropriately. The next step in the direction of a single or internal market—which aims to introduce not only the free movement of goods but also the free movement of people, services, and capital—further strengthens the need for such 'supranationalisation'. Economic integration of the single market requires a complicated process of national deregulation, and this will only work if re-regulation takes place at the European level. In turn, this requires a policy initiator and, again, a watchdog. In both cases, the European Commission is the most obvious institution. It monitors treaties and verifies whether they are complied with, and also ensures that states not only enter into credible obligations but also fulfil them. It is moreover the obvious link between 'the external dimensions of the EU's internal actions' and 'the EU's external actions', to put it in official, post-Lisbon Treaty jargon (see foreword). As an international trading partner, the EU follows a twofold system of delegation: the member states delegate what are called exclusive powers to the collective of the EU, and the Council of Ministers delegates powers to the European

Commission. The latter then takes up the negotiating mandate and makes contact with third countries. This also means that at least part of the technical expertise required to draw up trade agreements moves to Brussels. Over the years, much of that expertise has become concentrated in the powerful Directorate-General for Trade.[7] It should be made clear that although the European Commission has exclusive powers to conduct negotiations, this does not mean that it has the last word. At the end of the negotiation process, all agreements must be approved by both the Council and the European Parliament. During negotiations, therefore, the European Commission is constantly providing information and consulting with the two other European institutions. Therefore, the phrase 'single voice' used above should be nuanced, also institutionally.

The third ideal-type phase in the EU's economic integration process from customs union to internal market was accompanied by a real fear outside the EU that it could lead to a 'fortress Europe'. This fear turned out to be groundless, not only because (as we shall shortly see) the EU pursued an increasingly liberal policy—so-called commercial internationalism—but also because the fear was not theoretically compelling. The decision to create an internal market had absolutely no impact on the EU's external borders. At the most, the effect was indirect: by releasing internal market forces, European companies competed more with each other, thereby increasing their competitiveness and ultimately enabling them to operate more successfully on the world market. Foreign companies that wanted to profit in the same way from the completion of the internal market could invest in one of the member states and thereby reap the same benefits from this market expansion from the inside.

Closely linked to the issue of Europe's competitiveness was the discussion on the introduction of the euro and the realisation of the European Economic and Monetary Union (EMU), the fourth and last phase. The expectation was that more and more trade would be settled in euros (which would dramatically reduce the risk of exchange loss) but also that the single currency would lead to advantages of scale and competition. (In chapter 6 we will see that the completion of the internal market and the creation of the EMU via the mechanism of asymmetrical regulation also had an important internal effect in the form of so-called structural reforms in the member states.)

In an earlier publication, I introduced the term commercial internationalism (CI) to describe external economic relations, including the EU's trade policy, *and* to emphasise the interaction with the internal deepening of the integration process from the second half of the 1980s (our caesura in this book—see chapter 1).[8] CI is the dual policy of: 1) strengthening the competitiveness of the European business community via a process I termed extended relaunch i.e. with the single market and single currency, and 2) strengthening the European trading state (see below). One of the politicians who symbolised the liberal turnaround in the European integration process like no other was Britain's Sir Leon Brittan. Following a career in national politics, he was a member of the European Commission for a period of 10 years (1989-1999), during which he occupied various positions dealing with competition, trade, and external relations. Halfway through his stay in Brussels, he wrote: 'Creating the best environment for companies to thrive within Europe should go hand-in-hand with a commitment to open trading (...). Europe's top priority must be to create the climate most conducive to the growth of its economy beyond Europe's border' (Brittan 1994: 136). This internal-external link, which aimed to make the EU the most competitive economy in the world (the later Lisbon Strategy, see above) was characterised by another British politician, former Chancellor of the Exchequer and Prime Minister Gordon Brown, as a 'race to the top'.

3.2.1.   The EU as a trading state and as an external power: who are the principals and who are the agents?

The term trading state was first introduced by Richard Rosecrance to emphasise the increasing importance in the 20th century of economic relations between states. In contrast to territorial (or political-military) states, trading states try to increase national wealth through internal development and external trade (Rosecrance 1986: 28). To achieve this, they require open trade routes and export lines. Military power is no longer needed to conquer new territory but to guarantee trade areas. What we are actually dealing with here is a contemporary interpretation of the 'freedom of the seas' thesis developed by Hugo de Groot (or Grotius) almost 400 years ago to secure the commercial interests of the Dutch East India Company. Textbooks usually position Grotius within the neoliberal tradition of IR, and with a bit of good will we can also see him as the originator of the concept of civilian power.

   The similarity between Rosecrance's trading state and the more recent literature on Civilian Power Europe is evident. In his 1986 book, Rosecrance did not reflect on the EU but, entirely in line with his analysis of post-war Japan and Germany (economically strong but with its military wings clipped), he would have described the EU as a 'trading state by default' or a trading state in the absence of other means (ibid: 138). And this clearly corresponds to the EU as a civilian power, as we have seen above. Due in part to the post-war embedding of the defence of Western Europe within the collective security of NATO, and in part to the persistently strong national reflexes in relation to defence policy, EU decision-makers were (and still are) able to focus predominantly on securing open seas, air space, and markets, and on guaranteeing a sufficient supply of strategically essential raw materials. Behind the realism and rationalism of the EU as a civilian power, however, lies a more idealistic and normative side. The aforementioned Brittan often wrote and spoke about the positive ramifications of a world based on free trade for peace, security, democracy, and poverty alleviation. It would be too simplistic to dismiss these expressions of political idealism as empty concepts with the sole aim of disguising particularistic economic interests. We cannot rule out that politicians such as Brittan truly believed, or still do believe, in the civilising effect of free markets. Indeed, this may be why they entered politics in the first place and why they have not, as yet, pursued a better-paying career in the corporate sector.

Whatever the case may be, paradoxically the literature on *civilian* power concentrates, without exception, on the external manifestations of this power and, as we have already seen, almost always ignores the internal sources of that power. An additional problem is that while a correlation, and probably also a causal link, has been established between the remarkable relaunch of the European integration process in the 1980s and 1990s on the one hand and the significant increase in external economic power on the other, the question of how CI could be so successfully introduced and why this took place from the mid-1980s remains unasked.

An important exception to the way in which most studies on the EU's external economic relations, particularly its trade policy, give only cursory mention to non-state actors is the focussed literature on the role of lobby groups and/or national interests on the formation of EU trade policy. We can take as our starting point the debate between Andreas Dür and Cornelia Woll in *Key Controversies in European Integration* (Zimmermann and Dür 2012: 177ff). This controversy deals with the role of lobby and interest groups in the development of the EU's external economic policy. Woll defends the claim that the lobbying activities of organised economic interests take place according to a two-channel logic: protectionist tendencies can best be defended at the level of the member states, and liberal tendencies at the European level. From this she concludes that the European Commission can remain relatively autonomous vis-à-vis societal interests because its success is not determined by the intensity of the lobby but by 'the way it corresponds to Commission objectives' (Woll 2012: 188-9; see also Woll 2009). In other words, businesses can exert a certain amount of influence on the EU's trade policy as long as they embrace the European Commission's most fundamental free market principles. She suggests, however, that it is more likely that the influencing process works in exactly the opposite direction: namely that the EU's trade policy steers the behaviour, preferences, and wishes of the business community, partly because businesses often do not know what they want, and partly due to the complexity of the EU's decision-making structure. This makes it possible for the Commission to select its allies from kindred spirits. Woll uses the term *reverse lobbying* to describe the Commission's impact on businesses (Woll 2008). This interesting argument raises an important question: if business lobbies are only effective if they fall in line with the Commission's established and set preferences, how can we explain the post-1985 tendency of European decision-makers to express trade preferences in increasingly liberal terms? In other words, why was this neo-liberal turn initiated by European decision-makers, as the reverse lobbying concept would suggest?

Eugénia da Conceição-Heldt casts the theory of the Commission's relative autonomy within a *principal agent* setting. She contends that the Commission's negotiating mandate, granted by decree, can degenerate into agency slack (meaning that the 'representative', in this case the Commission, adheres less strictly to the substance and intent of its mandate) if there are strong internal divisions within the principal (the Council of Ministers) (Conceição-Heldt 2010), or if it does not have sustained formal or informal control over the actions of the agent (Conceição-Heldt 2013). In a comprehensive comparative study of the agriculture agenda of the World Trade Organization's Doha Round, Conceição-Heldt concludes that the EU was the sole actor whose position was only marginally determined by private economic interests because of its relative autonomy as a delegated negotiator (Conceição-Heldt 2011a: 19ff; see also Conceição-Heldt 2011b).

This argument is pursued to its conclusion by authors such as Sophie Meunier and Kalypso Nicolaïdes. In her oft-cited *Trading Voices* (see also above), Meunier argues that the 'delegation of trade policy-making authority (...) facilitates the insulation of the process from domestic pressures and, as a result, promotes trade liberalization' (Meunier 2005: 8). This implies that the more protectionist business lobbies initially take place at the national level, thus effectively shielding the EU's trade policy from these (atavistic?) preferences via the practice of delegation. This double delegation of authority (from the member states to the EU, and from the Council to the Commission), along with the relatively complex mix of exclusive and shared competencies, creates an institutional balance of power between national governments and European institutions within which there is no room for private economic interest groups (Meunier and Nicolaïdes 1999, 2006, and 2011).[9]

Regardless of whether this bold denial of the role of the business lobby in matters of external trade holds water (of which more later), what is striking in the above quote from *Trading Voices* is the apparently casual addition of 'as a result'. This is perhaps not as obvious as it sounds. Trade liberalisation can very well be the outcome of socio-political contestation (or not, as we shall see in the next sub-section) rather than delegation. This opposing view can indeed be found in other parts of the literature on the EU's trade policy, which see it as the result of action by powerful business lobbies at various institutional levels (Dür 2012). Alternatively, it is argued that businesses have a finger in the pie, simply because member states still have much say over the EU's trade policy; according to this point of view, businesses primarily influence their national governments (Ehrlich 2009). The common denominator in these studies is the simple conclusion that the most powerful stakeholders have the most influence on the EU's external economic relations. And these just happen to be the biggest companies.

The problem with many of these analyses is that it remains unclear how and by which mechanisms this private influencing of public decision-making takes place. For example, Andreas Dür at one point writes that there is 'business support', and at another that trade policy 'reflects business preferences'. The difference is important but remains unexplained (Dür 2008 and 2012; see also Dür and Elsig 2011). Cornelia Woll, on the other hand, has a point when she contends that this interest-group-focused approach tends to see this influence as a one-way street—that is, coming from one direction only, and primarily from the corporate sector (Woll 2012: 188). Finally, and in addition, the problem is that this approach assumes a general relationship between EU trade policy and private interests but still offers no explanation for the clear liberal turn in the 1980s and 1990s. More specifically, this literature does not establish any links between trade policy on the one hand, and the completion of the single market and the concomitant rise of the competitiveness discourse on the other.

The next sub-section develops a middle ground explanation, introducing a literature that both emphasises reverse lobbying and top-down Europeanisation to shield the EU's external economic relations in general, and its trade policy in particular, from protectionism and economic nationalism, *as well as* the privileged access to European decision-making headquarters enjoyed by a special group of top European businesses that are united in the European Round Table of Industrialists (ERT). In doing so, the difference between lobbying and agenda-setting will be discussed in greater detail. The emphasis will be on the importance of the public-private partnership between the European Commission and the ERT, which is based on a political programme aimed at strengthening competitiveness and CI. This partnership was of vital importance just prior to the relaunch of the European integration process in the mid-1980s, particularly as it saw structural reforms at the state level and external economic expansion as two sides of the same coin. The relaunch of European integration from the mid-1980s, which started with the completion of the internal market and culminated in the establishment of the EMU, brought the completion of these twin objectives so close that, paradoxically, it also gave rise to a richly diverse group of counterforces.

3.2.2. The partnership between the European Commission and European business: *commercial internationalism* explained

As indicated in chapter 2, we can only fully understand the rise of a 'neo-liberal Europe' or 'market power Europe' (Damro 2012) if we try to approach it from a heterodox political-economic perspective. Without going into too much detail (for those interested, see Ryner 2012), the essence of this approach is that we first take the interaction between politics and socio-economic processes seriously, and second, that we try to find underlying (and shifting) power configurations between public and private, state and non-state actors at various interwoven decision-making levels. In what follows, it is categorically *not* my intention to claim that the partnership between the Commission and the ERT overshadowed all other possible and actual interest communities and condemned them to irrelevance. It is furthermore incorrect to suppose that there is a simple causal relationship between on the one hand the liberal turn in the EU's internal and external policy and, on the other, the burgeoning cooperation between the Commission and the business community on the basis of mutual interests. The emergence of CI most certainly did not take place without a struggle and was not even broadly accepted within the ERT (see Van Apeldoorn 2002: 115ff, and Holman 1996). In the following, my aim is modest: to look for an explanation for the moment at which the change came about, somewhere in the 1980s, and to determine which actors took the initiative. Recalling what was said in chapter 2 about the formation of coalitions and in chapter 1 about the crisis in the integration process prior to the relaunch, we can probably assume that a number of enlightened minds came up with roughly similar ideas at the same time about how to get out of the impasse. We can further assume that these 'minds' had the strategic sense to realise that a unified force might be essential to either convince other actors and get them on board or present them with a fait accompli. And that this alliance could, in a specific historical context and as part of a complex, multidimensional, and multilevel whole—what I call a power configuration—take the lead and determine the direction and content of the recent European integration process.[10]

The public-private partnership between the European Commission and the ERT is probably one of the most influential alliances in the history of the EU.[11] The European Commission is the European institution that proposes legislation and thus plays a central role in policy planning. An important part of this planning process is setting the policy agenda. What topics are important and urgent enough to be transferred to the European level? And which elements of a broader interpretation of a topic should be taken on board and which should be left to be dealt with at the national level? For example, we could decide to put the completion of the single market on the agenda, which would intensify competition between European businesses, but simultaneously decide to have accompanying social measures—to provide some degree of compensation to the losers—fall under national sovereignty.

It is thus important who determines the topics that are added to the European agenda and how. It goes without saying that the Commission does not operate independently. To begin with, every idea has to be accepted and approved by the member states, and their opinions can best be gauged at an early stage. Second, the Commission does not initiate policy in a vacuum but usually in reaction to societal problems and challenges. It is always on the lookout for so-called windows of opportunity.

And it is precisely here, and in the context of the 1980s and 1990s, that the ERT gained a particularly privileged position as the Commission's co-partner in agenda-setting. This was apparent in three main areas: the neo-liberal redesign of the common European market; the specific details of the economic and monetary architecture surrounding the introduction of the euro; and the global market focus of the CI strategy. It is important to reiterate that these three topics were part of an all-embracing and integrated strategy that can most effectively be described as competitiveness.

The ERT was set up in 1983 as a joint initiative of the then European Commissioner for Industrial Affairs, Etienne Davignon, and Pehr Gyllenhammer, the CEO of Swedish carmaker Volvo. The founding members were businesses in the electronics, automobile, and steel industries, all companies that by their own account were facing strong competition from the US and Southeast Asia in particular (in the 1980s primarily from Japan). The stated aim of these 'knights' of the European business community was to provide a platform for dialogue between European industry and policymakers at both the European and national levels. In turn, this dialogue had two aims: to find a joint solution (i.e. political and economic) to the alleged loss of competitiveness vis-à-vis their most important competitors, and to secure political support (particularly from within the Commission) for the internal market project (Cowles 1994). In the years that followed, particularly during the Delors Commission, this symbiosis reached a peak (although one could argue that its influence remained incommensurate until the 2005 referenda in France and the Netherlands on the European Constitution which plunged the EU into a long-term political and institutional crisis, and the financial-economic crisis of 2008-2013).

The partnership can be described as a symmetric, interdependent alliance in as much as that neither party directed or dominated the other and that they had a mutual interest in working together. Both partners needed the other to achieve their largely overlapping goals. Even at an early stage, a member of Delors' cabinet said of the captains of industry united in the ERT: 'We see this group as a very useful bunch of people. These men are very powerful and very dynamic. They seed us with ideas. And when necessary, they can ring up their own prime ministers and make their case' (cited in Merritt 1986: 22). In other words, the Commission was very well aware of the opportunities offered by its alliance with the ERT in its own attempt to strengthen its position vis-à-vis the member states. Conversely, the ERT had an interest in developing a good relationship with the Commission, given its executive and co-legislative power. The fact that the Commission has a quasi-monopoly in the areas of policy planning and innovation as well as delegated power in the area of external trade makes it an obvious political target for a large number of interest groups. And with hindsight we can clearly state that the ERT had a clear *primus inter pares* role in these three areas. And that is hardly surprising if we look closely at the ERT's clout. It is comprised of a group of around 50 CEOs representing internationally operating European industrial enterprises, with a joint turnover of more than 2,250 billion euros. These companies generate 6.8 million jobs in the EU and annually invest more than 50 billion euros in research and development (see https://www.ert.eu).

The neoliberal approach introduced in the 1980s, which I briefly mentioned in the foreword (see also chapter 6), sought to resolve the perceived disadvantage the EU had with its main trading competitors by drastically adjusting the supply side of the EU economies. It was agreed that none of the other decisions taken in the context of European integration should be in conflict with this one overarching aim of restoring competitiveness. That is why, in 1994, the ERT suggested setting up the Competitiveness Advisory Group (CAG) which would act as 'a watchdog, by subjecting policy proposals and new regulations to the test of international competitiveness' (ERT 1994: 3). The CAG, composed primarily of representatives of the European business community, was established in 1995. As this group directly advised the European Commission, we can justly describe this as the institutionalisation of the partnership between the Commission and the European business community, with the primary aim of putting—and keeping—the question of competitiveness high on the European agenda.

Alongside this concrete example of the CAG, the ERT regularly found a willing ear among both national and European politicians. At strategic moments—and preferably just before European summit meetings—the ERT often published reports and memoranda with concrete priorities and suggestions for European policy. These reports were sent to national and European decision-making bodies. At the same time, the ERT discussed these ideas with the president and various members of the Commission, and contacted ministers and the prime minister of the country holding the six-month presidency of the European Council. This became a fixed ritual within the ERT: at least twice a year, just before a European Council meeting, ERT members would come together for a plenary session to which they would invite the prime minister of the presiding country for an 'informal exchange of ideas'.[12]

An important number of key decisions taken at the European level can thus be traced back at least partly to initiatives taken by members of the ERT. We should not be shocked or surprised by this. To begin with, European integration until its relaunch was primarily an economic integration. Secondly, during the 1970s and the beginning of the 1980s, European industry fell into a state of deep crisis. Thirdly, the integration process was stagnating during this period, as evidenced by several moves to renationalise crisis management policies. Fourthly, there was a growing conviction, justifiable or not, that the post-war welfare state had in at least two aspects reached its limit: budget deficits and national debts were growing, and unemployment levels and benefit payments were increasing. And in the fifth place, vulnerable European industries such as shipbuilding, steel, automobiles, and electronics felt threatened by the penetration of imports coming primarily from Asia. National governments faced significant pressure to protect national sectors in crisis from 'unfair' competition from non-European countries. It was clear that the risk of disintegration became real in this context (after all, European integration was, to repeat it once more, primarily economic integration). From this vantage point, and in hindsight, it makes perfect sense that the two parties with the most to lose from such a scenario—namely the Commission and that part of the business sector whose main market was the EU—would join forces and take the offensive by championing liberalisation, deregulation, and privatisation through single market integration—all of which would be underpinned by the EMU and with a key role for the Commission—as well as expansion on the world market via multilateral and bilateral trade agreements, through the strategy of CI.

And the neoliberal turn cut both ways. On the one hand, the completion of the single market and the introduction of the single currency strengthened the role of the EU as a global actor, enabling it to become one of the main driving forces behind a phenomenon that from the 1990s came to be known as globalisation. In contrast to what politicians such as Margaret Thatcher would have had us believe, namely that there was no alternative and that globalisation forced us to implement internal reforms, the EU became a proactive player in a global economy that was becoming more open, complex, and interdependent. As Sir Leon Brittan put it, the EU's external trade policy 'converted the single European market into a vast negotiating lever to win global access for European exports and investment by challenging our partners to be as open as we are to them' (cited in Meunier 2005: 21). On the other hand, granting access to the largest internal market in the world was a massive instrument of power for the EU in international negotiations. This was reinforced by the change in the EU's trade strategy in the 1990s (and still in effect today) from managed multilateralism to open bilateralism, partly due to the failure of the WTO Doha Round of free trade negotiations, and partly as a reaction to the growing markets offered by emerging economies.[13] After all, the power of an actor is felt more directly and is more effective in bilateral contacts than in the complexity of multilateral negotiations.

A good illustration of what we have thus far discussed is the establishment of the Trans-Atlantic Business Dialogue (TABD) in 1995. This transatlantic network included representatives of the American government, the European Commission, and American and European businesses. Members of the ERT played a prominent role in this latter group. The aim of the TABD was to deregulate trade between the US and the EU within the framework of the so-called New Transatlantic Agenda, which was signed with great fanfare in Madrid in 1995. It is important to note here that the TABD largely belies the generally accepted idea that trade agreements are a matter for and between governments. One example is the Transatlantic Mutual Recognition Agreement (MRA) dating from 1997-98. The then US Secretary of Commerce, William Daley, plainly stated: 'I also want to give credit to the TABD. The TABD said the MRA was important; we heard them and acted'.[14] In Europe, too, the TABD was a public-private partnership that, in the words of Maria Cowles, effectively amounted to a 'Europeanisation of business-government relations' (Cowles 2001: 159). According to Cowles, this Europeanisation also had a top-down component. As top companies gained privileged access to the Commission via the ERT and the TABD, so the traditional national relationships between governments and businesses also changed character. 'As large companies discredited the "national route" of EU policymaking in favour of direct negotiations with European institutions, domestic business-government relations were challenged' (ibid: 178). This brings us back to an earlier concept, reverse lobbying, but with a slightly different twist, that of reverse agenda-setting. The US and the EU wanted to use the 1997-1998 MRA not only to steer the global trade agenda—an aim that was explicitly reiterated at the launch of the TTIP, as we will see shortly—but also to determine de facto the agendas of less dynamic governments and companies at the national level. CI thus incorporated several Europeanisation effects, both upwards and downwards, as well as external Europeanisation of policy and the consequences thereof.

The TABD in fact lost much of its power in the years following the MRA. Likewise, very little of its ambitious deregulation agenda was realised. It was only with the election of Barack Obama as US President in 2008 that the transatlantic dialogue came back to life, but the reason for this was, initially at least, a negative one. Obama had given priority to his pivot-to-Asia strategy, instilling in Europe the fear that the US would drift away. It is this fear that is often cited as providing the inspiration to the EU to re-open the transatlantic agenda via the Transatlantic Trade and Investment Partnership (TTIP).

3.3.   Case study I: the TTIP as a source of (trans)national conflict

At the height of the 2008-2013 crisis, researchers and commentators whose work involved studying and analysing the EU were briefly distracted from the paramount issue of the member states' austerity programmes. The reason for this was a series of international events related specifically to external trade relations.

First, the EU and China were embroiled in a number of trade disputes, such as a dispute related to solar panels in the first half of 2013. Accusing the Chinese government of subsidising solar panels which were then sold cheaply on the growing

European market where they competed unfairly with products made in the EU, the then European Commissioner for Trade, Karel De Gucht, at first tried to punish these Chinese dumping practices with import levies. This provoked countermeasures by China, leading in July of that year to a compromise that did not turn out well for European producers. De Gucht was put under pressure by a coalition of EU member states under the leadership of Germany. The German government was, in turn, under pressure from the *Bundesverband der Deutschen Industrie*, the umbrella organisation of employers, which feared a serious disruption to Germany's trade relations with China. There are three points to note here: German industry successfully managed to lobby its own government; unity within the EU was in short supply; and the supranational authority of the European Commission on trade issues was called into doubt.[15]

Secondly, a few months after the Brazilian Roberto Azevêdo was appointed Director-General of the WTO on 1 September 2013, Brazil announced that it would press for a bilateral trade agreement with the EU. Confronted with serious internal economic problems and difficult relations within its regional trading block, Mercosur (which the EU believed should be its negotiating partner), Brazil made a conscious decision to give regional and multilateral frameworks lower priority. Brazil was not alone in this; partly because of the continuing impasse within the WTO, more and more emerging (and developed) economies have sought refuge in bilateral agreements. The EU itself has played an active role in this erosion of trade multilateralism by concluding a large number of trade agreements since the failure of the WTO Doha Round.

A third event was triggered by the start of negotiations in the first half of 2013 regarding what initially promised to be the most spectacular trade agreement ever made. In the words of José Manuel Barroso, then President of the European Commission, the completion of the TTIP would be nothing short of a game changer and 'a boost to our economies that does not cost a cent of tax-payers' money' (cited in the *Financial Times* of 14 February 2013, page 1). De Gucht too made it clear that the importance of the TTIP transcended purely economic interests. Such an agreement would certainly be in the interests of 'our industries' but was also a political weapon of the first order. He rightly stated that there was no longer any 'low-hanging fruit'; after all, free trade between the two trading giants on either side of the Atlantic Ocean had already been largely realised. The emphasis now would be on the removal of non-tariff trade barriers and the mutual recognition of standards. And since together these two giants make up approximately half of the global economy and one-third of global trade, the TTIP would determine the rules of the game for the rest of the world (ibid).

This was one of the original arguments with which the supporters of the TTIP justified their position. The other important reason was the expected positive effect on economic growth and the creation of extra jobs (incidentally, this was exactly the same reasoning used for the completion of the internal market in the 1980s). Ferdi de Ville and Gabriel Siles-Brügge were two of the first authors to criticise these formal justifications in book form. They clearly showed that the power of the emerging economies was now so great that they would not unquestioningly accept a game-changing dictate from the old West. They also showed that the idea of the TTIP as a motor for job creation was grossly exaggerated and had been called into question by a number of authoritative studies (De Ville and Siles-Brügge 2016). If this analysis is correct and no substantial advantages could be achieved in either area, the question arises as to why national and European politicians stubbornly held on to the TTIP and initially did all in their power to protect the bilateral negotiations from any form of interference by civil-society actors. Was it ignorance, or worse, incompetence? Was it the result of ideological tunnel vision that ruled out any empirically substantiated argument from refuting the sacred belief in the benefits of free trade? Or did the efforts of politicians on both sides of the Atlantic Ocean serve other interests—and if so, what interests?

We can also look at this issue from another angle. As the reputed advantages of the TTIP came to be increasingly called into doubt, more attention was paid to its suspected negative effects. Three themes were central to the criticism of the negotiations: two technical, and one political.

Firstly, opponents of the TTIP feared that the principle of mutual recognition of regulatory measures, the acceptance of regulatory equivalence, or even the harmonisation of regulatory measures could lead to a downward adjustment of European standards in the fields of labour, health, and food safety. The advantages for businesses was obvious: they would no longer have to conform (or at least to a much lesser extent) to two different sets of regulations. The fear arose, however, that the more flexible regulations in the US would lead to the European market being flooded with chlorinated poultry; industrial, hormone-treated meat; and genetically modified food.

Secondly, there was a significant though not always legitimate aversion to the introduction of an Investor-to-State Dispute Settlement, a system of dispute resolution whereby private investors could lodge an appeal against the supposed arbitrariness of public authorities. Opponents of the TTIP saw this as a confirmation of what they considered to be the unbridled power of big business. Companies would be able to take a democratically elected authority to court before an in-dependent (read: secretive and entrepreneur-friendly) tribunal if they disagreed with a democratically taken decision. The criticism had, of course, much to do with the overarching political argument against the TTIP, namely the allegedly undemocratic negotiations, specifically the unequal access of non-state actors to the European Commission. Initially, information was exclusively shared under strict confidentiality (for example only with members of the relevant commission of the European Parliament), and it was only after Greenpeace put many of the relevant negotiating documents online in 2016—in what became known as ttipleaks—that the Commission actually started working on the transparency of the EU's trade policy that it had announced earlier (see https://trade-leaks.org/ttip/).

This third theme, the supposed democratic deficit regarding the state of affairs surrounding the TTIP, was in the period between 2013 and 2016 soon reduced to a simple juxtaposition of the big and powerful business community and the various one-issue movements operating within European civil society. The former group was seen as a collective evil genius, responsible for all the negative aspects of the trade agreement which, behind the smokescreen of complicated technical details, would eventually be forced down citizens' throats. At its presentation of the leaked TTIP documents, Greenpeace stated that while the environment and consumers were being threatened, businesses could get whatever they wanted, with the whole process amounting to 'opening the door for corporate takeover'. Over the course of the TTIP negotiations, the second group (i.e. European civil society organisations) became more and more assertive and active, organising massive demonstrations and mobilising as many citizens and politicians as possible. It thus became gradually obvious that opponents of the TTIP would not be convinced by any technical arguments raised by the supporters, however well-founded they might be. The feeling gradually prevailed that citizens had to resist the practices of 'the' Americans, 'the' business community, and 'the' European elite in order to defend fundamental European values. In this way, the countermovement gave a whole new meaning to the concept of Normative Power Europe (unintended by the original creator of the term): it was a concentration of power to defend threatened values rather than to actively promote them. In the end, it was also an indictment against that 'other' normative Europe: that of the neoliberal ideology and the Anglo-Saxon model of capitalism, including the mantra of privatisation, liberalisation, and deregulation.

The principal point here is not to determine whether the proponents or opponents were (or are) intrinsically right but to ascertain whether the opponents' claim that the business community is the most dominant player in the negotiation game is correct. In the first place, it should be stated that if corporate Europe really was as powerful as its opponents claim, every form of opposition would be more or less futile. Secondly, the categorisation 'the business community' is too generic; the definition needs to be specified and honed if it is to be politically and strategically effective. And thirdly, the economic determinism in the assumption that the CEOs of European business take national and European politicians (and negotiators) by the hand and tell them what to do and what not to do is a clear oversimplification. It really is important for European institutions, particularly the Commission, to continue to play an active role in the aforementioned 'open bilateralism'. And it cannot be ruled out that the politicians concerned really do believe in the adequate protection of all sorts of civil interests and in the positive effect of further free trade, be it for geopolitical or geo-economic reasons. The picture that emerges from the coverage of the negotiations and from ttipleaks clearly shows that there was constant consultation between the Commission and businesses, and that the latter certainly played an important role in the *co*-determination of the negotiating agenda and negotiating positions. Furthermore, as the aim of the TTIP always was to make transatlantic trade easier for companies, it is not entirely surprising that such a partnership arose.

But something has been overlooked. The unprecedented mobilisation of counter-forces at every conceivable European decision-making level was, at first, seen as an inconvenient but temporary sidestep off the (neoliberal) path. It was not until the protests continued to grow and even found political response that it became clear that proponents of the TTIP would also have to defend and/or present their case better. One may well wonder whether such a reaction in defence of a transatlantic trade deal was not too little too late and was, in fact, doomed to failure, particularly because the most important socio-economic and political repercussions of the euro crisis in 2013-2016 had not yet been fully dealt with. There was still a very deep mistrust of European elites, capitalists, and Americans.

It is impossible to say what would have happened had Donald Trump not pulled the plug on the TTIP negotiations, but we can make a reasoned, step-by-step hypothesis. In the first place, we can assume that the mass demonstrations against the TTIP would have slowly fizzled out, in the same way the protracted demonstrations and protests again the recent austerity policies did. Secondly, in the case of the TTIP, the analogy with the protests against austerity measures is largely flawed due to another important point. Trade agreements in general, and the TTIP in particular, are nowadays no longer solely concerned with the removal of tariffs or even non-tariff barriers. They often include clauses that directly or indirectly touch on issues of environmental protection and health care—issues that also often fall under national jurisdiction. This means that it is no longer accurate to speak of exclusive competencies at the European level when discussing trade agreements. And this in turn means that national governments, and thus national parliaments, also have a voice. And thus, thirdly, a successfully completed TTIP treaty would have been submitted not only to the European Parliament but also to 28 (for the time being) national parliaments, and in the case of some member countries (Belgium for example), to regional parliaments as well. In some member states, the mood was already so hostile to the TTIP that there was a real likelihood that somewhere within the EU (and probably in more than one place) a parliament would have blocked it. And then there were the spontaneous actions already taken by local authorities in the EU to protect themselves from a possible agreement under the motto TTIP-free zones.

It has been suggested that over recent years (specifically, since 2008), civil society organisations have had a greater impact on European decision-making. The alleged reason for this is the fact that the single market, including all kinds of measures to increase the competitive edge of European businesses, has to a large extent been achieved, which creates more room for civil society. Furthermore, such civil society organisations tend to select high-profile or eye-catching themes to bring to the attention of the general public. Due to populist and Eurosceptic forces, the public is already more sensitive to European issues. This is an opportunity for the European Commission to listen to voices that do not, for a change, have competitiveness at the top of their agenda and that do not originate in the echelons of the powerful and wealthy top layers of society.

We can draw two conclusions from all this. If the TTIP negotiations had been continued and brought to a successful conclusion, it would have considerably increased the likelihood of a democratic veto, or the final deal would have been amended to such an extent that a majority of the opponents could have agreed to it after all. Secondly, and going beyond the specific example of the TTIP, it is clear that in such cases, large transnational companies do not necessarily always have the upper hand. Thanks to the system of checks and balances that are built into our multilevel governance system, it is apparently possible to mobilise counterforces and to make use of the (national and European) parliamentary routes available to us.

In the next example we will see the rise of a totally different power configuration since the 1950s, which has had a decisive impact on how European trade policy has been worded but which has come under increasing external and internal pressure.

3.4. Case study II: the Common Agricultural Policy and the Janus face of the EU

We noted earlier that although the partnership between the Commission and the ERT played an important role in situating competitiveness at the heart of the European agenda, this did not mean that every interest group could be rendered ineffective or that the liberal trend, initiated by the partners, would not face any opposition within the EU. We dealt with one such reasonably effective opposition movement in the previous section. Another example is the EU's Common Agricultural Policy (CAP) which, since its inclusion in the Treaty of Rome, has been one of the most unruly and problematic, and thus most criticised, policy areas. It shows that there are apparently vested interests at work in the EU that have thus far managed to prevent the complete dismantling of the CAP despite the dominance of industrial interests at the European level. The export-oriented industry has a clear interest in further liberalisation of global trade. Given that the ongoing protectionist agricultural policy of the EU (and, incidentally, of the US) continues to form one of the biggest stumbling blocks to a new round of WTO negotiations, we can only conclude that the agricultural lobby within Europe still has the upper hand on this issue.

The EU's founding treaty listed explicit reasons for fulfilling France's desire for cooperation in the area of agriculture (art. 39 of the Treaty of Rome). To begin with, the Second World War was still fresh in the mind, which meant that the fear of food shortages had not completely disappeared. Guaranteeing a sufficient supply of food was therefore specifically mentioned as an aim. A second general aim was market stabilisation: excessive fluctuations in the demand, supply, and prices of food had to be avoided at all costs. This was closely related to two other aims: guaranteeing that the consumer had access to sufficient food at a reasonable price, and ensuring that the rural population had a reasonable standard of living 'in particular by increasing the individual earnings of persons engaged in agriculture'. In the short term, these latter two aims could not be realised simultaneously—low consumer prices did not go hand in hand with higher earnings for agricultural workers. The solution was found in increasing agricultural productivity. This policy was already being implemented in several of the founding member states, particularly in the Netherlands, where the spiritual father of the CAP, Sicco Mansholt (who later became European Commissioner), had held several important political posts related to agriculture since 1945. Research at agricultural colleges and universities resulted in the technical advancement of the agricultural sector, which led to the optimal use of the agricultural labour force, and to greatly increased production, thus meeting the double aim of reasonable prices and incomes. Furthermore, the 'optimum utilisation of the labour force' was necessary because the post-war industrial expansion in Western Europe had led to labour displacement to better paying industrial enterprises.

During the reconstruction phase immediately after the Second World War, Western European countries had introduced measures to protect their national agricultural sectors. It was this that gave Mansholt the idea of creating a common market for agricultural products that would stop protectionism at the national level but introduce it at the EU level—a perfect example (and historically the first of its kind) of deregulation at the national level via re-regulation at the European level. The single market was one of the three principles of the CAP. The second principle was financial solidarity with the agricultural sector. Government subsidies would have to help this neglected sector get back on its feet. The third principle is what is referred to as community preference: the preference for and emphasis on agricultural products produced within the EU had an important effect on the relationships that the six original EU (then EEC) members had with other countries. Taking the objective of 'our own products first' seriously meant that the common market had to be protected from external competition. In order to better understand the external consequences for the EU's trade policy, a short explanation is necessary to clarify how these three principles were jointly realised in a system of price support and market regulation.

Target prices for essential agricultural products such as dairy, beef, and grains were set annually. These were prices that farmers had to receive for their products in order to guarantee the objective of a reasonable standard of living. EU agriculture ministers set these target prices jointly during what often amounted to difficult negotiations with conflicting national interests. Completely in line with the sector's accepted mores, this political horse-trading went on into the small hours of the night, often with a steady supply of alcohol, until it was finalised. The artificial target price led to a second, lower price—the intervention price. If the actual price in the common agricultural market—that is, the internal market price resulting from the natural progression of supply and demand—dropped below the intervention price, European agencies would intervene and buy up products, i.e. remove products from the market. This would increase demand and consequently increase the price again. Two additional challenges remained: how to prevent the import of cheap agricultural products from keeping internal market prices low and the need for intervention correspondingly strong, and what to do with the products bought up by the intervention agencies. The first challenge was met by introducing import levies. If the world market price for a particular product from a third country was lower than the price in the internal market, then an import tariff was imposed that brought the price to just under the target price. The result was the so-called threshold price which was set at the level of the target price minus the necessary transport costs needed to get the product from the EU's external borders to its final destination. This threshold price effectively kept cheap agricultural products from outside the EU away from the internal market. The second challenge was met by introducing export restitutions: subsidies to exporters of agricultural products with the aim of bringing the export price in line with world market prices and thereby making EU agricultural products artificially competitive. This system of export subsidies also meant that the products bought up by the intervention agencies could be dumped onto the world market.

Clearly this system of price support and market organisation was to sooner or later meet its limits, both figuratively and literally. As a result of the alarming reports coming from the Club of Rome (particularly the *The Limits to Growth* report, published in 1972), some politicians (including Mansholt) and researchers were already expressing their reservations about the CAP in the 1970s. This criticism grew stronger and stronger throughout the 1980s and 1990s with what would prove to be far-reaching consequences. At first, the focus was on the overproduction of certain agricultural products and the negative environmental effects resulting from this. How could it be otherwise: the CAP paid a premium for increased scale, efficiency, and productivity, and it did not matter how much you produced or whether the market became saturated, as the intervention price (the social safety net) was always there as a guarantee. This stimulated farmers to expand and the intervention agencies to buy up even more surpluses from farmers. The result was the 'butter mountains' and 'milk lakes' that captured Europe's imagination in the last decades of the 20th century.

The costs associated with maintaining the CAP grew and took up an ever-increasing part of the EU budget. Furthermore, the system was susceptible to fraud and worked to the advantage of large-scale agricultural industries in some member states and to the disadvantage of smaller businesses in other member states (the so-called anti-regional impact of the CAP).[16] And finally, and importantly for this discussion, the CAP became an increasing liability to the further development and intensification of the EU's external relations. As the industrial interest in CI started to grow during the 1980s and 1990s, so the calls for radical reforms of the CAP grew louder. To reproduce a few of the comments from that time: 'the fatal success of the European farmers'; 'the crazy system that cannot be explained'; 'our agrarian politics is immoral'; and 'the EU is the only remaining institution in the post-Cold War period that still honours the out-dated Soviet system'. All these comments were about the CAP.

All this eventually led to a series of changes, beginning with the MacSharry reforms in 1992 which were named after the then European Commissioner for Agriculture. These measures, which included a gradual shift from price support to direct income subsidies, primarily affected the internal working of the CAP. Later reforms were increasingly directed towards dismantling the CAP's market-distorting effects, which put export subsidies and import levies in particular under pressure. The EU was seen as a Janus face—an outward-looking trading power with two faces and double standards. On the one hand, the EU was a fervent advocate of open markets and multilateral free trade frameworks, but on the other it kept CAP alive behind high tariff walls. Moreover, this became increasingly incompatible with the EU's attempts (and those of the US) to strike new deals on the further liberalisation and deregulation of world trade during the WTO Doha Round.

During the Doha negotiations, which started in 2001, the EU and the US quickly found themselves diametrically opposed to countries that would benefit from the opening up of Western agricultural markets as a result of the dismantling of protectionist structures such as the CAP. This stumbling block, along with other points of difference, initially caused the negotiations to fail. This led to the drawing up of 'negotiation modalities' in July 2008, which consisted of three main themes. First, the internal support that the EU, the US, and Japan provided to their own agricultural sectors was a thorn in the side of those who supported a fair playing field. Second, market access became a central theme in the negotiations. This boiled down to the issue of reducing customs tariffs (in the case of the EU, the aforementioned import levies) and whether certain exemptions from the general reduction could be accepted. For example, special or 'sensitive' products might be excluded, temporary measures could be taken to avoid excessive market disruption (as a result of a dramatic increase in imports), and limited tariff reductions could be accepted for developing countries. And finally, under the third theme of export competition, negotiations focussed on the removal of export subsidies and all sorts of indirect subsidies such as the provision of export credit (for a useful summary of the course of events during the Doha negotiations in relation to agriculture, see Massot 2017).

In general, since 2008 the most progress has been made on this third theme of export subsidies. For example, the EU has abolished most of its export restitutions. There has also been some progress on the other two themes, although in practice this has been more difficult than the partial agreements reached so far would suggest. All in all, this means that while the EU still prefers comprehensive, multilateral trade agreements aimed at unleashing market forces (in line with CI), the stagnation of the Doha Round has made the EU move into the second-best direction of 'open bilateralism'.

Alongside the ever stronger call for far-reaching changes to the CAP, there are also those who have sounded a note of caution in recent years against overly drastic changes for fear that the proverbial baby will be thrown out with the bath water. Recent slogans that are diametrically opposed to the criticism of CAP include: 'we must stand behind the CAP'; 'calls for radical reforms of the CAP are misplaced and outdated'; 'the CAP is a cheap way to ensure our future'; and 'without subsidies, our food security will be in danger'. These statements stem from very different interests than those of the dreaded agricultural lobby and can be divided into roughly two categories. The first group stems from the age-old aim of guaranteeing a sufficient supply of reasonably priced food. Since the major international food crisis of 2008 (which was repeated on the eve of the Arab Spring in 2011), we know that sudden increases in the price of basic needs—sometimes the result of failed crops and/or periods of drought but at other times, and more cynically, the result of financial speculation on futures markets—may not only lead to outbursts of spontaneous popular anger but also threaten the availability of supplies. Seen in this light, food security in a globalised economy is not necessarily self-evident. Together with the realisation that both the global population and global purchasing power will rise sharply, the warnings issued by the Food and Agricultural Organization should spur the EU to give even more thought to the future of the CAP (FAO 2009). According to some, this argument is strengthened by the realisation that dismantling the CAP would not necessarily be to the advantage of the least developed countries (and their farmers) in the international system (see the next chapter); and this was, after all, one of the primary *moral* arguments on the basis of which the protectionist CAP had to be abolished.

Secondly, the argument for a CAP (albeit in amended form) is motivated by a relatively new definition of the term food security that, to some extent, takes us back to the opponents of the TTIP. This argument is based on the growing interest in organic food. There are some who argue that if we want to maintain the quality of our food, we will have to keep its production at least partly in our own hands. If we give up production, we also relinquish control. And production will disappear if the European consumer can choose between widely differing prices for food as a result of the total liberalisation of global trade. It does not matter whether these arguments for the maintenance of the CAP (partially and/or in another form) are valid. What is important is that the EU's external relations are influenced, now more than ever, by considerations that are not primarily technical or related to the profit and loss accounts of imports and exports. Environmental, health, geopolitical security, and social considerations, to name but a few, play an ever-increasing role in politicians' considerations.[17] And these considerations are ever-changing, kept in motion by changing internal and external, political and socio-economic power relations.

3.5. Conclusion

This chapter has presented an unconventional perspective on EU trade policy. Conventional perspectives begin with a historical description (what are the most important developments, and what internal and external events have played an important role in them?) and an institutional analysis of the most important responsibilities, decision-making procedures, and actors at the European level in order to eventually arrive at some moderate theoretical conclusions. By contrast, this chapter started with a lengthy analysis of what the EU as a power actually means (i.e. independent from the adjectives attached). We established that all three of Lukes' dimensions of power are relevant to the analysis of European trade policy. This policy terrain is seemingly extremely materialistic in nature and the strongest expression of EU actorness in its most effective form. However, it is also a policy terrain to which the notion of Normative Power Europe applies, not as a proclamation of universal norms but as an extension of specific European interests and their projection onto the world market. These external projections by the EU are not uncontested. Indeed, looked at more closely, the EU's trade with the rest of the world is one of the most important internal and external battlegrounds in which state and non-state actors collide at various levels of analysis. This is clearly evident in the now defunct TTIP, which brought supporters and opponents increasingly to blows until President Trump unilaterally broke off negotiations. And we have seen that increasing external pressure on the Common Agricultural Policy—formally a separate area of policy that originally had primarily internal aims—has led to a considerable modification of this form of trade protectionism. In the next chapter we will *inter alia* consider whether such trade liberalisation—and the politics of commercial internationalism more generally—has contributed to bringing an officially stated goal any closer: reduction of economic disparities in the international system.

Suggestions for further reading

Unlike most of the other chapters, this one has many literature references. The cited publications can, of course, be found in the bibliography. (Meunier 2005) provides a nice analysis of the EU's trade policy; Young and Peterson offer a more recent analysis in (2014). Even more recent and more comprehensive is (Khorana and García 2018).

Neoliberalism has been described and analysed by many researchers, from left to right, without, incidentally, reaching a more or less universally accepted conclusion. A nice introduction with a focus on Europe is (Schmidt and Thatcher 2013). See also (Glyn 2006) and (Harvey 2005). A critical treatise on the austerity policies of Western countries is (Blyth 2013).

Later in this book I will look more specifically at the effects of neoliberalism, particularly at increasing socio-economic inequality. A great deal has been written about inequality, particularly in recent decades. Almost every author who deals with this subject refers to the French economist Thomas Piketty and his unsurpassed *Capital in the Twenty-First Century*, which caused a flood of reactions when it first came out in 2014. Another author who enjoys much publicity, and who has written a number of important books about global inequality, is Branko Milanovic. This World Bank economist does not agree with Piketty on all fronts but largely shares his conclusions about developments after 1980 (for the connoisseur: Milanovic 2014 and 2016).

The European Commission's website on trade is very informative. It shows what trade agreements were reached with which countries and in what context and what the most important aspects of the bilateral relationship are. It also provides information about ongoing negotiations, and a range of documents dealing with the EU's trade policy can be downloaded (see http://ec.europa.eu/trade/). The home page has a link to Transparency, which provides the most important negotiation texts (including 'the mandate') and progress reports on the various negotiation rounds.

4. Decolonisation and enlargement: The European Union's development policy

The previous chapter demonstrated that global trade in agricultural products continues to be plagued by various distortions that can be traced back to government policy, which chiefly serves concrete local, national, or— in the case of the EU—regional interests. As a result, in the biannual ministerial conferences held as part of the WTO Doha Round, different groups of countries often find themselves diametrically opposed to each other: the EU and its member states, the US (which also has diverging interests per state), the so-called Cairns group made up of 19 countries that together represent more than 25 per cent of global exports in agricultural products, and finally the group of developing countries. The latter group is large and heterogeneous, and within this group we can differentiate between various coalitions. The WTO identifies as many as 16 different coalitions that each take a common position in the negotiations on topics concerning agriculture. The EU does not belong to any coalition, and most coalitions are made up exclusively of developing countries (see https://www.wto.org/english/tratop_e/agric_e/negoti_groups_e.htm).

For a long time, the EU's Common Agricultural Policy (CAP) was the cornerstone of European integration policy, and not only because almost two thirds of the EU budget initially went on agriculture-related expenditure. Almost every other policy domain at the European level was linked to, or suffered the consequences of, the CAP. And though the original aim of the Europeanisation of agricultural policy was to provide a reasonable standard of living for Europe's farming population and to simultaneously safeguard internal food supplies, in the course of the integration process the CAP began to have an increasingly significant impact on the EU's external relations. The previous chapter explained the CAP's relationship with EU trade policy; the CAP's relationship with the EU's development policy was—and still is, albeit to a lesser extent—also often an adverse one. A notorious episode from the end of the 1980s and beginning of the 1990s was the EU's financial aid, via its development budget, to West African farmers to build up their local livestock, while at the same time frozen beef from the EU was being dumped on their local markets via the CAP's export restitutions, which resulted in the West African farmers and their budding businesses being undercut by European producers. A similar story can be told about the poultry sector. Partly in response to these kinds of alarming contradictions in the EU's external relations, the EU has gradually reduced its export subsidies and more recently abolished most of them.

More generally, there is a growing awareness among policymakers at the European level of the possible adverse effects of European policy on the development prospects of the least developed countries in the world. In the case of the CAP, this has led not only to a removal of export subsidies, a reduction of import-restrictive measures, and a shift from price-supporting subsidies to direct income support but also to a strategy known as *Everything But Arms* (EBA), announced in 2001. The European Commission's 2015 report, optimistically titled *Trade for All*, also mentioned Europe's responsibility towards the least developed countries (European Commission 2015). The question, however, is whether trade is the most appropriate and effective means to reach a more equitable distribution of income in the world. I will return to this point at the end of this chapter, where I will also elaborate on the added value of the EBA programme and whether overblown slogans such as *Trade for All* have any pertinence. But first I will give a brief overview of the most important phases in European development policy since the Treaty of Rome. It will become apparent that the EU's original interest in former colonial ties gradually made way to a stronger emphasis on the least developed countries in the international system. I will also show how attention has shifted in recent decades to countries more closely located to Europe, certainly since the end of the Cold War, in a reflection of the saying "Charity begins at home". In the subsequent section, two traits of the EU's more recent development policy will be explained: the so-called trade-development nexus, and the political conditionality that has been tied to development aid. This will be prefaced by some theoretical reflections. Various theoretical points of view on the importance of free trade will form the basis of the analysis here of the European Commission's trade and development strategy based on neoliberal principles. As with the other chapters, this one will end with a short conclusion and some suggestions for further reading.

4.1.   A brief history of the EU's development policy

European development policy commenced with Part IV of the Treaty of Rome which dealt with 'the association of countries and territories overseas'. Except for territories such as the Belgian Congo and Dutch New Guinea—territories that became independent in 1960 and 1962 respectively—this referred primarily to France's colonial possessions. In the somewhat cryptic wording of Article 131, the association was to further 'the interests and prosperity of the inhabitants of these countries and territories in such a manner as to lead them to the economic, social and cultural development which they expect'. This was to be achieved in two ways. First, the six founding states were to open up their economies to all non-European countries and territories. Vice versa, these countries and overseas territories were supposed to 'apply to [their] commercial exchanges with Member States ... the same rules which [they apply] in respect of the European State[s] with which [they have] special relations'. This part of the association thus implied a clear reciprocity in the trade relationship, a symmetry that was to only be removed later. And second, the mother countries would make a special contribution to investments in the concerned territories. This was to become a type of collective financial assistance via a fund that was to be set up especially for this purpose, with all member states depositing a 'specific amount'. It was emphasised that this collective aid was to serve as a supplement to already existing bilateral aid. All of this was to be stipulated in a convention that would be applied for a period of five years.[1] This last-minute insertion of Part IV was allegedly a precondition on the part of France for signing the treaty, for it was thought that the contribution of the other member states, notably West Germany, would to some degree lessen the financial burden of sustaining the French colonial empire. Comments made by the then Dutch government bring another reason to light: the reciprocity of the association would offer other member states access to the markets of French overseas countries and territories, and France wanted to be compensated for this. This is how the European Development Fund (EDF) was born.

In 1963, after some of the associated countries had become independent and the first period of five years had elapsed, a new convention was deemed necessary to give shape to the relationship between the EU and eighteen former French colonies in Africa. On 20 July 1963, the first Yaoundé Convention was signed in the capital of Cameroon; a year later the treaty entered into force for a period of five years. A second Yaoundé Convention was signed in 1969 and entered into force on 1 January 1971. Apart from the unmistakable mark left by the French on both agreements, Yaoundé confirmed the traditional division of labour: countries that received development aid exported for the most part agrarian products, and the European donor countries mainly exported industrial products. Trade was still based on the principle of reciprocity, with agrarian products from African countries allowed to freely enter the European market unless they directly threatened European producers. The EDF's financial means were almost entirely bestowed on infrastructure projects, with no conditions attached to trade and financial aid. In the period between 1957 and 1975, Europe paid scant attention to political modernisation—despite it being a key component of the EU's alleged civilian or normative power.

In the course of the second convention, at the beginning of the 1970s, the context in which EU development policy was implemented changed to such an extent that a new generation of conventions was considered necessary. In the first place, in 1972-1973 an international economic crisis broke out that, for the first time since the Second World War, confronted the world with a combination of stagnating growth, rapidly growing government deficits and national debts, and rising inflation fuelled by surging oil prices. This crisis had three effects. First, Western governments began to consider introducing measures that were initially aimed at protecting ailing sectors and reining in their government deficits. It was only later—from the end of the 1970s—that this policy took on a more structural, reformist bent with the rise of neoliberal ideology (see chapter 6). The emphasis on global liberalisation, deregulation, and privatisation also had an impact on the so-called Third World. The international debt crisis confronting these countries—which was the second effect and which was in a sense the mirror image of the crisis of the Keynesian welfare state in Western Europe—was addressed through liberal *and* repressive measures via what were called Structural Adjustment Programmes from the IMF and the World Bank (better known as the Washington Consensus, a reference to the place where both international organisations are located; see below). A third effect stemmed primarily from the oil crisis and the fact that the cartel of oil-producing and exporting countries (the Organization of Petroleum Exporting Countries, or OPEC) could reduce oil production and thus raise the price of oil at short notice. This instilled the fear in the West that other commodity producers would decide to form a similar kind of cartel. Given the West's import dependency on essential commodities, such a development would have further deepened the crisis.

A second factor that influenced the EU's development policy was the growing awareness both within and outside the EU that relations between the EU and its former colonies were still highly unequal and that the EU's development strategy had had little effect in the associated countries. Three manifestations of opposition and protest can be mentioned here, beginning with the Club of Rome's warning in its report *Limits to Growth*. The conclusion of this report was both simple and alarming: it argued that if we continued to grow at the same pace in terms of industrial production and global population, the planet would be destroyed as a result of environmental pollution and the depletion of natural resources (including food). One didn't have to be a rocket scientist to see the connection between this doom-and-gloom scenario and the position of the Third World: industrialisation and population growth there would only bring the Club of Rome's prognosis one step closer. A global solution based on a more equitable distribution of prosperity and natural resources was the logical plea that followed, even if it was a plea that went largely unheard. A second countermovement came from the rising influence of Marxism (and neo-Marxism) at Western universities in the 1960s and beginning of the 1970s and the subsequent radicalisation of the debate on development (see the following section). Finally, the group of non-aligned countries—which in the course of the 1960s had made their voices heard, particularly through the United Nations Conference on Trade and Development (UNCTAD)—drew up a declaration for the establishment of a New International Economic Order (NIEO).[2] This 1974 declaration aimed to bring the period of decolonisation to a definitive close and to create a NIEO that would focus on the following aspects: the sovereignty of, and equality between, states; the removal of all remaining practices of colonialism and neocolonialism; national self-determination; sovereign control over a country's own natural resources such as raw materials, including the right to nationalisation or transfer of ownership to national citizens; the regulation and supervision of the activities of multinational enterprises (so-called codes of conduct); better and fairer prices for commodities; development aid in the form of financial transfers and technology diffusion; and a strengthened South-South cooperation between developing countries. Here again, it did not take much political acumen to realise that this package of measures, if implemented, would result in a threat to existing Western interests and in any case would put an end to what was referred to in the declaration as a gross inequality: that 'the developing countries, which constitute 70 per cent of the world's population, account for only 30 per cent of the world's income' (United Nations 1974).[3]

A third factor that had an indirect influence on notions about development was the emergence of what was called the New International Division of Labour and the related rise of the group labelled Newly Industrialising Countries (NICs). Seen somewhat schematically, and perhaps put in rather exaggerated terms as well, the phenomenon of the capitalist division of labour entered a new phase. In the seventeenth century, the staple market of Amsterdam symbolised the budding division of labour between 'national' economies within Europe (a phenomenon identified by Immanuel Wallerstein as the creation of a modern world economy based on a core-semiperiphery-periphery division of labour). At the beginning of the twentieth century, the intra-company division of the production process via the introduction of the assembly line and the division of labour between 'brains and brawn' formed the basis of what was later to be coined Fordism (see chapter 6). At the beginning of the 1970s, this intra-company division of labour got a geographical and transnational dimension. Partly set in motion before the 1970s crisis and amplified as a result of it, industrial enterprises moved the labour-intensive parts of their production process to so-called low-wage areas. This geographic, in-company labour division could take place within a country (such as Fiat's investments in Southern Italy) or within a region (such as Ford Europe's investments in Spain). An important effect of this development was that the 'old' division of labour between highly developed industrialised countries and countries that supplied commodities and agricultural products was breached. Moreover, the rise of Asian, Latin American, and Southern European 'tigers' resulted in the group of developing countries becoming more heterogeneous and diffuse, and it also invalidated the assertion that the poor countries were becoming increasingly poor and the rich countries increasingly wealthier—in other words, that there was no way out of the neocolonial division of labour of the 'old' international economic order.

A fourth and final factor affecting the EU's development policy was the EU's first round of enlargement, in particular the accession of the former global power Great Britain on 1 January 1973. With this new member state, the number of developing countries with which the EU had historical ties expanded drastically. French Africa could no longer claim a monopoly; henceforth countries in the Pacific Ocean and in the Caribbean were also among the recipients of EU development aid. It was clear that a new convention had to be approved, which was the Lomé Convention, named after the capital of Togo where the signing took place. From that moment, a new acronym became part of the EU's development policy: ACP, which refers to the three aforementioned regions—Africa, the Caribbean, and the Pacific Ocean. More important than the naming was the substantive—and, to a certain extent, ideological—changes that became a reality with the accession of Great Britain. At the signing of the Treaty of Rome, there was already a difference of opinion between so-called regionalists (which in actual fact was represented by France alone) and globalists (Germany and the Netherlands). The latter wanted to focus more generally on all underdeveloped countries instead of exclusively on 'overseas territories and countries' with which Europe had historical ties (Carbone 2011: 326). Added to this difference of opinion (and interests), in the course of the 1970s a difference between French paternalism and the British approach, which was focused on respect for national sovereignty and open trade relations within the Commonwealth, emerged. In the words of Holland and Doidge, the new convention had to 'protect French sensitivities yet meet British demands' (Holland and Doidge 2012: 53).

The Lomé Conventions I to IV + IV (bis) (1976-2001)
It was against this background that the first Lomé Convention was signed in 1975 between the EU and 46 ACP countries. The Convention came into force a year later and was ultimately renegotiated and updated three times and also extended once (in the case of the fourth Convention) after a so-called mid-term review had taken place. By the end of the 1990s, the number of participating ACP countries had risen to 70.

The Lomé agreements consisted of several main components: a preferential trade system, specific facilities to support and stabilise ACP exports of a specific series of goods, and of course actual development assistance via the EDF (see Dent 1997: 198-204; and Holland and Doidge 2012: 53-69). While the magnitude of this last component increased in absolute terms during the Lomé period, this increase was much less significant when corrected for inflation, and even declined when stated in real per capita terms. Of course, this had to do with the sharp increase in the number of ACP countries, but also with the economic crisis that had hit the EU donor countries and the gradual emergence of 'donor fatigue'. Despite the fact that new (potential) donor countries had joined the EU in two rounds of enlargement—in particular with the 1995 enlargement that led to the accession of Sweden, Finland, and Austria—the 1980s and 1990s were characterised by a greater degree of indifference on the part of the Union: not only towards the demands of APC countries to make more financial funds available but also initially with regard to the call for (partial) debt write-offs for developing countries' foreign debts.

Very little political or socio-economic conditionality was applied in the first three Lomé Conventions, which led some to surmise that this new generation of development agreements no longer bore the marks of neocolonial dependency. This changed, however, in the fourth Convention, which started to couple aid with such things as human rights, the position of women, and environmental objectives. Also during the 1990s, demands were made regarding the type of economic policy that recipient countries should pursue, in line with the Structural Adjustment Programmes (SAPs) resulting from the aforementioned Washington Consensus. These structural reforms often boiled down to reducing the government's role in the economy and encouraging development through export promotion (see below). The formal aim of aid from the European Development Fund was to contribute to the industrial development of ACP countries, for example by investing in infrastructure which in turn served to support export-led growth. However, the partially tied nature of the aid resulted in European companies being the main beneficiaries of the orders and contracts financed by the EDF. Moreover, the supplementary nature of EDF financing resulted in member states scaling back their bilateral aid. More generally, the reality in many ACP countries was not exactly favourable to a development strategy focused on industrialisation. As a result, the traditional division of labour remained largely intact, and by the end of the Lomé Conventions, agricultural products and raw materials were still the most important export products for most ACP countries.

As partial concession to the drafters of the NIEO declaration—who, after all, had made a case for better prices for primary export products—two new arrangements were devised to introduce safeguards for ACP countries for their exports: Stabex and Sysmin. The first mechanism, Stabex, was meant to stabilise the agrarian export income of ACP countries, on the condition that the product in question had to be of considerable importance for the balance of payments of the country concerned. Many ACP countries were dependent for their exports and their prosperity on only a few products, which meant that they were very vulnerable to a decline in the production of—or sharp price fluctuations in the world market of—coffee or cacao, for example. If the price or the harvest of a particular product fell under a particular threshold, the country (as well as the domestic producer of that product) was eligible for a Stabex payout. In the second Lomé Convention, a similar system was introduced but this time for minerals. In the same way as Stabex, countries could be compensated if the production or export of particular minerals declined to under a particular level. There was widespread criticism of both mechanisms: the available means were insufficient and were furthermore unevenly distributed across the ACP countries. Moreover, Stabex did not apply to industrial products and Sysmin was applicable to only a limited number of minerals. And finally, both systems were blamed for rewarding inertia instead of more efficient production methods. Nonetheless, the EU's good intentions must be recognised, along with the fact that the ACP countries generally considered these innovations under the Lomé Conventions to be positive.

It was a different situation with the third component of the Conventions: the preferential trade system that favoured ACP countries non-reciprocally with regard to their export penetration of the European market. This created a certain degree of asymmetry in the EU-ACP trade relationship that had not existed before Lomé. In order to clarify why this became a problem in the course of the conventions, a brief detour is necessary. As stated earlier, there were calls at the outset of the EDF to replace the old policy based on colonial ties with a more global approach targeted at the poorest countries in the international system, and these calls only increased following the accession of Great Britain to the EU. One consequence of the first approach (adhered to by the French) was that the geographic emphasis lay primarily on Africa. As a result, the EU had virtually no external development relationship with countries in Asia and Latin America. To start to put an end to this situation, a Generalised System of Preferences (GSP) programme was introduced in 1971 that offered developing countries non-reciprocal, preferential access to the European market. The GSP was an exception to the Most Favoured Nation principle enshrined in the General Agreement on Tariffs and Trade (GATT, the predecessor to the WTO) that required GATT members to grant the trade benefits it offered to one country (or group of countries) to other countries too. Favourable treatment towards developing countries, so went the argument, could be accepted for this reason alone—that is, to combat stark inequalities in the international system. The problem, however, was that the GSP programme did not offer the same preferential access as the conventions with the ACP countries, which meant there was a difference in favourable treatment between developing countries that were often at similar levels of development—and this difference was based purely on old colonial or alleged cultural-historical ties. Some years later, in the course of the 1990s (in particular after the successful conclusion of the Uruguay Round of trade talks and the formation of the WTO in 1995), the protests became louder, leading to the repeal of both non-reciprocity and the ACP trade preferences in the Cotonou Agreement. And thus the system once described as 'collective clientelism' came to an end (Ravenhill 1985).

Another reason ACP countries viewed the trade component of the Lomé Conventions with mixed feelings was the limited impact of 25 years of preferential treatment. In the first place, both the share of ACP countries in the EU's total imports and the share of EU exports to ACP countries in the EU's total exports halved to under 3 per cent over those 25 years. Secondly, very little change occurred in the traditional division of labour between the two groups of countries, and there was no increase in ACP industrial exports to the EU whatsoever (a situation that became increasingly awkward as more and more countries participating in the 1971 GSP system became newly industrialising countries). What's more, every tentative attempt to facilitate a take-off towards industrialisation was made difficult by two separate clauses in the conventions: the rules of origin clause and the safeguard clause. The first clause determined that if an ACP country wanted to sell its industrial product preferentially on the EU market, it had to be produced for the most part in that particular ACP country. This was meant to block so-called screwdriver plants, where all the product parts come from an industrialised country and the ACP country serves as the place where the product is assembled. The second clause allowed the EU to activate protectionist measures if an ACP export product were to cause severe damage to a sector in one of the member states. This measure, which often took the form of quantitative import restrictions, was not uncommon in the textile industry.

4.2.   The most important characteristics of EU development policy since the Cotonou Treaty (2000)

Just as with the transition from the second Yaoundé Convention to the Lomé Conventions in the first half of the 1970s, key international and European events played a role in the transition from the Lomé to the first Cotonou Agreement (named after Benin's largest and economically most important city). Having said that, most of these changes already began to determine the agenda in the 1990s, at the time of Lomé IV. To begin with, the Mediterranean enlargement of the EU towards Greece (1981), Portugal and Spain (the latter two joining the EU on 1 January 1986) had a concrete impact on the EU's development policy, comparable to the first round of enlargement. Spain in particular broadened the development agenda by calling for more attention to be paid to Latin America. In the first half of 1989, when the social-democratic government under the leadership of Prime Minister Felipe González held the EU presidency, Spain raised the need for a transatlantic agreement given the imminent establishment of the Mercosur trade bloc. In this case, historical ties clearly played a decisive role. That was plainly not the case following the subsequent enlargement round in 1995 which included countries with no colonial past and thus bolstered the camp of the globalists (see above).

Secondly, the end of the Cold War ushered in an entirely new European geopoliti-cal architecture. The fall of the Berlin Wall and the transformation processes in Central and Eastern Europe had not only an important security component, given the new position of the Russian Federation in post-Cold-War Europe, but also a socio-economic and political development dimension. This time around, however, all of this was taking place right on the external borders of the EU (see also chapter 5). Shortly after 1989, the first reactions in diplomatic circles were already being voiced: the EU's external relations—i.e. the previously mentioned actorness or external power of the EU—would have a much more direct and tangible effect on Central and Eastern European countries than in the case of the ACP countries. Moreover, it was said that the EU had a more direct interest in stable external borders than in laboriously acquired changes in countries located further away, where it was unclear whether such changes would be lasting. Once again, the emphasis was on the saying "Charity begins at home".

Thirdly, as a result of the Maastricht Treaty from 1991-1993, serious efforts were made to establish a Common Foreign and Security Policy (CFSP). In concrete terms, this meant that the two most important pillars in external relations up until that point—namely trade policy and development policy—suddenly gained a 'competitor'. From this point onwards, foreign policy and security considerations became more important, if only because the (in retrospect) relatively stable Cold War bipolarity had come to an end and because the threat of waning American leadership—or a decline in US involvement in European affairs—became increas-ingly real (see chapter 6).

Fourthly, from the second half of the 1980s and particularly in the 1990s, the outlines of what we have thus far called the neoliberal turn started to become visible. As will become clear in chapter 6, this had an important internal effect in the form of a rationalisation of the structures and practices of the welfare state (or, seen from another ideological perspective, a dismantling of these structures/ practices). But it also had an effect on external relations. The previous chapter dealt with the phenomenon of commercial internationalism (CI), which entailed that internal liberalisation, deregulation, and privatisation became mantras in the EU's relations with third countries. Also in relations with developing countries, the importance of trade liberalisation began to play a more dominant role.

The aforementioned four elements were integrated into the Cotonou Agreement to a greater or lesser degree (with Lomé IV acting in a certain sense as an advance notice). Before examining this agreement in more detail, it is necessary to take a brief look at the debate within postwar development theory regarding the position of the market and that of the state—or free trade and intervention—in the process of socio-economic and political modernisation of undeveloped or lesser developed territories and countries in the international system.

4.2.1. The development of development theory: From hope to nihilism?

Just as realism served as a reference point within IR theorisation from which alternative theoretical approaches were developed (see chapter 1), there is a starting point within development theory to which all subsequent approaches more or less explicitly had to react, namely the theory of comparative advantage, which dates back to the British political economist David Ricardo (1772-1823). The cornerstone of this theory is the assumption that countries participating in an international system of free trade will eventually specialise in the goods that they can produce most efficiently or economically on the basis of their specific factor endowments (qualities or characteristics such as the availability of technological knowledge, land, capital, labour but also geographical traits and things such as climate). This is what all countries would do in an optimal situation of free trade, which would lead to a product and export specialisation that is to the advantage of all participants. Often this theory is explained in textbooks with the help of a simple example with two countries and two products: there is country A and country B, and both produce grain and computers. Even if country A can produce both computers and grain more efficiently than country B, it will still be to country A's advantage if it concentrates on the product that it can produce most efficiently or cheapest, which in this simple example is computers. Country B would then apply itself to producing grain, and at the end of this story, everyone is happy. But as is often the case with these kinds of ideal-typical scenarios, reality is considerably more complicated.[4]

Nonetheless, after the Second World War, economic liberalism, on which the theory of comparative advantages is based, received a sequel in the form of modernisation theory. An important founder of this theory was Walt Whitman Rostow, an American political scientist and political advisor to the Democratic presidents John F. Kennedy and Lyndon B. Johnson. Rostow was convinced that if developing countries had sufficient capital at their disposal, rapid economic growth and democratisation would follow. The underlying assumption was that such countries would automatically end up—and remain—in the Western sphere of influence as a result of this economic and political modernisation.[5] And in his perception, that sphere of influence consisted of free markets and open societies. The problem of underdevelopment was mainly a problem of tradition, of cultural values and social institutions that remained stuck in the past. On the opposite side of tradition was modernity, and to make the leap towards a modern society—and for this Rostow used the term take-off—developing countries had to go through various stages of economic growth. International contacts (as well as capital) were essential for this; it was only through such contacts that eyes could be opened and atavistic views abandoned. The fifth stage, that of mass consumption, was also explicitly seen as a last one in order to indicate its difference with the main adversary of the day, Marxism, which saw the development and modernisation trajectory as a sure way to achieve a classless society. That Rostow wanted to have nothing to do with this was explicitly expressed in the subtitle of his most-cited book, which reads *A Non-Communist Manifesto* (see Rostow 1960).

The undertone in both the theory of comparative advantage and modernisation theory was the idea that the unleashing of international market forces would solve the problem of underdevelopment. It was thought that if the recipes of economic liberalism were followed precisely, the considerable development gap between countries could be eliminated. Already at an early stage—a decade before the publication of Rostow's *The Stages of Economic Growth*— Raúl Prebisch, the Argentine development economist and director of the United Nations' Economic Commission for Latin America, came to the conclusion that the difference between poor and rich in the international system was not narrowing but rather widening. He had intuitively come to this conclusion in response to the Great Depression between the two world wars, but in 1950 he formulated his thesis of the worsening terms of trade as part of a theory that has come to be known as structuralism (Prebisch 1950). In his analysis, Prebisch presumed the existence of two more or less structural developments: global rises in productivity and in wages. Given that the international division of labour was still largely complementary, with poor countries supplying agricultural products and commodities and rich countries producing industrial products, the deteriorating terms of trade between the two product groups (and thus between the poor and the rich countries) occurred on both the supply/production side and the demand side. Higher productivity in the industrialised countries led to lower production costs but not necessarily—or much less so—to lower prices. The explanation for this limited downwards price elasticity lay partly in the increasing concentration of industrial sectors in the hands of a few market leaders, which reduced price competition between them; lower production costs did not lead to lower prices but to higher profits and wages. In developing countries, technological development and rising productivity led to a sharp rise in the supply of agricultural products and commodities and—in the absence of monopoly or oligopoly formation and strong labour unions—to a decline in prices. Consequently, on the supply side, the division of labour between rich and poor countries resulted in a decline in the price of agricultural products but not in the price of industrial products. A global rise in wages further worsened these terms of trade. In general, higher wages tend to lead only partially to a higher consumption of food, while the demand for industrial products is less easily satisfied. Globally rising wages thus had the net effect that relatively more industrial products and fewer agrarian products were purchased worldwide. When added up, the developing countries were much worse off than the industrialised countries both on the supply and the demand sides, at least according to Prebisch. Focusing primarily on his own region, the logical conclusion he drew was that countries in Latin America had to tear themselves away from this detrimental division of labour by embarking on a process of industrialisation.

This short summary of the main argument of the deteriorating terms of trade thesis does not do justice to this very well thought out and highly influential discourse. In less than 60 pages, Prebisch outlines the problem in a dazzling way that reads like a major indictment of the simplistic assumptions of the theory of comparative advantage. It is perhaps for this reason that Prebisch is sometimes portrayed as a Marxist (for example by those students who prefer to think in terms of ideologically 'good' and 'bad'). Nothing against Marxism, but Prebisch was not a follower. In the 1960s and 1970s, however, his analyses were partially subsumed by representatives of an approach that has come to be known as *dependencia* theory (from the Spanish word for dependency). This theory, which in all its diversity often came down to a sharp criticism of the capitalist system, stated unequivocally that economic development in the existing centre-periphery division of labour was impossible for the periphery. Worse still—and here is where the full societal implication of the economic analysis of the deteriorating terms of trade becomes clear—what is at stake here is the development of the underdevelopment. Underdevelopment is no longer the effect—albeit unintended—of trade relations and the division of labour but rather the result of a dependent relationship based on exploitation whereby state and non-state actors in the West, supported by local elites (the so-called *comprador* bourgeoisie), are responsible for a surplus transfer from the periphery to the centre, resulting in development in the centre. Put in stronger terms, development in the centre implies underdevelopment in the periphery; development and underdevelopment are two sides of the same coin.

The lack of development is therefore not the result of an absence of capital or entrepreneurship, as the modernisation theory would have us believe, but occurs under the influence of the centre-periphery division of labour in the international system and is therefore externally rather than internally determined. This conclusion has direct consequences for a possible way out of the almost deadly neocolonial or neo-imperialist embrace. Inasmuch as underdevelopment is the result of linkage to the centre, disassociation from the world market and the pursuit of self-reliance can be the only solutions. Given that the existing inequality is partly the result of the intimate relationship between local elites and Western governments and businesses, revolutionary political changes are necessary. The only thing that can lead to development—which is construed as industrial development—and to greater equality (both internal and external) is the elimination of external and internal as well as political and socio-economic obstacles.

Dependencia theory has been put into practice in varying degrees in a number of countries. In a study dating from 1984, Blomström and Hettne tried to demonstrate that this theory served as a source of inspiration for decision-makers not only in Latin America but also in the Caribbean area (Jamaica), Africa (Tanzania and Kenya), and Asia (India, where it largely failed). Their core argument, however, was more interesting: as the subtitle of their book *The Dependency Debate and Beyond: Third World Responses* suggests, the concrete application of the theory— which became well-known as a result of publications by academics such as Andre Gunder Frank who studied and taught at Western universities—was the response of the Third World itself (i.e. beyond academia), as an attempt to pull itself out of underdevelopment (Blomström and Hettne 1984). However, this primarily occurred in developing countries in an uncoordinated manner and independent of each other. The policy that sought to give shape to this attempt has become known as the strategy of import substitution. This term can be taken quite literally: by closing off the national market to industrial products from abroad, Third World countries hoped to create space domestically to kick-start industrial development. Subsequently, regulation and legislation had to see to it that foreign businesses (whose activities were not unwelcome per se) adapted their behaviour to the new objective, for example by reinvesting their profits in the developing country where they were made. Nationalisation could be deployed as a last resort. The role of the state was considered essential, particularly in two areas: central economic planning and government stimulus. A successful take-off could not be left to the market alone. Finally, for industrialisation to succeed, it was necessary to redistribute national income progressively. After all, the nationally produced industrial goods had to be sold on the domestic market.

As Geoffrey Kay, a former participant in the development debate, said somewhat bitterly in the 1970s, the dependencia *practice* mainly consisted of 'an eclectic combination of orthodox economic theory and revolutionary phraseology' (Kay 1975: 103). There is some truth in this. The radical anti-system twist deemed necessary was not pursued in any country. Indeed, if there was any kind of class struggle or revolution, it came after a while from the political right, in reaction to the failed import substitution policy. The economic policy of the Chilean government led by Salvador Allende at the beginning of the 1960s was Keynesian more than anything. It was only when the 'democratic path to socialism' resulted in the nationalisation of several foreign—mainly American—companies that the Chilean army staged a coup d'état in 1973. The result was a revolutionary policy shift (see below) that the (in)famous American economist Milton Friedman called the 'Chilean wonder' and has otherwise come to be known as the laboratory of neoliberalism.

So what went wrong with the policy of import substitution? To begin with, the countries that implemented such a policy were dependent on capital goods and on imports for raw materials, particularly oil. A country can systematically prepare its great leap forward, but without technological expertise and technologically advanced machinery, it is impossible to set up industries. These products have to be imported. To pay for these imports, the country needs to export. This is one side of the story. The other side concerns wage developments that are necessary to stimulate domestic demand for locally produced industrial goods. This sparks inflation, which leads to an increase in export prices. As a result, the country's competitiveness on the world market declines. Government investment and demand stimulation are certainly necessary at the beginning of this process of change, but the financial means must come from somewhere. Put simply, government deficits and deficits on the balance of payments—two things that are inextricably linked to the economic ambitions of the policy of import substitution—can ultimately only be paid for via external debt financing. Loans can be obtained from private institutions, foreign governments, and/or international organisations such as the World Bank and the IMF. But these loans must be paid off and interest must be paid on them. If a country does not generate enough export income, it could eventually find itself in payment problems or even outright insolvency. This could lead to a debt crisis and subsequently to the restructuring of its debt position, ultimately resulting in a package of new policy recommendations often imposed as a condition for debt refinancing.

From the 1970s and 1980s, this spiral of deficits to debt to further deficits led to a new form of external dependency that ultimately compelled countries to adopt a radical policy change. This policy change came to be labelled as Structural Adjustment Programmes, alternatively known as the Washington Consensus. The main component of this export-oriented policy was external and internal liberalisation: externally via trade liberalisation and internally via the reduction of state interference in the economy. The free market was restored, along with the privileged position of foreign businesses. New regulation had to ensure that companies encountered as few obstacles as possible. In addition, the new develop-ment strategy included elements such as a favourable tax climate, the installation of an export-oriented infrastructure, and additional investment subsidies for multinational companies to locate their business in the country. As is no doubt clear by now, the new export orientation ran counter to the 'old' policy that was focused on the redistribution of national income. Wage restraint was important for attracting foreign businesses and for a successful export strategy. This became the new mantra in the developing world. Obviously, all of this was not blindly accepted by workers and labour unions. More often, as indeed was the case in Chile but also in Argentina and several African countries, the policy turnaround was accompanied by a return to authoritarian rule and repression. In a cynical twist to the story, it was at this point that some former *independentistas* began to stockpile large nest eggs in foreign bank accounts.

Holland and Doidge draw a nice parallel between the aforementioned phases in the evolution of development theory and the succession of conventions in European development policy (Holland and Doidge 2012: 23-27). Confidence in the benefits of international trade and capital movements, which formed the basis of modernisation theory, was reflected in the first Yaoundé Convention, which explicitly stated that its goal was industrialisation of the associated states. The adjustment in the EU's development policy in the form of the first Lomé Convention to a certain extent reflected the popularity of the dependencia theory and the rise of the NIEO movement at the time, as well as calls for a more equal and equitable development relationship. The new turnaround in the course of the 1990s, from Lomé IV and continuing on into the Cotonou Agreement, took place within an international context typified by an increasingly sceptical attitude towards grand theories, by the negative experience of the developing countries' debt crisis, and by the neoliberal solutions put forward by international organisations and private financial institutions. At the same time, a virtually silent revolution was taking place in ways of thinking about development and the possibilities thereof. In fact, the goal of putting a country on the map, industrially speaking, subtly began to give way to an increasing emphasis on poverty reduction and so-called basic needs. Instead of investing in productive activities or facilitating these activities via investments in infrastructure, for example as a foreign incentive to self-help, aid came to be targeted at alleviating the need for food, water, clothing and shelter, or embedded in a broader strategy to improve things such as healthcare and education. A good example of such a basic-needs strategy is the Millennium Development Goals adopted by the United Nations in 2000. The idea was that the following eight goals would be realised by 2015: eradication of extreme poverty and hunger (more concretely: halving, between 1990 and 2015, the number of people living on less than one dollar a day); achieving universal basic education; promoting gender equality and empowering women; reducing child mortality; improving maternal health; combating HIV/aids, malaria, and other diseases; ensuring environmental sustainability; and devising a global partnership for development.[6]

Since Lomé IV, a paradoxical development has arisen that can be summarised as a decoupling of the two most important components of the EU's development strategy: aid and trade. Just as the confidence in grand theories—major theoretical constructs that claim to be right, ontologically and epistemologically speaking— started to wane within the broader social sciences, a postmodernist and postpositivist nihilism began to appear within the field of development studies. More importantly, this turnaround in thinking did not fail to have an effect on the practice of development policy. The idea is that aid has long since stopped to serve the holy purpose of industrial take-off which, in combination with an active, modernising role of the government, would result in social and political change in the country concerned.

In today's world, aid is, as indicated, predominantly about poverty relief. At the same time, the neoliberal belief in free trade as the solution to extreme global inequality is preached like never before. Proponents point out the success stories of the NICs in the 1970s and 1980s and the BRICs in the first decade of this century. The lonesome scholar who argues that countries that have successfully started a catch-up race have all been through a period of increased state intervention and some measure of closing off their domestic market, and that the neoliberal recipe of liberalisation, deregulation, and privatisation basically boils down to kicking away the ladder towards a higher development level, remains the proverbial voice crying in the wilderness (see Chang 2003). In other words, it seems that there is a reality behind this paradox that allows the philanthropy of aid to survive, while at the same time allowing the developed countries to pursue their self-interest of further global trade liberalisation.

This is also reflected in the formulation of the overall objective of EU development cooperation in Article 208 of the Treaty on the Functioning of the European Union:

> Union policy in the field of development cooperation shall be conducted within the framework of the principles and objectives of the Union's external action. The Union's development cooperation policy and that of the Member States complement and reinforce each other. *Union development cooperation policy shall have as its primary objective the reduction and, in the long term, the eradication of poverty.* The Union shall take account of the objectives of development cooperation in the policies that it implements which are likely to affect developing countries [italics added].

The reference in this Article to the principles and goals of the Union's external actions could not send a clearer message. In sections 2d and 2e of Article 21 of the Treaty on the European Union, the following two goals are mentioned in virtually the same breath:
- foster the sustainable economic, social and environmental development of developing countries, with the primary aim of eradicating poverty;
- encourage the integration of all countries into the world economy, including through the progressive abolition of restrictions on international trade.

4.2.2. Trade and aid: Two sides of the same coin?

As mentioned earlier, EU aid dispensed via the EDF has increased in absolute terms but not in real per capita terms. This is due to various factors on both sides of the relationship, such as an increase in the number of participating countries, growing populations, periods of sharp rises in inflation, and reluctance among EU governments to put more money into hopeless development projects in territories far away—the so-called 'bottomless pit'. With respect to this last consideration, a number of developments close to home played an important role—including the end of the Cold War, the growing importance of security and stability in the EU's own backyard, and, more recently, the euro crisis and the migration crisis—as well as global developments like the rise of so-called emerging economies, which to some extent became competitors to the EU in their development relationship with the poorest—but often resource-rich—countries in the international system.

A persistent problem in the EU's development aid is its fragmentary nature. Development aid via the EDF within the framework of the series of conventions has traditionally been the most important EU component. However, this is strictly intergovernmental and is financed by the member states via an allocation ratio. On top of this, the European Commission has a role through the EU budget, and more specifically the Development Cooperation Instrument (DCI) from which the Commission can finance projects. In addition, most of the member states have their own national development policy as well as their own financial resources, which they can spend in three different ways: bilaterally, multilaterally (through international organisations), or via companies and non-governmental organisations. If we add everything up, then it is indeed the case—as is often stated in handbooks and official EU brochures—that the EU is by far the largest donor in the world, with well above half of the world's total official development assistance (ODA), which refers to the government aid of all countries that are part of the OECD. The implicit idea behind this observation is that the EU derives actorness from its donorship. This would be true if the previously discussed concept of Europeanisation were also applicable to European development policy, i.e. if a clear movement could be observed towards member states opting for a common policy on the basis of the efficient bundling of resources and forces. Despite attempts to do just this—and despite a limited degree of progress—there are very few signs of any substantial Europeanisation (see Orbie and Lightfoot 2017). This is largely due to the fact that so many different practices and interests continue to exist within the EU. Member states still see development policy in terms of national sovereignty and as a part of their foreign policy based on national interests. The partial or complete transfer to the Commission, or even better coordination with or through it, remains a thorny issue.

An important difference between the member states is how much weight each member state carries individually in terms of its ODA in absolute terms. Figure 4.1 shows clearly that it is mainly the big three—Germany, Great Britain, and (albeit to a lesser extent) France—that belong to the largest donors within the OECD's Development Assistance Committee (DAC). The further right we move along the graph, the smaller and less prosperous the EU member states become. Indeed, some of the latter member states still benefit considerably from the internal development aid that the EU dispenses through its structural funds.

Looking not only at the absolute amounts but also at the net official development aid as a percentage of national welfare (see Figure 4.2), we get a completely different picture. To the left of the figure is tiny Luxembourg, while France suddenly drops to somewhere in the middle of the rankings (notice also how the US moves from first position all the way to a meagre 22nd place). Most countries in 2016 did not meet the UN target of 0.7 per cent; only six countries fulfilled this norm, three of which were interestingly enough Scandinavian countries (and two of which are members of the EU). The Netherlands' dip under this norm and Great Britain's recent movement towards this norm are particularly noteworthy.[7]

Apart from these financial-economic differences between member states, there are also significant strategic and policy differences between them. Each member state differs, for example, in the percentage of national aid it disburses bilaterally or via multilateral frameworks. Generally speaking, we can presume that a higher percentage of bilateral aid correlates with a stronger interweaving of a donor country's development policy with its national interests. What is closely related to this is the relationship between tied and untied aid as a percentage of total assistance. An example of tied aid is when the recipient country must purchase products or services produced in the donor country. It should be obvious that the higher the share of bilateral aid in a donor country's total ODA, the greater the likelihood that this aid will be tied via a specific conditionality imposed on the recipient countries. In addition to the relationship between tied and untied aid, national preferences and interests also come to the fore in the choice of projects or subsectors supported. Some countries pay particular attention to the theme of 'women and development', some concentrate more on micro-finance, and other member states give relatively large amounts to humanitarian aid. What may seem like a charitable, interest-free prioritisation is on closer inspection the result of a broader assessment of interests in the donor state. For example, where is the boundary between French philanthropy and self-interest if child illiteracy is combated via language education which at the same time serves to preserve the French-speaking world? Finally, national interests also show up in the geographical priorities in member states' development policies, which, in some cases, have historically been strongly linked to old colonial ties.

And now on to the EU itself. The European Commission can finance development projects on its own or in collaboration with the European Investment Bank via the aforementioned DCI. The DCI was established in 2007 in order to bundle and streamline the fragmentary aid to countries that do not belong to the ACP group—in 2017 that meant some 47 countries in Latin America, the Middle East, Central Asia, and southern Africa. The funds come from the EU's multi-annual budget known

Figure 4.1.   Net Official Development Assistance, 2016 (in billions of US dollars)

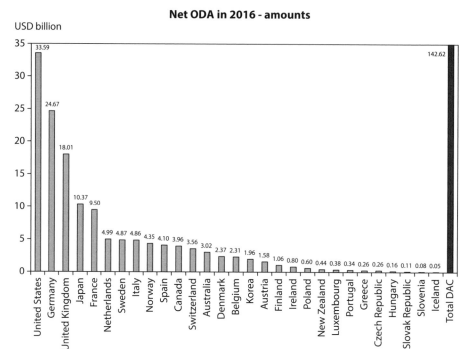

Source: OECD 2017: 6

as the Multiannual Financial Framework (MFF), from the fourth category called Global Europe. For the most recent period of 2014-2020, a total of 19.7 billion euros was reserved in the MFF (in current prices, see Table 5.1 in the following chapter).

Through its involvement in the DCI, the Commission has taken on the role of donor in the international system, but in the last quarter of a century it has also been given a greater coordinating role. In the jargon of development cooperation, this has come to be known as the three Cs: coherence, coordination, and complementarity. The Commission plays a pivotal role in all three. *Coherence* refers to the EU's aspiration to ensure that there is sufficient alignment between the various policy areas that might have an effect on poor countries, with the development goals as formulated in the treaties serving as a key focus. The impact of the CAP on developing countries, discussed in the previous chapter, is a good example of this. *Coordination* aims to ensure alignment between the EU's policy and member states' activities. The exchange of information plays a crucial role in this. The term also refers to coordination between the three European institutions—the Commission, the Council, and the European Parliament—and between the EU, its member states, and international organisations and multilateral initiatives

Figure 4.2. Net Official Development Assistance, 2016 (as % of GNI)

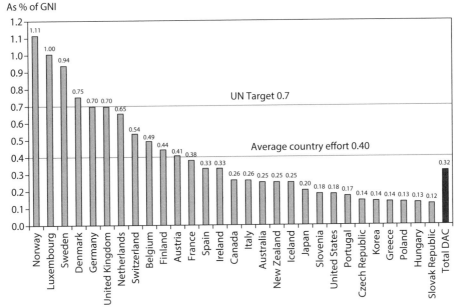

Net ODA in 2016 - as a percentage of GNI

Source: OECD 2017: 6

such as the Millennium Development Goals and its follow-up, the 2030 Agenda for Sustainable Development. Over the years a number of plans were launched to improve coordination, such as the European Consensus on Development (2005), the EU Strategy for Africa (2005), the Agenda for Change (2011), and most recently the New European Consensus on Development (2017). But the existence of various players, interests, and decision-making levels remains too complicated to bring about a clear and irreversible Europeanisation of development policy (see Orbie and Carbone 2015). *Complementarity* stands for the EU and its member states' ambition to complement each other in terms of policy priorities and programmes and in any case to not work against each other. In view of this, the European Commission's coordinating role has gained in importance.

And finally, the third component in the total package of the EU's development assistance is the funds made available to ACP countries via the Cotonou Agreement. Besides the observations made above regarding this EU development aid—and in particular the intergovernmental nature of the EDF with which this aid is financed—I would add two elements that are new in the post-2000 generation of conventions. To begin with, the aid now comes in the form of what are known as partnership agreements, which the EU negotiates with the ACP countries. Despite the name, in reality there is no question of a partnership, as the EU largely determines the substance of these agreements as before. This is reflected in what we could quite rightfully describe as a divide-and-conquer strategy, for the EU makes a distinction between the least developed countries in the group and other ACP countries, and moreover concludes partnerships with separate subgroups of countries. This makes it possible for the EU to offer development aid tailored to particular countries, and to impose conditions almost on an individual country basis. Moreover, the partnership approach weakens the negotiating position of the ACP group as a whole—a position that had already been weakened by the increasing focus of the EU and its member states on the group of poorest countries (i.e. independent of any colonial ties from the past). Secondly, the Cotonou Agreement foregrounded a political dimension to aid, which had also been raised during the Lomé years. In EU jargon, this was called a 'renewed partnership with a stronger political basis'. This so-called political dialogue—a term that suggests equality and reciprocity, just as with the notion of partnership—meant that recipient countries would henceforth be assessed on their upholding of human rights, respect for the rule of law, democratisation in general, and good governance (the new buzzword that emphasises, among other things, the fight against corruption). With the introduction of the partnership agreements, aid was granted on the basis of not only needs but also a country's achievements. The non-execution clause was introduced for this purpose, which allows for aid to be frozen or discontinued—partially or completely—if recipient governments fail to comply with European democratic principles. In addition to good governance, an element of new governance was also incorporated: the involvement of civil societies, local authorities, and non-state actors in the recipient countries were to be actively stimulated. The emphasis was placed on the decisive role of the private sector in the development process.

The two traditional pillars (or two sides of the same coin) of EU development policy—aid and trade—thus acquired a third, to some extent unifying, pillar in the Cotonou Agreement: the political dimension. But the implication of this addition is broader and less stripped of specific EU self-interest than it appears to be, for can we really say that the political conditionality is monitored well and, perhaps more importantly, that it is consistently applied in all cases that arise? And isn't the emphasis on democratic governance structures primarily intended to facilitate the private sector and to free it of meddlesome and corrupt (representatives of) government? Some will say that these are rhetorical questions. Others will emphasise the EU's good intentions based on the idea that it involves the spread of universal norms and values—proof that the EU takes its normative power seriously. There I would defend the claim that the further away from the EU the developing country in question is located and/or the less it plays a role in the immediate security of the EU or its member states, the more thoroughly and more consistently the EU adheres to its own political principles. In other words: as soon as a trade-off must be made between the idealist goal of democratisation on the one hand and realist interests tied to one's own economy and security on the other, it is likely that the EU will choose the realist position. To this rule of thumb, which can be quite easily verified if one examines the EU's external relations since the end of the Cold War, we should include an important exception: as soon as there are signs of genocide, all interests are set aside and the EU responds. Nevertheless, recent history—from the humanitarian crises in Bosnia and Kosovo to Rwanda in the 1990s and Myanmar in 2017—has demonstrated that in such situations the EU has little or no ability to act. Without military means, economic or diplomatic means do not have sufficient impact to deter certain regimes from committing crimes against their own populations.

The limited clout of the EU also has to do with changing perceptions of Europe within developing countries. The EU's willingness to provide assistance is under pressure; the amount of aid is falling in real and per capita terms, and is increasingly focused on poverty reduction instead of industrial development; and development assistance is now being tied to political conditions. In addition, stronger emphasis is put on trade liberalisation as a development strategy, as part of what is known as the 'trade as development' approach. And in the EU's experience this means that, certainly after the launch of the Everything but Arms initiative in 2001 and the entry into force of the Cotonou Convention a year later, trade relations with developing countries should be based on reciprocity and on a stronger orientation toward the least developed countries, whether or not they are members of the ACP group (see Young and Peterson 2013).[8] The move away from relations with former colonies—or rather away from an underlying motivation based on a misplaced (or valid) sense of historical responsibility—has done the EU's normative power no good. As these colonial ties became looser, emerging countries such as China and India stepped into the breach that was created. The 'no questions asked' approach regarding fundamental democratic rights adopted by the new players on the global development cooperation scene is considered an added benefit for many developing countries.

4.3. EU actorness and the position of development policy in EU external relations: Challenges or contradictions?

The European Commission recently outlined the contours of a new European trade policy in a report entitled *Trade for All*. In the foreword written by the Commissioner, it is immediately clear what 'for all' is intended to mean: 'a stronger trade policy for a stronger European Union' (European Commission 2015: 5). The report makes no mention of an ambition focused on the development of the poorest countries. The document emphasises that, in addition to realising intra-European goals (such as the creation of jobs, increased security for consumers, and transparency), trade is not only about interests but also values. Sustainable development, human rights, and the fight against corruption are of great concern to the EU. Partnerships that the EU enters into with other countries must therefore represent these norms and values. This ambition is fully in line with EU treaties. The first section of Article 21 of the Treaty on the European Union leaves no doubt about the most important aims of Global Europe (a label that refers to the eponymous category in the EU's multiannual financial framework):

> The Union's action on the international scene shall be guided by the principles which have inspired its own creation, development and enlargement, and which it seeks to advance in the wider world: democracy, the rule of law, the universality and indivisibility of human rights and fundamental freedoms, respect for human dignity, the principles of equality and solidarity, and respect for the principles of the United Nations Charter and international law.

At the end of this chapter, questions are posed about whether the EU can realise this ambition through its interventions on the global stage, and whether its actorness has been strengthened since the end of the Cold War. For this, it is necessary to look at the entire process rather than a snapshot of the EU's external relations. This chapter focuses more specifically on external action towards the traditional group of ACP countries on the one hand and the group of poorest countries in the international system (the Least Developed Countries or LDCs) on the other.

Turning back to the discussion about IR theories in the first chapters of this book, the dichotomy between rational choice institutionalism and constructivism can also be applied to the problems of the EU's development policy. An approach that says that policy is chiefly based on rational choices and a complex system of interest representation and mediation offers a credible explanation for why a gradual shift took place, particularly at the end of the Cold War, from a policy based on old colonial ties (and historical obligations) towards a more self-interested policy based on economic priorities and security policy objectives. This has, roughly, to do with the following, closely connected developments. Firstly, what was (somewhat irreverently) referred to above as basic needs nihilism—i.e. the emphasis on poverty reduction and on alleviating the most elementary humanitarian needs—was the result of waning confidence in the ability to externally guide internal development processes. It is like the old saying that everyone knows how an egg can be hatched and grow into a chicken but that it is impossible to make a stone undergo the same transformation. This scepticism is evident in the EU's treaties and in the most recent documents regarding EU development policy. None of them specify what the precise definition of development is, what end goals are being pursued (except for the eradication of poverty or, more generally, the realisation of the aims of the United Nations as articulated in the Sustainable Development Goals), let alone how these end goals can be realised. A clear vision of development seems to be lacking, for example in terms of the importance of social cohesion in political and economic processes of change, the link between political and economic modernisation, and the fundamental difference between modernisation and Westernisation.[9] While confidence in grand theoretical projections appears to have eroded considerably, little has taken its place. What has become clear is that 'development fatigue' is increasing at a time of economic decline in the European donor countries. The sensitivity of development budgets to crises has meant that many countries have reduced their ODA as a percentage of national wealth in reaction to the recent euro crisis (see Heinrich et al. 2016).

Secondly, political and socio-economic changes in the EU's immediate surroundings after the end of the Cold War have played a decisive role. As mentioned earlier, attention rapidly shifted to the transformation processes in Central and Eastern Europe and, in the wake of the big bang enlargement in 2004-2007, towards the new neighbours, i.e. the countries that after 2004 became part of the EU's Neighbourhood Policy (see chapter 5). More recently, the fear (whether realistic or not) of the increasing geopolitical assertiveness of the Russian Federation, as for example reflected in its relations with Ukraine, as well as the sharp rise in refugee flows, were added to these post Cold War concerns. Even back in the 1990s, at the time of the fourth Lomé Convention, it became clear that the EU's attention was shifting to the new democracies in Central and Eastern Europe. The chances of success—'value for money'—were considered greater in this other Europe, where communism had already laid an important industrial foundation. Moreover, the prospect of membership was a crucial incentive for candidate countries to undergo their double transformations successfully (see chapter 5). For its part, the EU benefited from stability and security on its direct borders and—albeit to a lesser extent—from new markets and business locations for labour-intensive production processes. From the turn of the millennium, the problems of stability and security have become multidimensional and above all more urgent. This phenomenon is referred to in the academic literature as the security-development nexus, a term that is generally used in an institutional sense (Furness and Gänzle 2017; see also below) but first and foremost receives its importance, of course, from the underlying problems as well as the growing awareness of these problems, which are often disguised as 'challenges'.

The theme of 'development and underdevelopment' in the EU's external relations is increasingly tied to—and often made secondary to—measures aimed at addressing direct security threats, whether supposed or real. A good example of this is the mounting interest in sustainability in external relations in general and in the EU's development policy in particular. We are continually told—quite rightly—that it is in everyone's interest for development in the twenty-first century to be sustainable. At the same time, however, this increases or complicates the 'challenge' for the least developed countries to put themselves socio-economically and politically on the map. The emphasis on sustainability effectively means that for today's developing countries, a second ladder towards a higher development level—the ladder of environmental pollution—has been kicked away (see the analogy used above of the 'kicking away the ladder' effect of the neoliberal prescription for development). A second, and recently most compelling example, is the refugee problem. This is a clear instance of what has been dubbed the securitisation of development aid (Orbie and Lightfoot 2017: 211). Refugee flows are increasingly seen as an internal security problem of the EU, and this has had repercussions for policy. On the one hand, a part of the development budget is being used for the reception of refugees in the receiving EU member states, and on the other hand the development policy of the EU and its member states is being determined by the need to restrict immigration and the desire to send back immigrants to their country of origin.[10]

Thirdly, as part of commercial internationalism (discussed in chapter 3), the EU has an increasing interest in the continued liberalisation of global trade. The idea is as simple as it is effective: with the rise of new growth centres in the world economy, any future increase in economic demand will take place for the most part outside of the EU. Therefore, the EU has everything to gain from new and potential markets remaining accessible for European products and services, also in the future. In the language of the European Commission's *Trade for All* report mentioned earlier, it is said that 30 million jobs within the EU—one in seven jobs—originate from the export of goods and services (European Commission 2015: 8). These jobs are, moreover, highly skilled and well-paid. The rise of new growth countries and the importance of external trade in generating internal growth thus go hand in hand with, and move in the direction of, further globalisation. This occurs at the expense of the poorest countries in the international system. We could call this the great paradox in that other 'nexus', the trade-development nexus: a number of studies have shown that recent decades of economic opening have been accompanied by a narrowing of the gap between poor and rich countries but that on closer inspection this so-called convergence can largely be attributed to the success of countries in Asia in catching up (see, for example, Milanovic 2010). The poorest countries have seen little or no benefit from this trend but are meanwhile confronted with the emphasis put on trade liberalisation in the EU's development strategy (Young and Peterson 2013; see also the various contributions in Carbone and Orbie 2015). Hence it can be deduced that 'trade for all' does not necessarily apply to the poorest in the world. Assuming that this is something that policymakers at both the national and supranational level are aware of, we can only conclude that, also in the field of trade relations, an enlightened self-interest has prevailed in the EU's development policy.

In contrast to this analysis—which is based on rational choices being made in a changing environment—there is another approach that places emphasis on ideas and social interaction and the common values and norms that ensue from this. In the case of EU development policy, the added value of such a perspective can be made clear using a number of examples. Since the relaunch of European integration in the mid-1980s, the persuasiveness of a discourse focused on market forces and a lesser role of the state in the economy has increased considerably and has, three decades later, reached a peak. As we saw in chapter 2, ideas or ideologies such as neoliberalism do not emerge out of thin air, but rather have their basis in concrete interests and identifiable actors, even if much digging is often needed to find them. But forceful ideas also have a mobilising effect, in that they can change (groups of) people's minds. The spectacular paradigm shift from Keynesianism to neoliberalism has supposedly 'opened the eyes' of many politicians, commentators, academics and voters on issues ranging from the welfare state and ownership structures to market forces. This same change has occurred regarding the form and substance of development cooperation. Back in 2001, Gorm Olsen concluded that the impact of public opinion on governments' development aid was crucial when it came to poverty reduction and direct humanitarian aid, but that otherwise a certain aid fatigue had set in (Olsen 2001). This is confirmed by the answers given in a recent Eurobarometer survey in which respondents were asked what the three most important reasons were for the lack of development in Third World countries. By a wide margin, the three most important reasons given were corruption, misgovernment, and conflicts in the receiving countries (European Commission 2017: 54 and further).[11] This mirrors research that is being conducted into the so-called aid-corruption paradox: corruption has a demonstrable effect on donor fatigue in public opinion, even though it is precisely in countries that are relatively more corrupt and that suffer from misgovernment and conflicts where the humanitarian needs and thus the necessity for humanitarian aid is the greatest (see Bauhr et al. 2013). This perhaps explains why opinion polls such as Eurobarometer show rather stable public support for development aid among EU populations but also an increasing scepticism regarding the prospect of sustainable development. In this sense, public opinion and the aforementioned trends in the EU's development policy since the 1990s appear to be converging. In this process of convergence, public perception seems to play an important role—with regard to how the EU should respond to both heart-rending states of emergencies and political-administrative wrongdoings.

Public perception also plays an important role in a completely different sense, certainly when viewed from the perspective of EU actorness. Here it is not only public opinion in the EU member states that is important but also public opinion in the recipient countries. To use Christopher Hills' notion of a capability-expectations gap once again, what was said before can be repeated: this gap can be reduced in different ways, among others by a downwards adjustment of expectations outside the EU. Public perceptions outside the EU of European commitment to the development of the poorest countries has suffered a blow for several reasons. The role of countries such as China and India—who are not members of the OECD DAC and are inspired by their own, non-Western convictions with regard to development aid—in developing countries has contributed to adjust the image of the EU as a DAC superdonor. This image has further changed as a result of the European responses to the euro crisis and the refugee crisis. The gradual changeover from the EU's emphasis on old colonial ties to poverty reduction and then to restricting migration has meant a subtle shift in priorities, and corresponding discourses on development, taking place within Europe. This is something that has not gone unnoticed in recipient countries.

A third example of the significance of ideas for the genesis and further de-velopment of the EU's development policy is the various foreign policy cultures and corresponding public opinions in the different member states. These vary from deeply rooted commitments in the northern member states to remnants of neocolonial grandeur in countries such as France, Spain and Great Britain, as well as enlightened economic self-interest in, for example, Germany. The new member states of Central and Eastern Europe represent a special category of member states in this respect. The big bang enlargement led to the balance being tipped even further towards member states that historically have had no colonies and thus were relatively open-minded and impartial towards the heterogeneous group of least developed countries (LDCs). Moreover, this enlargement brought the EU face to face with its new neighbouring countries, adding a new dimension to the relationship between the EU and Russia due to these neighbouring countries' role in the former Soviet Union (see the next two chapters).[12] At the same time, these are member states that are mostly net receivers of internal EU aid; they have yet to join the DAC or, if they have done so, have such a limited development budget that the aim of achieving the EU average percentage of 0.7% is unfeasible for the time being. There is thus a genuine divide within the EU: a Europe of different speeds. The recent position of the new member states with respect to receiving refugees is a potentially explosive element of this divide. Their refusal to take on a proportionate number of refugees can partly be explained by their self-perception as 'developing member states'.

This last aspect offers a much clearer perspective on another theoretical discussion conducted in previous chapters. An almost automatic spillover to a supranational development policy is absolutely out of the question. Put in other words, persistently significant differences in terms of interests, priorities, and discourses continue to impede the Europeanisation of member states' development policies. In a prelude to the next chapter, the conclusion is that such Europeanisation has become more difficult with every round of enlargement. Each new entrant—Great Britain in the 1970s, Spain in the 1980s, Sweden in the 1990s, or Poland in the first decade of this millennium—brings along with it a new perspective and a long-standing tradition (or a lack thereof) as well as a reluctance to see a drastic strengthening of the exclusive powers of European institutions in the field of development policy. Although the European Commission has gradually taken more initiatives since the turn of the millennium, the EU's development policy remains predominantly intergovernmental in terms of aid, with the principal responsibilities (and financial means) remaining at the level of the member states. At best, it can be said that in the last 20 years, particularly since the Treaty of Lisbon came into force in 2009, the Commission has been given a coordinating role. But finding the right balance between global free trade, the sustainable development of poor countries, and the EU's own security remains too great a 'challenge' for the time being.

4.4.   Conclusion

This chapter has made clear, first, that a common European development policy has become more ideologically specific since the 1990s. In line with changing ideas within the EU on government intervention, the emphasis has come to rest on economic liberalism, also with regard to development issues. Governments in developing countries should focus on export promotion, on the one hand, and on the realisation of a political investment climate that can best be described as good governance, on the other. Second, the EU's development policy has increasingly been targeted at the poorest countries in the international system, which has partly been at the expense of a policy focused on good relations with former colonial territories. Third, grand ideas about development and underdevelopment have made way for a stronger emphasis on poverty relief and the fulfilment of basic needs. This appears to be a reflection of a certain degree of pessimism about the likelihood of development, which is both industrial and sustainable, succeeding in the poorest countries. And finally, development policy has been 'polluted' by two considerations that have little to do with a global and altruistic perspective on inequality. Since the end of the Cold War, priority has been given to developments in Europe's immediate neighbours, while security considerations with regard to the EU itself have received a more prominent place on the political agenda.

Another conclusion that can be drawn is that the Europeanisation of development policy still has a long way to go. The differences between member states remain too significant. The larger member states in particular continue to see development policy as an extension of their national foreign policy; other countries have a national development culture that is largely based on non-material interests. And still other countries, in particular the new member states that joined in the 2004-2007 period, are yet to start developing a full-fledged policy of development aid.

Though there are traces of convergence to be found, especially since the turn of the millennium, there are two reasons to believe that such a convergence will ultimately be found wanting. Firstly, this convergence is a convergence of interests based on a common (or at least perceived to be common) external threat and not one based on mutual cooperation conjoined by beliefs—i.e. not based on functional spillover and upward Europeanisation. Secondly, not all member states are a part of this convergence. If the big bang enlargement of the EU—covered in the next chapter—has shown anything, it is that the various external 'challenges' are perceived and appreciated in different ways by old and new member states.

Suggestions for further reading

(Holland and Doidge 2012) cited in this chapter is an informative introduction to the EU's development policy. The publications of Young and Peterson (2013 and 2014) cited here are also very much worth reading. A recent book about the Europeanisation of development policy is (Carbone and Orbie 2017).

The OECD's annual Development Report contains statistics and analyses of the development policies of members of the DAC. These reports are available going back multiple years and can be downloaded from the OECD's website. Other interesting publications can be found on the OECD website, as well as a wide range of statistics on official development assistance (ODA). The website of Oxfam International (https://www.oxfam.org) offers a number of often critical reports about the substance and effects of Western development policy. There is also a wealth of information on the website of the EU's Directorate-General for International Cooperation and Development.

The following books about development theory complement each other nicely: (Rist 2014), (Chang 2003), and (Acemoglu and Robinson 2012).

5. The end of the Cold War, the enlargement strategy, and the European Union's Neighbourhood Policy

The previous chapter showed that the end of the Cold War and the implosion of the Soviet sphere of influence led to a gradual shift in the geographical orientation of the EU's external relations. The most pressing challenges were now closer to home—around the corner, so to speak, in that 'other Europe'—and the problems appeared to be solvable according to the initially optimistic way of thinking about a new global order and the end of history. That is, they seemed more solvable than the years of struggle against underdevelopment and poverty in more distant countries. Cultural factors certainly played a role in this. From the first steps towards national self-determination in countries such as Poland, Czechoslovakia, and Hungary, developments in the former Eastern Bloc were seen as a *European* matter. The double transformation that began with the Velvet Revolutions of 1989—from authoritarian rule to parliamentary democracy and from command economy to free market economy—became part of the EU's 'historic duty' towards the new democracies. The establishment of a sizeable aid operation—which included financial, technical, and other kinds of support—was accompanied by overblown slogans such as 'the return to the European house' of democracy and a market economy. As a result, in the course of the 1990s, the EU's relations with the non-European underdeveloped world were soon overtaken both in a quantitative and qualitative sense (quantitatively all the more so if we consider the difference in numbers of countries and inhabitants).

Table 5.1 shows the most up-to-date ramifications of this development that began in the early 1990s, at the time of Lomé IV (and is furthermore an accurate summary of the importance of the subject matter of this chapter, i.e. enlargement strategy and neighbourhood policy, for the EU's external relations). We see here the section of the EU's multi-annual budget for the period 2014-2020 that focuses on 'Global Europe' (see also the corresponding table with the breakdown of the entire Multiannual Financial Framework in chapter 1). The order of the categories presumably does not indicate any overt prioritisation, but the first two expenditure items together account for more than 40 per cent of the total amount of more than €66 billion, while the development cooperation instrument takes up slightly less than 30 per cent. This chapter will show that the first two instruments are inextricably linked to each other and to the end of the Cold War; both have their origin in the 1990s and were initially focused on the new democracies in Europe. Previous enlargements prior to 1989 did not involve coordinated and integrated aid programmes. The contrast with the accession of Spain, Portugal, and Greece in particular is significant—as will become clear later in this chapter.[1]

Table 5.1.   Multiannual Financial Framework (2014-2020) – 'Global Europe' (millions of EUR – current prices)

Commitment appropriations for 'Global Europe'	Total 2014-2020
1. Instrument for Pre-accession Assistance (IPA)	11,698.6680
2. European Neighbourhood Instrument (ENI)	15,432.6340
3. European Instrument for Democracy and Human Rights (EIDHR)	1,332.7520
4. Instrument for Stability (IfS)	2,338.7190
5. Common Foreign and Security Policy (CFSP)	2,338.7190
6. Partnership Instrument (PI)	954.7650
7. Development Cooperation Instrument (DCI)	19,661.6390
8. Humanitarian Aid	6,621.6960
9. Other	5,882.4080
Total commitment appropriations for 'Global Europe'	66,262.0000

Source: http://ec.europa.eu/budget/mff/index_en.cfm

The end of the Cold War also had major institutional and policy-related consequences for the EU. New candidate countries applied to join, or quietly joined. The latter was the case with former East Germany which, as a result of the reunification of East and West, automatically became part of the EU without so much as a stroke of a pen. To a certain extent, the 1995 enlargement round that included Sweden, Finland, and Austria also took place without problems and almost without notice. This was not the case for the candidate countries from Central and Eastern Europe that had belonged to the former Eastern Bloc. A new policy area within the broad external relations of the EU was created for them, which made this a genuine enlargement strategy. The key element of this strategy was the concept of 'conditionality', which was divided into two parts corresponding to the aforementioned double transformation. For the first time, the EU formulated explicit political and economic criteria that candidate countries had to meet before accession could take place.[2] This issue will be elaborated upon in this chapter using the concept of transformative power. It turns out that the EU has much more influence on other countries if the remuneration is not limited to financial assistance. The prospect of full membership of the EU appears to be an important weapon in bringing about structural changes in those candidate countries that are politically and economically at a lower level of development than the EU member states. The situation is altogether different for countries that do not have such prospects, such as the more distant developing countries that are eligible for financial support from the EU, or for what are termed the neighbourhood countries, which are those countries that suddenly bordered the EU as a result of the 2004-2007 big bang enlargement round, whose prospects for accession are limited (as is the case with Ukraine, for example) or simply non-existent.[3] The second part of this chapter will discuss this group of countries in more detail as well as the EU policy that was specifically created for these countries in 2004.

This chapter is structured as follows. The first section (5.1) will deal successively with the interaction between enlargement and deepening of the European integration process, with previous enlargement rounds (i.e. prior to the big bang enlargement towards Central and Eastern Europe), and more extensively with the big bang enlargement itself. This will be wrapped up with a discussion about the limits of enlargement in the light of external and in particular internal impediments. Subsequently, the term transformative power will be introduced in section 5.2 as an element connecting the first and second parts of this chapter. It has long been assumed, both in politics and academia, that the most successful part of the EU's external relations after the end of the Cold War was its enlargement policy. It was precisely the close-knit combination of the stick (the accession criteria) and the carrot (the ultimate reward in the form of membership) that triggered structural transformations, which developing countries were unable to realise, or only realise with much difficulty, as discussed in the previous chapter. Now, more than a decade after the actual big bang enlargement, many things have become significantly more nuanced (or, to put it another way, less unambigiously positive). Both the internal and external consequences of enlargement will be explained in section 5.3, under the heading 'beyond conditionality'. One of the external consequences of enlargment is that the EU has shifted its boundaries to countries that are not entitled to membership. In this light, section 5.4 will examine the effect of the EU's Neighbourhood Policy on countries that will never be able to join the Union but that are geographically close enough to affect EU stability and security. The chapter will end with a short conclusion and some suggestions for further reading.

5.1.   Deepening or widening, enlargement and disintegration?

Enlargement has a longer history than the policy that has been pursued as part of the EU's external relations since the 1990s. From the early beginnings of European integration, the founders were confronted with the question of which countries could and should participate and which countries should not. On the one hand, this issue was settled on grounds of principle. For example, European integration was limited to countries that were geographically part of the European continent, even if the boundaries of that continent were never clearly demarcated. (The previous chapter showed that European states' overseas territories initially formed an exception to this territorial inclusion and exclusion, simply because they were considered to be part of the motherland. Later in this chapter, I will note that in the current enlargement debate, political rather than geographic arguments prevail.) A second argument used to refuse countries was political in nature. The assumption was that successful and stable supra-state integration on a voluntary basis could only take place between countries that were democratically governed. This principle meant that the countries of Central and Eastern Europe that became part of the sphere of influence of the Soviet Union after the Second World War could in any case be excluded from membership, if they even had such ambitions. The same was true for the authoritarian regimes in Southern Europe.

In addition to exclusive, fundamental arguments of a geographic and political nature, there were of course also non-participating countries that met the afore-mentioned conditions but decided, for reasons of their own, to stay outside the original integration projects. This was very specifically the case for the so-called neutral countries of Sweden, Finland, and Austria, which under the influence of the Cold War threat could not—or did not want to—make a clear choice for one of the two spheres of influence. These countries were not to join the EU until 1995. And Switzerland to this day remains outside, cherishing its policy of calculated detach-ment. But by far the most important country that excluded itself after having given ample consideration to the matter was the United Kingdom. Generally speaking, the literature mentions three considerations that together led to this decision (see, for example, Dinan 2010). In the first place, British foreign policy was still steeped in times of yore, when this island kingdom could rightly claim world power status. In an echo of the famous words of Winston Churchill at a conference in The Hague in 1948, the British still considered themselves to be a bridge between the US and an integrating western part of continental Europe. This was, of course, based on the notion of the infamous special relationship between the British kingdom and the new hegemonic power. Closely linked to this, a second factor played a role in the United Kingdom's decision not to become a member of the integration project: the British relationship with the Commonwealth countries. This voluntary partnership between Great Britain and most of its former colonies and mandate areas, dating back to 1949, guaranteed the British an influx of cheap agricultural products. Membership in an economic community including a common agricultural policy might have brought an end to this preferential trade relationship. This would certainly have been the case if the intended move from a free trade zone to a customs union was taken, which implied that national trade policy would be subordinated to a common policy led by a supranational body, i.e. the European Commission. And this brings us to a third factor: from the outset, the British were afraid that the idea of an 'ever closer union' as stated in the preamble to the Treaty of Rome would lead to a supranational construction in the hands of supra-state technocrats. From the first deliberations about European integration, the British were in favour of a strict free trade zone without further complications in the form of what they saw as an unnecessary or even undesirable transfer of sovereignty. The island mentality proved to be stronger than the idea of Western European unification.

Moreover, the British were not very convinced of the European economic community's chances of success as an initial integration project. They were soon to be proved wrong, but by then it turned out to be too late to get on board the moving train. Retrospectively, more than half a century later, it remains difficult to imagine that only three years after the Treaty of Rome entered into force in 1958, the United Kingdom made an attempt to join the EU. It must have realised that its special relationship with the US might not have been as equal as it thought—the end of the Suez Crisis of 1956 must have been an early warning sign of this—and that the first intiatives towards European integration may not have been so supranational after all. Moreover, membership would allow Great Britain to influence the gradual transition from a free trade zone to a customs union from within. Whatever the case, in 1961 the British applied for membership. But they had not considered one thing: two years later, the French President Charles de Gaulle submitted his first veto on British accession.[4]

5.1.1.   Previous enlargement rounds and the dynamics of deeper integration

The fact that the British had been mistaken about the dynamics of European integration and subsequently wanted to join the project points to a historic connection between what is referred to as the link between deepening and widening. There are four different ways to substantiate this. Firstly, and to some extent referring back to the example of Great Britain, the relationship between deepening and widening can be summarised by the concept of geographic spillover (see also chapter 1). This term refers to the fact that a successful deepening of integration between two or more countries may be sufficient reason for third countries to apply for membership. This can be based on positive grounds, purely and simply because of the appeal of the project and/or a rational cost-benefit analysis of membership. It may also be based on the negative consideration that not joining an integration group of neighbouring countries might have irrevocable consequences, without the country in question being able to co-decide on the further course of cooperation. This appears to have been an important reason for Sweden, Finland, and Austria, once stripped of their Cold War yoke, to apply for membership soon after the acceleration of the EU integration process through the Maastricht Treaty (and for the governments of Switzerland and Norway to repeatedly and unsuccessfully take the case for membership to their own people).

Secondly, the link between deepening and widening lies in the historical observation that the first always preceded the second. A successful step in the deepening of the integration process was, in fact, a condition for enlargement. In 1969, the summit of European government leaders and the French head of state (then George Pompidou, who had replaced the stubborn De Gaulle) paved the way for accession negotiations with the United Kingdom, Ireland, and Denmark, but only after the six founding states had decided that the predecessor of the Common Foreign and Security Policy—the European Political Cooperation, which was a kind of rudimentary EU foreign policy , as explained earlier—would come into force and that a monetary union would be realised by 1980. The accession of Spain and Portugal on 1 January 1986 was preceded by the decision to complete the internal market. The enlargement towards the so-called neutral countries took place after the ratification of the Treaty of Maastricht marked a new phase of deepening. And the 2004-2007 big bang enlargement was preceded by an agreement on a European Constitution. Based on the idea of an ever closer union, there was a certain logic behind this specific historical sequence. Since every new step in the integration process would become more difficult with more members, certainly if there were to be a necessary treaty change that could (and can) only be decided on the basis of unanimity, it was important to move further on deepening before new members could express any possible objections. Candidate members would then be confronted with a new integration package that they would either have to accept or reject. The importance of this sequence of events will be illustrated below.

Third, the link between deepening and enlargement can also go in the opposite direction: enlargement can also prevent further deepening or at least make it considerably more difficult. The well-known German political scientist Fritz Scharpf has rightly argued that every new round of enlargement in the direction of less developed countries makes it even more difficult to take a step towards a so-called social Europe (Scharpf 2002). The reasoning goes as follows. Countries in Europe not only have different traditions and different views on the role of the state in society but also significantly different development trajectories. As a result of the big bang enlargement—and to a lesser extent the earlier Mediterranean enlargement or, even earlier, the accession of Ireland in 1973—the difference between rich and poor, developed and less developed member states has increased enormously. This is reflected in the widely varying social practices and circumstances that exist in Europe, such as differences in wage levels (especially minimum wage levels) and in social provisions such as benefit systems and healthcare. Existing differences make it virtually impossible from a political point of view to achieve a substantial harmonisation of social policy at the European level.

This is just one of countless examples. Consider, for example, European agricultural policy. Some new member states such as Poland have a relatively large and inefficient agricultural sector that was already eager to participate in the Common Agricultural Policy in the years before its accession. Elsewhere, however, in the old member states, the call for a (partial) dismantling of this money-wasting policy is getting stronger. For years, attempts have been made to reform the CAP and to make it more financially sustainable.

In external relations as well, the differences have widened as a result of the respective enlargements, and the different opinions and voices have become increasingly difficult to unite. Some countries are full members of the Development Assistance Committee (DAC), while others are net recipients of EU internal development aid. The importance of international trade in the national economy varies greatly between member states, as does the geographic origin and destination of their imports and exports (and therefore the priorities of member states). And among the new member states, there is a far greater willingness to subordinate national foreign and security policy to transatlantic loyalty towards the American leader (and patron) within NATO, as well as a far deeper fear of renewed Russian aggression than elsewhere in the EU. In short, in almost every policy area—be it internal (with external consequences) or external—national interests, traditions, values and norms, and sensitivities have diverged considerably under the influence of successive rounds of enlargement, with big bang enlargement being the most cogent example. Divergence is at odds with cohesion, and cohesion is necessary to reach the desired consensus for the next phase in a process of ever deeper integration.

This last observation irrevocably leads to a certain differentiation among member states in order to ensure that the aforementioned process of ever deeper integration is not brought to a standstill. This is the fourth and last point I would like to make regarding the link between deepening and enlargement. Here too, there are plenty of examples. The Treaty of Maastricht announced the establishment of an Economic and Monetary Union, but two of the three countries that had joined the first enlargement round—namely the United Kingdom and Denmark—managed to obtain an exception for themselves (the so-called opt-out) and therefore remained outside the eurozone. Of the sixteen countries that have joined the European Union since 1991, seven are not yet members of the eurozone, although they are required to become members in the long term. Another example of de-facto differentiation is the recent resistance that the so-called refugee agreement has met from member states in very different ways—and more generally the issue of the free movement of people. And also in the area of the CFSP, a dichotomy has emerged, with a core group of member states deciding to integrate at a deeper (or higher) level. And this completes the circle, bringing us back to a small (or smaller) group of countries that have chosen to take on a new initiative in the area of supra-state integration that could in the long run be sufficient appealing to other countries. The latter countries can then still try to join the initiative if that is what they want and if they meet all the conditions. This was the opportunity that was introduced with the notion of 'enhanced cooperation' as a way to break through any impasses in the integration process. The possibilty of enhanced cooperation was first included in the Treaty of Amsterdam (1997) and further institutionalised in the Treaty of Lisbon (2009) but was already suggested as an option in the 1970s by leading European politicians such as Leo Tindemans. Whenever an increase in socio-economic and political-cultural differences would result from a new enlargement round, proposals in line with the notion of 'differentiation in integration' were made. Various names for this differentiation have been suggested, including 'a Europe of multiple speeds', 'Europe à la carte', 'core Europe', and 'variable geometry'.

As mentioned, enhanced cooperation is the institutionalised variant of this way of thinking about integration between unequally developed and dissimilar entities. Article 20 of the Treaty on European Union and Articles 326 to 334 of the Treaty on the Functioning of the European Union state the substantive and procedural conditions for closer cooperation and the conditions under which non-participating member states can still join at a later stage. Three elements are important to state explicitly here. Enhanced cooperation between at least nine member states in areas that do not fall within the exclusive competence of the EU can only take place if it does not affect economic, social, and territorial cohesion within the Union. Moreover, enhanced cooperation must in no way conflict with the CFSP and more generally with the Union's external action. A special provision has been included in the Treaty of Lisbon that regulates the possibility of closer defence cooperation within a smaller group of member states.

Enhanced cooperation aims to strengthen the integration process when diverging interests as a result of enlargement make unanimous deepening impossible (at least for the time being). Although enhanced cooperation is not allowed to have a negative impact on socio-economic cohesion within the Union, differentiated integration as a historic necessity and treaty-based option has certainly been the result of diminishing cohesiveness. And with the most recent big bang enlargement, this issue has only become more relevant. A comparison between the Mediterranean enlargement and the accession of the countries of Central and Eastern Europe shows this clearly.

5.1.2.   Big bang enlargement in comparative perspective

This is not the place to elaborate on the individual enlargement rounds. The purpose of this chapter is to indicate how the EU's enlargement strategy fits into its broader external relations and what impact this strategy has had on countries that had (or have) expressed their ambition to join. In addition, one can legitimately wonder why—given the possible consequences—the EU is prepared to include new countries at all. This last issue will be discussed later in this chapter.

The big bang enlargement of the EU occupies a unique place in the history of the Union in terms of its preparation, size, and scope. This is made clear when one makes a comparison between the enlargement that included Spain, Portugal, and Greece in the 1980s and the 2004-2007 enlargement to include countries that belonged to the former Soviet bloc. Such a comparison is interesting for several reasons. In the first place, both the Mediterranean countries and the former Soviet bloc countries clearly lagged behind the existing EU member states at the time of their accession. But this similarity cannot hide the fact that the differences between the two groups were and are extremely significant and still resonate in the way things work in Brussels today. Secondly, not only were the two groups of candidate countries different but also the EU itself had undergone a radical transformation in the twenty years between the two enlargement rounds. To use a metaphor: it really does matter how fast the train is going at the moment you decide to jump on it. Partly because of this, the consequences of both rounds of enlargement are also signficantly different.

The countries in both regions—henceforth referred to as SPG (Spain, Portugal and Greece) and CEE (Central and Eastern Europe) respectively—started from quite different positions. This had national, historical, and international, European dimensions. The national dimension can be explained by introducing a difference between transition—the term that is often used to indicate the transition to democracy in SPG in 1974-75—and transformation. The first term refers to the formal institutional changes necessary for the *establishment* of a democracy and a market economy, while the term transformation also refers to the structural and behavioural changes necessary for the *functioning* of the new system, in accordance with the rules of democracy and a market economy. The first consequence of introducing such a difference is immediately noticeable. In order to determine whether a transition has been successfully completed, one only needs to proceed with mathematical precision to answer the following questions. Is the separation of powers anchored in the new, democratic constitution? Are free elections held (including monitoring by foreign observers)? Is there a rule of law in which minority rights are respected and freedom of expression guaranteed? And so on. Such an assessment is significantly more difficult when it comes to structural, behavioural, and mindset changes. When can we speak of a consolidated democracy in which the basic rules are observed by political, military, and economic elites and accepted by the vast majority of the population? When can we say that a well-functioning market economy exists, and who determines that? When can it be established that a metamorphosis from *homo sovieticus* to *homo oeconomicus* has actually taken place, and on what criteria can such a determination be made at all? We will see later that these questions are also important in assessing the enlargement strategy that the EU developed for CEE in the course of the 1990s.

For now, it is important to note that after the 'fall of the dictatorships' in 1974-75—with the Carnation Revolution in Portugal, the end of the colonel regime in Greece, and the death of General Francisco Franco in Spain—a transition to democracy was started in SPG that in fact constituted a formal conclusion of a process of social change that had begun much earlier. Moreover, this was a single transition because the three countries had undergone an economic development process from the beginning of the 20th century on the basis of market-driven industrialisation and the primacy of private ownership. If the state played a dominant role, this was due to a lack of private initiatives and private entrepreneurship and not for political-ideological reasons.

How different the situation was in CEE. Attempts at cautious internal democratisation were suppressed with violence until the very last minute—as in Poland in the 1980s—and the abrupt transition to democracy under the influence of the 1989 Velvet Revolutions came as a big surprise, if not as a shock, instead of an already long-anticipated process as in SPG. Furthermore, the change in CEE was a double transformation instead of the single transition in SPG. In addition to the transition to a parliamentary democracy, including the behavioural change that was necessary for the new system to function properly, the CEE countries also had to complete a transition from a command economy to a free and internationally oriented market economy. And here too, it was to be a transformation with far-reaching consequences.

The 1989 revolutions were to lead remarkably soon to a somewhat hasty privatisation of companies that had been set up by the state under communist rule and were considered state property. But the transfer of state-owned companies into private hands presumes the availability of sufficient private capital. In the absence of domestic private resources so soon after the fall of regimes in which private ownership was kept to a minimum, the financial resources had to come from elsewhere. And so it was that the privatisation of industrial companies and banks could only occur by virtue of the influx of foreign capital. This development—as part of the economic transformation— has been referred to as the introduction of a kind of 'capitalism without capitalists' (Gil Eyal et al. 1997: 61). That may sound good but it is actually incorrect. Capitalism was introduced from the outside, and the private property of private entrepreneurs— as an essential characteristic of capitalism—came from abroad in the absence of domestic alternatives. This touches on an important point: if Western Europe (seen here as the interplay of state and non-state stakeholders in the then member states, and at the European level) was of the opinion that the political and economic systems in CEE should be shaped along the same lines as the prevailing systems in the West—and that was, indeed, the general opinion—then active participation on the part of the EU would be indispensable. This necessity was recognised at a very early stage by the well-known

German political sociologist Claus Offe: 'The only circumstance under which the market economy and democracy can be simultaneously implanted and prosper is that one in which both are forced upon a society from outside and guaranteed by international relations of dependency and supervision for a long period of time' (Offe 1991: 874). And this was precisely what happened from the early 1990s, in a process that will be explained later using the concept of transformative power.

The international relations of dependence and supervision to which Offe refers in the quotation above had a dual nature. In the first place, CEE countries became heavily dependent on the influx of foreign direct investment as their economic transformation progressed. This requires a brief explanation. The transition to a market economy implies internal and external economic liberalisation. Internal liberalisation involves the abolition of price control, among other things. If prices become dependent on the free play of supply and demand, this will initially result in a severe money depreciation, otherwise known as inflation. After all, prices are no longer set from above by the state but are made dependent on real—and in the case of CEE often inefficiently high—production costs. For ordinary citizens, this means that although the supply of goods may be increasing, the possibility of purchasing these goods is reduced (the long lines for poorly stocked state stores are replaced by people who look in shop windows at products they cannot buy). External liberalisation essentially means trade liberalisation. Since foreign products can be produced more efficiently and more cheaply, this form of liberalisation leads to trade deficits, certainly in the short term. More money flows out of the domestic economy than into it. In this context, attracting foreign direct investments is crucial, i.e. in addition to the aforementioned need for foreign capital to make privatisation schemes a success. The influx of foreign capital can to some extent compensate for trade deficits and in the long term also provide a boost to export-oriented growth. The dependence on foreign investments is therefore born out of necessity on the one hand, but on the other hand it can offer a (temporary) solution to structural economic problems.

However, this dependence also had a downside. Foreign capital initially flowed mainly to those sectors where growth was to be expected; and primarily companies that belonged to what were termed diamonds in the former state (or command) economy were targeted. Banking and insurance, telecommunications and utilities were among the favourite investment objects, often strategically important sectors in a country's economy. But this meant that the decision-making centres were moved elsewhere, namely to the headquarters of banks and industrial companies abroad.[5] After 1989, CEE also became an interesting greenfield investment area for the labour-intensive manufacturing industry due to the unique combination of cheap and relatively well-educated labour.

In a recent study on the role of foreign direct investment (FDI) in CEE, a few critical comments are made in this light. The relocation of labour-intensive production processes from Western Europe to CEE meant that the latter became part of so-called global value chains on the basis of its 'comparative advantage' of cheap but skilled labour. Such an overreliance on foreign capital can cause additional problems for a national economy during a global economic downturn. This was the case for many CEE countries during the recent euro crisis: decreasing investments were the direct result of the crisis in capital-exporting countries. Furthermore, an overreliance on external financing and productive investment can hamper the development of local technology and knowledge. The negative influence of FDI on local initiatives and locally inspired development projects is further accentuated by the fact that the region has low value capture. This means that the profits of domestic establishments of foreign companies do not remain in the region or are not reinvested there—and therefore are not a source of further and deeper development (Szent-Iványi 2017).[6] The dominant position of foreign capital in certain sectors and the practice of repatriating profits to the country of origin, together with the recent economic downturn, have led to the emergence of anti-multinationalism in many countries which, as part of growing nationalism and populism in the region, sometimes also has a strong Eurosceptic undertone.

Secondly, CEE countries were confronted with European institutions that kept the new reformers' activities under ongoing external supervision. That this was accepted without protest—certainly initially—was, of course, primarily due to the ambitions of the respective post-communist governments, supported by a large majority of the CEE population. For CEE countries that had not been part of the Soviet Union, a return to Europe was synonymous with joining the EU. Some countries applied for membership just five years after the 1989 revolutions.

Above, I mentioned that the SPG and CEE countries had clearly different starting positions. The first difference concerns the aforementioned distinction between single transition and double transformation. A second difference is related to the drastically changed international context—and the changed nature of the EU in particular—in the period between the two enlargements (1981-1986 and 2004-2007). This is a frequently forgotten dimension in reflections on successive rounds of enlargements. The differences between candidate countries are covered extensively, but that an apparently similar sequence of events or formally similar political and social processes can have very different implications or consequences in different phases of 'world history' (see Giddens 1981: 167) is less frequently discussed. The formal enlargement procedure of the EU can serve as a good example here. The transformation processes that CEE countries underwent from the 1989 revolutions coincided with a phase in the development of global and European structures that was fundamentally different from the world scene of only 15 years earlier, i.e. the moment the SPG started their transition. Three aspects of this 'new' phase can be distinguished.

First, it cannot be emphasised enough that the revolutions in CEE and the subsequent collapse of the Soviet Union sealed the end of the Cold War. These events were not so much the start but rather the necessary breakthrough in a previously initiated gradual shift from the post-war bipolar world order to a multipolar constellation in which the struggle for spheres of influence was waged by more parties in a more chaotic way; a struggle that, moreover, was largely stripped of its former ideological content—the struggle between capitalism in the West and real existing socialism in the East. The immediate consequences for CEE countries were twofold: on the one hand, they had to reconcile their recently regained sovereignty with the need for mutual cooperation (the principle of good neighbourliness as a condition for joining the EU) and shield this sovereignty from a potential threat from what was now reduced to the Russian Federation. On the other hand, they were confronted with an EU that, partly under the influence of the new European architecture after the Cold War, had become internally divided over its own deepening and over the speed and the way in which rapprochement with the new democracies and market economies in CEE should take place. This division had already surfaced virulently at the European Council of Maastricht in December 1991 and had led to a split over monetary unification (the United Kingdom and Denmark managing to negotiate an opt-out).

Secondly, and in spite of this internal division, the EU had taken an important final step immediately after the fall of the Iron Curtain in the ideal-typical phasing of economic integration (see chapter 3), although not with all member states. The decision to move towards economic and monetary unification was therefore taken well before the start of accession negotiations with CEE countries. The latter were, it goes without saying, not involved in the conception of the EMU at the Maastricht summit nor in its eventual entry into force, and therefore had no influence whatsoever. However, with the signing of the Accession Treaties—and in accordance with the Treaty on the Functioning of the European Union—they took on the obligation to adopt the euro, a fact that the European Central Bank does not refrain from repeatedly emphasising in the biannual convergence reports it publishes, which monitor the progress of macroeconomic convergence of all non-members of the euro area (excluding the United Kingdom and Denmark). In addition, the new member states were confronted with the planned deepening operation preceding the big bang enlargement in the form of the European Constitution, which eventually entered into force as the Treaty of Lisbon in 2009—that is, five and two years respectively after the enlargement round of 2004-07. This last step generated an integration dynamic that came perhaps too soon for the respective populations after the regaining of their sovereignty and too soon after their actual accession. It appears possible that this speed—from forced to voluntary integration and from regained freedom to renewed loss of self-determination in just one-and-a-half decades—has played a role in the recent revival of patriotism and Euroscepticism in countries such as Poland, the Czech Republic, Slovakia, and Hungary. The contrast with SPG is significant. Spain, Portugal and Greece became members of the EU or concluded their accession negotiations in a time of eurosclerosis and were therefore able to decide as members —i.e. from the inside, in an EU where treaty changes must be approved unanimously—on the completion of the internal market and the development towards monetary union. Moreover, the conditions attached to their accession were far more flexible, often implicit, and fewer in number (see below for the so-called Copenhagen criteria that were required of CEE countries to be able to accede). Finally, these southern European countries and their populations were already used to cooperating within Western organisational settings.

Thirdly, the transformation processes in CEE coincided with an unprecedented liberalisation and globalisation of economic structures. This development was accompanied by a major restructuring race between national economies and unbridled policy competition between governments with the aim of optimising the functioning of the supply economy (see next chapter). Cutbacks in government spending and the flexibilisation of labour markets translated into a gradual dismantling of the welfare state and a downward adjustment of social protection schemes in the West. The disciplining effect of global financial markets and company relocations also reverberated in the transition economies of CEE. The policy adjustment in CEE was in any case difficult to reconcile in the short term with the construction of a social safety net for large sections of the population. In the words of the Hungarian political scientist Attila Agh (1998: 56-57), the specific nature of the economic transformation process resulted in a 'new social crisis' in CEE: a drastic deterioration in material living standards (falling real wages, skyrocketing unemployment rates, declining life expectancy, a poverty trap in which an increasing number of people had to live below subsistence level); an intensification of social polarisation—i.e. an increasing gap between the winners (often in urban areas) and losers (usually in rural areas) of the double transformation; and a psychological crisis due to rapid economic and social changes. At an early stage, the World Bank signaled a similar development but stated that:

> greater disparity of wages, income and wealth is—up to a point—a necessary part of transition, because allowing wages to be determined by the market creates incentives for efficiency that are essential for successful reform. More efficient workers must be rewarded for their contribution to growth. But increased inequality can raise poverty in the short run because some people [...] inevitably benefit more than others. But the 'losers' will not necessarily be forced into poverty; it depends on whether governments restructure social safety nets to provide effective poverty relief. (World Bank 1996: 66)

What the World Bank failed to mention is that the governments in CEE had no autonomy to 'restructure their social safety nets' due to the many restrictions imposed on them by international organisations such as the World Bank itself and the IMF as part of the conditions that accompanied the necessary refinancing and restructuring of the huge debt positions in the region (see the discussion on the so-called Washington Consensus in the previous chapter). These requirements for 'creditworthiness' were entirely in line with (and perhaps even tailored to) the requirements imposed by foreign investors for a favourable investment climate as well as the general direction and content of the conditionality that the EU attached to its rapprochement strategy.

In the case of Spain, Portual, and to a lesser extent Greece, external debt played a relatively insignificant role in the transition to parliamentary democracy. Moreover, this transition occurred at a time when belief in Keynesian government steering of the economy had not yet given way to the neoliberal beliefs of the late 1980s and 1990s. It is significant both for the consolidation of the democracies in SPG and probably also for the continued positive attitude of the respective populations towards the EU (which in the case of the Greek population only came to an end under the influence of the euro crisis and the draconian austerity measures imposed on them) that governments could postpone overly rigorous and aggressive economic restructuring and policy adjustments and, especially in the initial years after 1974-75, concentrate on the actual political transition while maintaining a certain degree of socio-economic cohesion and stability.

5.2.   The EU as *transformative power*?

External debt played an important role in the first years of the double transformation in CEE, as did the mandatory and non-mandatory recommendations from international organisations and experts. However, with hindsight it is clear that the mutual rapprochement between the CEE governments and the institutions, member states, and civil society organisations of the EU has been of critical importance for its successful conclusion. The first countries to apply for EU membership after 1989—Poland and Hungary—did so in 1994. Other CEE countries followed in successive years. This was a formal request that actually formed the final step in a pre-accession strategy that came into play in the immediate aftermath of the fall of the Iron Curtain. Firstly, from 1991, what were termed Europe Agreements were concluded with CEE countries. These agreements aimed to create a free trade area for non-agricultural products between the EU and CEE over a ten-year period. However, the initial exception made for agricultural goods, and the import restrictions on steel and textile products, showed that while the EU had good intentions, these would not be at the expense of member states' vested interests. In fact, the intended trade relationship between the two parties was asymmetrical from the outset. On the one hand this was due to the fact that market liberalisation predominantly benefited the efficiently producing exporters in the EU; this resulted in considerable trade deficits in CEE, at least in the short and medium term. Besides, trade with the EU was much more important for CEE countries than vice versa; trade with these countries formed just a fraction of EU member states' total imports and exports. On the other hand, trade liberalisation was an important element of Western European companies' internal strategies: by relocating labour-intensive production processes such as in the automobile industry to CEE countries, they could cut costs without losing market share. As we have already seen, a side effect of this strategy was that CEE economies became dependent on the cyclical developments in the (member states of the) EU.

Secondly, a financial support operation was launched with the principal aim of facilitating the double transformation. Initially, the EU was accorded a coordinating role within the framework of the G-24, the group of 24 industrialised countries, in cooperation with relevant international organisations. In the period between 1 January 1990 and 31 December 1993, a total of 81.4 billion dollars was pledged, with the EU taking on the greatest share at 42.1 per cent, followed by the IMF, the World Bank, and the European Bank for Reconstruction and Development (26.8 per cent); the United States (13.3 per cent); the European countries united in the European Free Trade Association which was, and still is, allied to the EU via the European Economic Area (9.2 per cent); Japan (4.1 per cent); and Canada (2.9 per cent). The amount made available by the EU was for the most part (almost 70 per cent) bilateral aid, i.e. pledged by individual member states. Germany was the frontrunner by far, with a total amount of 13.1 billion dollars, followed by France (4.1 billion dollars), Italy (2 billion), the Netherlands (1.3 billion), and Great Britain (1 billion) (figures taken from the Atlantic Commission 1995: 28). This pattern is in line with established practices in European development policy: namely, the subordination of multilateral, communitarian policies to the priorities and interests of national member states (see chapter 4).

Thirdly, from 1989 onwards, and particularly from 1993, the most important part of communitarian assistance was organised within the Phare programme of the European institutions. The name Phare itself (*Pologne, Hongrie: Assistance á la Restructuration Économique*) makes clear that the programme was originally aimed at Poland and Hungary. However, *phare* is also the French word for lighthouse, and very soon the EU's symbolic financial light was shining on other CEE countries. The programme was funded from the EU budget and was officially tasked with supporting the political and economic transformation process. Inflated expectations of a new Marshall Plan were nowhere near met. In the eyes of the European

Commission, the Phare programme remained an 'incentive for self-help'; that is, a limited aid programme. For example, the total amount that was earmarked for Phare assistance in the period 1995-1999 was less than 7 billion ECU (European currency unit) for the entire CEE region. This stood in stark contrast to the sums that Spain, Portugal and Greece could expect to receive over the same period as part of the EU's structural and cohesion policies: these amounted to a total of 43, 18, and 18 billion ECU, respectively, in the multiannual budget (Holman 1999: 95). This imbalance between internal development aid to existing member states and external assistance to future member states was repeated in the next multiannual budget covering 2000-2006 (which included the last instalment of the Phare programme). All in all, it became clear that, in financial terms, the EU's quest for successful transformation in CEE was being paid little more than lip service. To the outside, the unfeasibility of an extensive aid plan for CEE comparable to the Marshall Plan—or a free lunch approach, as some have termed it—was legitimised by the EU on the grounds of a supposed capital shortage in the world economy, the need for the West to cut back on government spending (as a result of which extensive support to CEE would meet stiff opposition from their own populations), and the negative effects that such a financial injection could have on the macroeconomic and monetary discipline of post-communist governments.

Finally, the EU's comprehensive strategy with respect to CEE was given stature by its offer of a concrete prospect of accession. This was without doubt the most relevant point for the candidate countries, but at the same time the most problematic for the EU.

In the years immediately following 1989, the EU made no mention of enlargement. Following the pattern described above, priority was given to finding solutions to a number of internal EU problems such as the difficult ratification of the Maastricht Treaty (not completed until 1993) and negotiations for a new multiannual budget. Although the Europe Agreements referred to above were meant to regulate the association between the EU and the new democracies, the EU repeatedly made it perfectly clear that these agreements did not mean automatic membership (an analogy can be made here with the Association Agreement between the EU and Ukraine which entered into force in September 2017). This caution on the part of the EU came to an end in June 1993 when the European Council meeting in Copenhagen concluded that 'the associated countries in Central and Eastern Europe that so desire shall become members of the European Union'. Furthermore, for the first time in its history, the EU attached explicit conditions to the countries aspiring to join its ranks. Accession could take place 'as soon as an associated country is able to assume the obligations of membership by satisfying the economic and political conditions required'. These so-called Copenhagen criteria were subsequently set out in the following, oft-quoted passage from the conclusions of the European Council (as said, for the first time explicitly formulated; it was only with the Treaty of Lisbon that these accession criteria were also included in the EU treaties):

Membership
- *requires that the candidate country has achieved stability of institutions guaranteeing democracy, the rule of law, human rights and respect for and protection of minorities*
- *requires the existence of a functioning market economy as well as the capacity to cope with competitive pressure and market forces within the Union*
- *presupposes the candidate's ability to take on the obligations of membership including adherence to the aims of political, economic and monetary union.*

However, the accession of the associated countries in CEE did not merely depend on the extent to which they could meet these conditions. The criteria also stated that 'the Union's capacity to absorb new members, while maintaining the dynamics of European integration, is an important consideration too, in the interest of both the Union and the candidate countries'. In other words, it was essential that EU enlargement did not lead to a weakening of the integration process; widening should not be at the expense of further deepening. This clause implied that the EU should first get its own house in order and make all the necessary preparations before welcoming new members. Furthermore, the Copenhagen summit promulgated a structured relationship between the EU institutions, in particular the Council of Ministers, and the associated countries: a so-called 'multilateral framework for intensified dialogue'. In concrete terms, this meant that politicians from member states and candidate countries would come together periodically to discuss the progress of the transformation processes. This multilateral approach did not, however, alter the fact that a fundamentally bilateral approach was chosen for the assessment of the Copenhagen criteria. Each candidate country and each transformation process would be judged on its own merits.

This double trajectory did not change until the European Council meeting in Helsinki in 1999. The structured relationship was given substance one and a half years after Copenhagen, during the European Council in Essen in December 1994. Along with a number of economic issues—such as the internal market, the agricultural sector, trade and investment promotion—and cross-border themes such as organised crime, environmental pollution, and good neighbourliness, the parties also established that a 'structured relationship' in the area of the Common Foreign and Security Policy (CFSP) was paramount to allaying the widespread feeling of insecurity prevalent in CEE countries. Regular consultations between the respective foreign ministers on issues of mutual interest were meant to be the first step towards greater involvement of the associated countries in the procedures and measures related to the EU's CFSP. In theory, this broad and all-encompassing multilateral dialogue applied to all countries. It could not, however, hide the fact that the route towards membership had to be an individual one, and that the EU would evaluate the efforts on an individual basis. The Union's enlargement strategy was thus a differentiated one, and the possibility could not be ruled out that some countries would join earlier than others.

This was further accentuated by the fact that the European Commission started publishing individual 'opinions' and progress reports from the second half of the 1990s, a practice that is still in place today for current candidate countries. The Copenhagen criteria were used to assess the level of progress made and to judge whether there was a sufficient basis to start formal negotiations. The first political criterion was a precondition for the start of negotiations, mainly covering economic and legal matters. However, this fact-finding by the European Commission was primarily concerned with the political transition and much less so with actual transformation. No thought was given to developments beyond the formal institutional changes necessary for a 'functioning' parliamentary democracy. It was too easily assumed that decisions meant to constitutionally anchor such things as the separation of powers, the expansion of the rule of law, respect for and protection of human rights in general and that of minorities in particular, etcetera, would have a top-down emancipating effect.

To some extent, one could rightly argue that although this emphasis on transition—that is, on formal and institutional changes—leaves the underlying processes unidentified, this is only because such processes can practically neither be concretised in manageable terms, nor clearly operationalised and verified. What we are actually talking about here is the problem of democratic consolidation, i.e. a more or less successful completion of the political transformation, a topic that is strongly debated in the literature on democratisation processes. Opinions are deeply divided over the criteria that can be used to determine a consolidated democracy. In an effort to find such criteria, the following aspects are often mentioned: behavioural change among both the political elites and the populations at large, with an emphasis on informal democratic practices; the deepening of democratic values and norms; the generally accepted conviction that democracy is indeed not merely the best but the *only* game in town; the legitimacy of the democratic regime; and a certain level of trust in political leaders/elites. It can be added that the configuration of state and society must also be kept in balance by a strong and, where necessary, self-regulating civil society. Clearly these aspects are rather difficult to quantify, partly because here too (one could even say: especially here) the concept of *ceteris paribus* cannot be applied.[7] It is therefore difficult to determine the degree of transformation and consolidation, and this paves the way for speculation and interpretation. Once we start interpreting political transformation normatively, we risk moving down the slippery slope of subjectivity and political desirability. Constitutional changes can be checked, and fair elections can be fairly accurately confirmed with the help of foreign observers, but it is much more difficult to find convincing evidence to prove changes in peoples' mindset, i.e. in the direction of a favourable attitude towards democracy.

It could then be argued that the above also applies to the second Copenhagen criterion dealing with the establishment of a 'functioning market economy'. Here too, the text is very vaguely worded: how do we measure 'functioning', and how do we determine whether an economy has developed the capacity to cope with competitive pressure and market forces within the EU? In short, when is the economic transformation complete? Nonetheless, I want to give three arguments here to show that a distinction between the political and economic Copenhagen criteria can certainly be made. Firstly, as mentioned above, the political criteria are what we could call an entrance exam to the start of accession negotiations. This makes it a rather loaded 'political exam', but it also means that the examiner may be tempted—in the absence of hard evidence—to interpret and assess the criteria in a flexible manner. In the case of the economic criteria, there are many more safeguards in place against this kind of flexibility in assessing—which also has other consequences, as we shall see shortly. Secondly, the plausibility of alternative scenarios also plays a role. In the absence of concrete legal and administrative impediments, and associated sanctions, a political relapse *after accession* cannot be ruled out. Here too, the risk is much lower in the economic field, something not unrelated to the prevailing zeitgeist (considered separately from the EU itself, and the EU's decisions), namely that liberal economic principles appear to be indisputable and certainly not replaceable by real existing alternatives, whereas politics appears to be increasingly susceptible to nationalistic, populist, and authoritarian tendencies. Furthermore, there is an asymmetrical relationship here: as far as the EU is concerned, any change in mindset with regard to the economy is subordinate to—and, if anything, the result of—concrete treaty safeguards regarding free economic movements within a single market. And these guarantees are part of the EU's extensive *acquis communautaire*. This body of European Union law is primarily aimed at regulating the free movement of goods, people, services and capital. The EU is first and foremost a single market and not—or only to a limited extent—a supranational state. The primacy of economic regulation means that the negotiations between the EU and the candidate countries deal predominantly with the legal and institutional aspects of an optimal form of economic cooperation. This is the framework within which a 'market economy can function'. This reality is laid down in the first sentence of the third Copenhagen criterion: new members must be able to meet the obligations of membership. A cynic would also add that the ability to cope with the competitive pressure and market forces within the EU primarily requires new members to be receptive to the relocation of labour-intensive production facilities and to focus on their so-called comparative advantages, i.e. cheap, skilled labour.

When reference is made in the literature to the EU as a transformative power, it is the above conditionality that is generally being referred to. First and foremost: countries outside the EU—such as the new CEE democracies in the 1990s—are not obliged to become members. In other words, there is absolutely no obligation to join, and it is within the realm of each country's sovereign decision-making power to decide whether or not to apply for membership. Whether they do so or not depends primarily—if not decisively—on the attractiveness of the EU and the presence or absence of other attractive options. Once a candidate country has made the conscious decision to apply, there is no other choice but to meet the Copenhagen criteria. It is then up to the EU institutions and member states to determine whether the country in question meets the political criteria and, if so, whether the subsequent negotiations lead to the desired economic and legal-institutional results. To cut a long story short: transformative power is effective power to the extent that the political and economic structures of another country can be transformed into a material and ideational spitting image, in this case the spitting image of 'the EU' (see particularly Grabbe 2006; see also Börzel and Risse 2009).[8]

One problem with this political and academic belief in the power of the EU to fundamentally transform CEE countries is the implicit assumption of irreversibility. A second problem, closely related to the first, is the linear argumentation that underlies this assumption. Politics and economics are directly related to each other. Political transformation creates the preconditions within which the domestic economy can flourish: constitutional stability, transparent decision-making, minimisation of corruption and, most importantly, the protection of property. Economic transformation is believed to be the best guarantee for growth, and economic prosperity will further strengthen political transformation. This argument thus sees a linear relationship between economic liberalisation and political democratisation in what can best be described as a virtuous circle. Reality, however, is somewhat more complex. Rather than being linked directly to each other, both transformations (and their successful implementation) are connected to each other via an intermediate variable, often the missing link in the transformative power literature: the social repercussions of the transformation processes. Economic liberalisation often has winners and losers, and the starker the social consequences become in terms of income disparity, unemployment, and even poverty traps, the more political discontent we will see among the populations in CEE countries, along with an increased risk of political instability. If we recall the definition of social cohesion used in chapter 2, which links the objective reality of (present and future) socioeconomic differences to the subjective perception of these differences in the light of existing and/or announced measures to deal with them, it is clear that the emphasis on economic transformation in the EU's enlargement strategy has, *in the absence of any social criteria*, increased the socioeconomic disparities in CEE countries. In order to fulfil the EU's legal and institutional criteria, the respective governments were in effect forced to sacrifice the social measures that could have reduced the post-communist disparities on the neoliberal altar of macroeconomic adjustment and stability.

This did not, however, lead to major protests in the first decade after the 1989 revolutions. Although the initial euphoria about regime change gradually ebbed away throughout the 1990s, promises in terms of the restoration of growth and employment, EU membership and the increase in prosperity that would bring, and security within the framework of NATO all had a pacifying effect, at least temporarily. This was certainly the case when the decision on accession was finally made in 1999. At the Helsinki European Council in December of that year, the EU decided that no fewer than 12 countries could join in the foreseeable future (see endnote 3). Though Turkey was accepted as a thirteenth candidate country, it was not yet considered politically ready to start accession negotiations. Notwithstanding the EU's intended differentiated strategy, Helsinki decided on a catch-all approach. The geopolitical priorities of the existing member states varied so widely that in the end a compromise was reached that constituted a green light for all associated countries (apart from Turkey, that is): Germany demanded inclusion of the four Visegrád countries (Poland, the Czech Republic, Slovakia, and Hungary); France was pleased to see Romania and Bulgaria included; and the Scandinavian EU members ensured that the three Baltic states were allowed to join. In the years that followed, the Helsinki decision acted as a fait accompli, of which there was no way back, although the accession of Romania and Bulgaria was postponed by three years.

5.3.   Beyond big bang enlargement: dilemmas of a larger Europe

The second generation literature on the question of EU enlargement after the Cold War covers a theme that is often referred to as 'beyond conditionality'; that is, the situation in Europe after the big bang enlargement of 2004-2007. Conditionality refers to the Copenhagen criteria, or the conditions that the ten CEE countries plus Cyprus and Malta were considered to have fulfilled. The actual increase from 15 to 27 member states therefore constitutes a turning point that also had an impact on the academic literature (see, for example, Epstein and Sedelmeier 2008). In the remainder of this chapter I will look at four different interpretations of the notion of 'beyond conditionality'.

The first interpretation relates to the EU itself. What impact has this spectacular, almost twofold increase in the number of member states had on the functioning of the EU and on the social-political relations within the 'old' member states? Has the experience with the new member states led to a different approach to enlargement and to a change in the criteria as laid down in Copenhagen? In other words, have new explicit or implicit conditions been added?

The second interpretation relates more specifically to the new member states. The transformative power of the EU was based on the idea that candidate countries had to meet EU criteria before they could join. The ultimate threat, therefore, was delayed or even retracted membership. But what would happen to the political, economic, and legal measures implemented once the countries had actually joined, if the EU had little or no coercive means or persuasive power up its sleeve to rectify the situation? How would the new member states or their representatives conduct themselves within European institutions such as the Commission and the Council, and how quickly would they implement new EU legislation in their own countries? In short, how loyal would the new member states be, and to what extent would the European idea continue to live on among their respective populations?

Thirdly, we can add meaning to the notion of 'beyond conditionality' by including the current—that is, the post-big-bang—candidate countries in the analysis. Have they been treated differently by the EU, and if so, what effect does this have on the 'attractiveness' of the EU for these countries? Have they become more susceptible to advances from Russia and China over the past few years, partly as a result of a greater reticence on the part of the EU?

And finally, as will be discussed in section 5.4, 'beyond conditionality' also refers to the relationship between the EU and its immediate neighbours. In a number of cases, these countries became EU neighbours as a result of the big bang enlargement, but at the same time they can be fairly certain that membership is not on the cards for them. If membership is not an option for these countries, what remains of the EU's transformative power? Are the values and norms that underlie the European idea strong enough—as is claimed in the NPE literature (see chapter 3)—with or without the right amount of advice and financial resources, or are these neighbouring countries immune to European finger-wagging? In any case, how do these countries feel about this enlarging union of states at their borders, and how sensitive are the respective governments to their big neighbour's security concerns and dilemmas?

5.3.1.   Enlargement and Euroscepticism: incompatible quantities?

I stated earlier that in the history of the European integration process, 'enlargement' was usually preceded by 'deepening'. As I pointed out, there was a certain logic to this. An important exception is the big bang enlargement round. It may have been the EU's objective to first put its own house in order—a house that was comprised of fifteen member states at the time—by adopting a European constitution, among other things. In practice, this proved to be more complicated than expected. Following the fairly limited treaty amendment in the form of the Treaty of Nice in 2000, a Convention was very quickly set up which, under the leadership of the former French President Giscard d'Estaing, was tasked with drafting a full-blown European Constitution. The draft text was completed in 2003 and the subsequent Intergovernmental Conference was ceremonially concluded with the signing of a constitutional treaty by the government leaders and the French head of state (Rome, 29 October 2004), after which the parliaments of the now 25 member states had to ratify it. Things started to go wrong in 2005, first in France (in May), and soon after in the Netherlands (in June). Both countries called a referendum, and in both countries a majority—respectively 54.9 and 61.5 per cent—voted against the constitution.

Some of the most important changes described in the constitutional treaty were institutional and were aimed at making the decision-making process more efficient. The opponents in the French and Dutch referendum campaigns used this to conjure up the image of a looming European 'super state': an over-used term that was never precisely or substantially defined. In the end, people voted against the constitution for fear of losing sovereignty and identity; the fact that most citizens were little familiar with (the functioning of) the EU did not stop them from casting a negative vote. The EU turned out to be the ideal scapegoat for all social problems. It is to some extent the tragedy of the EU that at the very moment that the relaunch of the economic integration process after 1985 needed a political and institutional superstructure—for example in the form of a strengthening of the political union—Euroscepticism got the upper hand in the public discourse.

Alongside this political-institutional explanation, the big bang enlargement also played a role in the mood surrounding the voting on the European Constitution. Fear of the 'Polish plumber' as a symbol of the influx of cheap labour from the new member states played an important role in the campaign that preceded the French referendum. Following the extensive enlargement of the EU to include Eastern Europe, the question of 'who's next' also arose, with many looking askance at Turkey and the 'eighty million Turks'.

The term 'Euroscepticism' emerges here. Allegedly, it was first coined in the second half of the 1980s in the British debate on the desirability of further integration, and was used by Margaret Thatcher in a speech she gave in 1988 (Laconte 2010: 3). However, academic discussion of the term did not really get going until after the turn of the millennium, in particular after the surprising outcome of the French and Dutch referenda on the constitution. In a much-cited article dating from 2002, two British political scientists made a distinction between two types of

Euroscepticism: a hard variant and a soft variant (Taggart and Szczerbiak 2002). The first is a principled rejection of European integration on the grounds of sovereignty, national identity, and distinctiveness. The ultimate consequence of this position is withdrawal, as the British have now decided via a referendum. A hard Eurosceptic vision aimed at withdrawal can go hand in hand with a certain level of economic cooperation if the main bone of contention is the supposed loss of power to 'Brussels'. Soft Euroscepticism, on the other hand, is not necessarily directed against European integration but rather at its specific characteristics. A good example is the criticism of the EU's supposedly one-sided liberal, market-oriented approach. More emphasis on social policy and cohesion could make a big difference. It is clear that the discussion about Europe has hardened over the past two decades, with opinions on both extremes of the political spectrum turning away from the EU (and in some cases even away from membership).

The literature mentions several reasons for these manifestations of Euroscepticism (for an overview, see the various contributions in Hooghe and Marks 2007). The first explanation is the 'psychology of group behaviour'. A sense of alienation and threat emanating from open borders, from job losses, from the disintegration of traditional communities, and from foreign people and customs all translate into a search for new identities or a resurgence of old ones. If this turns into nationalism, the connection with Euroscepticism is quickly established. Secondly, Euroscepticism does not necessarily have to be the result of the European integration process but may be first and foremost related to a general political malaise or crisis, a lack of trust in political leaders or the functioning of democracy in general. The oft-repeated argument that the EU is undemocratic—that it has a democratic deficit—reinforces this mistrust, which can lead to people turning very quickly against the 'European elite' and backroom politics in Brussels. Thirdly, anti-European sentiments are 'activated' by populist politicians who cleverly frame social dissatisfaction as Euroscepticism and provide alienation and loss of identity with a focal point. Apparently, these populist leaders and their movements have a better understanding of the contemporary zeitgeist. Finally, there is a link between economic decline and an increase in nationalist (and protectionist) tendencies; tendencies that seem to reinforce each other across countries. And of course, in this context we must not forget that the old EU member states and their populations have also gone through their own transformation process—a transformation that not only broke down the formal and institutional certainties of the post-war Keynesian welfare state one by one but that also required a radical change in mindset. The success of populist movements in just about every EU country shows that this change has not yet been completed everywhere or been equally accepted by everyone.

The link between enlargement and Euroscepticism is therefore more indirect than direct; much more a result of deeper discontent and only partly an isolated cause-effect relationship. Although the unexpected increase in labour migration from CEE countries may have had a direct effect on the citizens of the 'old' member states, the discontent stems from deteriorating social circumstances. And the unsympathetic reception of new migrants is also partly a result of the more precarious position of some citizens in the West due to declining certainties under neoliberal regimes (see also chapter 6).

5.3.2.   Beyond conditionality: the spectre of populism

At the beginning of the 2000s—the decade that saw the increase and spread of Euroscepticism—the former German Minister for Foreign Affairs, Joschka Fischer, delivered a speech on the EU's *finalité politique* entitled *Vom Staatenverbund zur Föderation.*[9] Now that the economic deepening process with introduction of the euro had been completed, and in the light of the impending enlargement of the EU to the East, Fischer asserted that a constitutional treaty was needed that would move the EU towards a European federation. He provided an institutional argument for this plea: how could an EU with 30 members or more—Fischer apparently anticipated a further expansion after the big bang—function without institutional reforms that moved member states away from the national sovereignty towards which they were geared?

The answer to this pressing question was unintentionally and unwittingly given a few years later in French and Dutch polling stations. It turned out that a majority of the electorate was not ready for this and was much more concerned with two completely different end points: the *finalité géographique* and the *finalité sociale*. In response to this electoral uprising, the discourse on the limits of deepening the European integration process gradually became dominant among almost all politicians, only in a completely different sense than what was meant by Fischer. One Dutch social democratic politician at the time entitled his speech 'Beyond federalism'. He did not mean that a more attractive or deeper Europe was waiting beyond the horizon of federalism. On the contrary, he argued that the EU had more or less reached its end point and that there was even room to take a step backwards in some policy areas. In academic terms, the process of European integration was no longer a dependent variable but had become an independent one.[10]

Fatigue would have been a better word than *finalité* as a way of describing the general mood after the constitutional referenda and the subsequent impasse: enlargement fatigue and social sacrifice fatigue. In the case of France, a concrete consequence was initially attached to the outcome of the referendum: every new round of EU enlargement (after the planned accession of Croatia as the 28th member state) would have to be submitted to the French population via a referendum. This stipulation was changed in 2008: now the president can decide whether the population or the French parliament can decide by majority on any future enlargement—a clever solution that makes it possible to assess every enlargement on its political desirability. Be that as it may, the current candidate countries feel strongly that the 2004-2007 big bang enlargement round did not have a positive effect on their own chances of joining the EU quickly.

Yet this idea that the EU's experience with CEE member states has been unequivocally negative is unfounded. The new member states have since 2004 certainly not behaved in a less exemplary manner than the older members in terms of their institutional and legal loyalty and integrity. New European laws and regulations have been adopted and implemented at the same pace, decision-making within the European institutions has not been obstructed more than average, and cooperation in most policy areas has not been unilaterally impeded. As the vast majority of the *acquis communautaire* relates to economic integration, and as most of the new member states have put their legal and constitutional affairs related to the economy more or less in order, we can conclude that membership has been a success for both parties (see also Sedelmeier 2012; and *Journal of Common Market Studies* 2014). The same cannot be said for domestic policy areas.

The external discipline imposed on CEE countries—the combined result of the influence of foreign direct investment on the policies of the respective governments, the EU's enlargement strategy aimed at market integration, and the role of post-communist managerial elites in the countries themselves—led to a downside, which was the aforementioned 'new social crisis'. In this context, it is not surprising that citizens in CEE eventually got 'tired of endless demands for reform', as an editorial in the *Financial Times* in 2002 put it. It should not come as a surprise, continued the article, 'that they are now falling prey to the seductive voices of economic interventionism and of populism' (*Financial Times*, 4 June 2002). The newspaper was openly speculating about a political and policy relapse, unequivocally caused by the lagging change in mindset with respect to the ongoing processes of liberalisation, privatisation, and deregulation.

In a recent study, the German historian and specialist in East European studies, Philipp Ther, skilfully analysed the consequences of neoliberal policy over more than a quarter of a century since the 1989 revolutions. The sharp divide between the winners and losers of this policy, between urban agglomerations and rural areas, and between the young and old has certainly had a clear political effect. Ther focused particularly on the global crisis of 2008-2013, showing that many CEE countries went through a socio-economic downturn similar to what they experienced in the years immediately after 1989. He concluded that the authoritarian tendencies in the region are partly a result of these domestic crises (Ther 2016: chapters 5 and 7).

When the *Financial Times* was commenting on these developments back in 2002, one could only speculate about the effect of the social crisis on the process of political transformation in CEE. Now, more than one and a half decades later, we have a good impression of this effect, and we know that the democratic changes are not necessarily irreversible. Many of the new member states are experiencing emerging populism and authoritarian tendencies. In some member states such as Bulgaria, Romania, and Slovakia, corruption practices are rife. In other member states such as Poland and Hungary, governments ride roughshod over the EU's values and norms. The rule of law can no longer be taken for granted in these countries.

More recently, these internal political developments in CEE countries, particularly the stirring up of patriotism among their populations, have also had an impact on the formulation of new EU policy. A stark example of this is the attitude of the new member states towards the flow of refugees which, in the eyes of politicians and the media, has increasingly taken on the proportions of a crisis over the past decade. The situation was so acute in 2015 that the European Commission decided to take emergency measures to spread the refugees across the whole of the EU. The countries that until then had attracted the smallest number of refugees—probably because, in the eyes of the refugees, they were the least attractive—protested the most and refused to participate in the redistribution. Hungary and Slovakia even went to the European Court of Justice to try to have the compulsory reception of refugees by all member states declared illegal on procedural grounds. (The objection by both these countries was rejected by the Court in 2017).

This conflict over the reception of migrants is all the more disturbing when we realise that there has been a massive movement of workers from East to West which, particularly during the 2008-2013 crisis, took on proportions that, according to the previously cited Ther, far outstripped the refugee flows from war zones (Ther 2016: viii + 246 et seq). This massive labour relocation most certainly played a role in strengthening Euroscepticism in the 'old' member states. It is, for example, generally accepted that the free movement of people—as part of the EU's single market—played a crucial role in the outcome of the Brexit referendum in Great Britain.

The problem here is that the EU, in the shape of the European institutions, has few resources at its disposal to correct member states beyond conditionality for their politically deviant behaviour. Drawn out procedures in the Court do not have the necessary immediate effect; harsh penalties need to be approved by all member states; mutual solidarity among the new member states can in such situations take on surprising forms; and financial measures (such as the suspension or cancellation of EU subsidies from the structural funds) are more likely to make the situation worse than better. In short, the normative power so acclaimed by the EU itself—as well as the emphasis on stable institutions that can guarantee democracy, the rule of law, human rights, and respect for and protection of minorities—hinges primarily on the voluntary willingness of the member states to radiate this normative power inwards. How will countries outside the EU react to democratic finger-wagging if in some EU member states the 'democratic rule of law' is not taken all too seriously?

5.3.3.   Enlargement as security strategy: the EU and the Western Balkans

This question of how to deal with the internal and external consequences of illiberal political practices is, of course, particularly relevant in relation to the current candidate countries. Based on its mixed experience with the big bang enlargement round, one may well wonder why the EU, its member states, and their populations are even considering further enlargement at all. Whereas in the 2004-2007 enlargement round, the most stable post-communist countries were selected for membership, the countries that are now under consideration can hardly be called dependable in terms of their political and economic transformation.

In recent years, the EU has been too quick to assume that the political transformation in CEE countries was, if not complete, certainly moving in the right direction. It has then gone on to underestimate—or simply ignore—the long-term social and political exclusion that comes with economic transformation. In other words, the EU's enlargement strategy did not include a manual for the building up *and* long-term strengthening of the democratic state. In the words of Heather Grabbe, the EU realised too late that 'EU influence dwindles on politically hot topics' after accession (Grabbe 2014: 42).

This quote refers to one of the lessons learned more than a decade after the big bang enlargement. One could indeed argue that, since then, the EU has focused more explicitly on the development of democratic governance in the current candidate countries, especially those in the Western Balkans. One could also argue somewhat cynically that the administrative and legal problems—in combination with economic instability and, often, ethnic tensions—are so evident that even an EU focused principally on market integration would find it difficult to disregard the political dimension.

Be that as it may, in recent years a preliminary conclusion could be drawn: the enlargement strategy has clearly changed, with a greater emphasis on political transformation and a return to a more differentiated, individual approach. A geopolitically inspired catch-all strategy such as the 1999 Helsinki decision no longer seems to be an option for the Western Balkans.[11]

A second difference with previous enlargement rounds is the change in public opinion. Intra- and extra-European migration flows are an important source of Euroscepticism, whether or not in combination with socio-economic crisis and exclusion and, in the wake of this, enlargement fatigue. As it is probable that populations in at least some of the current member states will have a say in future accessions, it seems unlikely that a new enlargement round will be on the cards anytime soon.

Thirdly, a direct consequence of the declining prospect of accession is that the public mood in the candidate countries is also changing. Disappointment over limited national economic and political progress can easily turn into Euroscepticism, especially if this sentiment is fuelled by local elites who paradoxically were responsible for the limited progress in the first place.

Fourthly, and closely linked to this, there appears to be a changing pattern of expectations outside the EU more generally. The major internal tensions that have come to the surface as a result of the recent euro crisis have had an impact on the EU's persuasiveness as a normative power in general as well as the attractiveness of the EU as a future European safe haven where life is good for less fortunate countries in particular.

Finally, in this context it should come as no surprise that more and more politicians and citizens in candidate countries (as well as, incidentally, in some of the new member states) are intrigued by the recent approaches made by competing global players such as Russia and China (or by Turkey—that other, now sidetracked candidate country). The assertiveness of these major powers in their dealings with vulnerable countries neighbouring the EU has grown over the past decade and is unlikely to stop anytime soon. From the perspective of the European political elites, this is an important security threat (see also chapter 6).

How can the EU react to this perceived threat? The NATO expansion that brought CEE countries on board in the second half of the 1990s enabled the EU to fully concentrate on market integration. A similar scenario of a twofold enlargement of Western institutions to include the Western Balkans is unlikely. This creates a difficult dilemma for the EU: assuming it has learned from its big bang enlargement strategy, it will have to take political conditionality seriously. Ultimately, this means that at least some of the Balkan countries will not be able to join. On the other hand, continual postponement could push these countries into the arms of Russia (and to a lesser extent China), which may lead to the EU turning enlargement into a security project. And this in turn could result in the democratic conditions in the candidate countries being sacrificed on the altar of the EU's geopolitical interests.

So far, the EU has kept to its Stabilisation and Association Process which formally started in 1999 but in fact only really got going in the course of the following decade. In relation to the Balkans, a logical additional condition for accession was formulated in terms of intra-Balkan cooperation and good neighbourliness. A financial instrument with a budget of €11.5 billion for the 2007-2013 period (IPA I) and €11.7 billion for the 2014-2020 (IPA II, see also table 5.1) was to provide the necessary financial support.

At the beginning of 2018, the EU—or rather the Commission—changed its strategy towards the Western Balkans. In a communication, it indicated that its enlargement policy towards this region should be revived by formulating a number of ways forward and by suggesting 2025 as a possible year for accession. It explicitly mentioned three specific reasons for this new urgency, and one extra reason can be deduced from the comments to the plan. To begin with, it was necessary to ensure that the region did not regress into instability. A credible and realistic prospect of accession could help and would reverse the declining trust of the candidate countries in the EU. In the words of Commissioner Hahn, it is a choice 'between exporting stability or importing instability' (cited in *de Volkskrant*, 7 February 2018, page 1). Secondly, the issue of migration plays a major role. The Balkans are an important transit route for refugees and migrants from outside Europe, as the recent migration crisis has shown. They therefore play a key role in controlling these migration flows, thus making it essential for the EU to give new impetus to its relationship with these countries. And thirdly, there is the economic argument: EU businesses are the largest investors in the region and have significant commercial interests there (European Commission 2018b). The political and geopolitical urgency mentioned by Hahn, and echoed by High Representative Mogherini, combined with the reference to the region as a whole and the mentioning of a possible accession year, could paradoxically—and to some extent counter to the above—push the EU towards a revival of a big-bang-type enlargement strategy, this time involving the Western Balkans. Left unsaid in the communication and official statements, but nevertheless playing an important role in the decision-making process, is fear of the increasingly assertive role in the region played by Russia, China and even Turkey. The EU's new focus on the Western Balkans thus also encompasses enlightened geopolitical interests.

Time will tell whether this new strategy on the part of the Commission towards the current candidate countries is realistic. We would, however, be justified in asking why the EU wants to take on such extensive enlargement rounds at all. The costs in terms of financial and administrative support (not to mention the institutional and policy consequences of a major increase in the number of member states, and socio-economic differences) appear to outweigh any possible advantages. Ideological zeal and a strong belief in the normative power of the EU certainly play a role here. After the 1989 revolutions, countless statements were heard from concerned European and national politicians in the run-up to the big bang enlargement round, and we hear them once again in relation to the Western Balkans: we must export stability, security, and prosperity to the region so that the populations in those countries can benefit from the same advantages of cooperation and integration as our own populations have. Furthermore, politicians in the old member states are supported and, where necessary, triggered by their national civil societies. Trade unions, political parties, and all variety of NGOs—some subsidised by government funds—are active players in the promotion and promulgation of democratic and capitalist values and norms.

If we dig a little deeper, we see that there are also less idealistic considerations at play. Economic interests have always had a prominent role in an association that has, until now, been primarily based on market integration. It is clear that the business community in the old member states has profited from the wave of privatisations in the new democracies, from the improved investment climate due to market-oriented reforms, from cheap but skilled labour and low taxes on profits, and from new markets on the other side of the former Iron Curtain. Furthermore, Western European businesses have actively lobbied the European Commission and the new governments in CEE and the Western Balkans to emphasise the importance of the legal and administrative context of free entrepreneurship. Stability and security considerations clearly also play an important role alongside such economic arguments and interests.

Democratisation and market integration are the panacea that, together with good neighbourliness, are expected to achieve the desired results on the EU's immediate external borders. The EU has been described as an empire, for example by a former president of the European Commission, and one of the characteristics of an empire is that it attaches great importance to stable external borders. Closely linked to this is a fourth reason for enlargement—or at least for an effective foreign policy towards neighbouring countries—and that is the refugee problem mentioned above. Political-military and socio-economic instability on the EU's external borders can not only cause unwanted migration flows but also result in neighbouring countries becoming transit routes for people fleeing conflict areas further afield.

It is safe to assume that all these factors have been involved to a greater or lesser extent in the EU's enlargement policy since the Cold War. Economic interests were more important for the EU's strategy towards the big bang countries than they have been for the poorer and/or smaller countries in the Western Balkans. The opposite is true of stability and security considerations, partly because all the big bang countries joined NATO at almost the same time (in 1999 and 2004) and were not part of the bloody civil war that raged in the Balkans. And finally, considerations regarding security and migration flows play a dominant role in relation to the new neighbours—that is, those countries that, due to the recent expansion, are now on the EU's external borders but that have little or no chance of accession. Economic interests may sometimes also be involved, albeit more indirectly, for example via the external implications of the EU's energy policy.

5.4.   The new neighbours as friends: the Neighbourhood Policy

If the prospects of membership did indeed play such a major role in the start-up process of the double transformation, and if we are forced to conclude that the social-political completion of this process has come up against some hitches and is stagnating in the current candidate countries, then perhaps a final test for the

EU's transformative power lies in the success of its policy towards neighbouring countries that do *not* have any prospect of accession. Much has been written in recent years about the EU's policy on new neighbours, referred to in the Commission's jargon as the 'ring of friends'. None of the academic research examined refers to the European Neighbourhood Policy (abbreviated as ENP) in an unequivocally positive manner, and many studies are downright negative about the effectiveness of this form of 'external Europeanisation' (see, for example, Börzel 2010; and Lavenex 2017).

The ENP was launched at the same time as the big bang enlargement in 2004 as a new policy area within the framework of the EU's general external relations. Based on an earlier British idea for a wider Europe, this new initiative was seen by many member states as an alternative to membership. Countries on the other side of the external borders to the east or the shared border waters to the south of the EU were offered closer cooperation based on three objectives: to improve stability in neighbouring countries through the promotion of economic development; to promote important EU values such as good governance, democracy, the rule of law, and human rights; and to improve cooperation at the regional level through the Eastern Partnership and the Union for the Mediterranean. Initially, the ENP was formulated in generic terms and objectives and, at most, small adjustments were made to account for local conditions. At a later stage, the eastern and southern countries were treated as two distinct groups of neighbours, and again an emphasis was placed on an individual and thus differentiated approach. The following countries are part of the Eastern Partnership: Armenia, Azerbaijan, Belarus, Georgia, Moldavia and Ukraine. And the following countries participate in the Union for the Mediterranean: Algeria, Egypt, Israel, Jordan, Lebanon, Libya, Morocco, Palestine*, Syria and Tunisia.[12]

Strengthening friendships with new neighbours that could not qualify for membership but where social-political stability was of the utmost importance to the EU—new neighbours that must be guided towards political and economic modernisation and Westernisation, including the embrace of European values and norms—was no small task. And indeed, this endeavour had little chance of succeeding, for at least three reasons. To begin with, the ENP was from the outset characterised by a strong asymmetry between the EU and the participating neighbours, the objectives being imbued with perhaps well-intentioned paternalism but not always understood as such. Moreover, it was obvious that the EU was primarily concerned with its own stability and security and that it was the demanding or desiring party and had no other carrot to offer other than meagre—and moreover, conditional—financial support. Through the European Neighbourhood Instrument (ENI)—the most important instrument within the ENP—over €13 billion was spent over the period 2007-2013 and €15.4 billion reserved for the period 2014-2020 (see table 5.1; compare this amount, intended for 16 countries, with the EU's internal development assistance under the Structural Funds of more than €371 billion for the period 2014-2020, see table 1.1).

Secondly, little attention was paid, certainly in the first decade of the ENP, to the political uniqueness of the 16 participating countries and the political reality in the often authoritarian countries. As has been shown in some (potential) candidate countries (Bosnia-Herzegovina is a good example), it is virtually impossible to influence local elites who benefit from the political status quo and therefore have an interest in maintaining it and can, in short, only lose in an adjustment to ENP values and norms. Incidentally, a regime change offers absolutely no guarantee of stability, as demonstrated by post-Gaddafi Libya and the so-called Orange Revolution in Ukraine. The military regime of Egypt is firmly in the saddle after the failure of the Arab Spring, has considerable interests in the country's economy, and does not intend to exchange its own dominant position for the instability that an energetic adoption of the EU recommendations would probably bring about. Moreover, it is likely that many politicians within the EU believe that authoritarian stability in Egypt is greatly preferable to democratic instability. In this sense, it is often the case that the EU only pays lip service to its own objectives and normative mission.

A third and final reason for the general lack of results achieved by the ENP is the undervaluation and underestimation of the social dimension in—and as a result of—its own policy. As we saw earlier with regard to the double transformation, social processes are an important intermediate variable between economic liberalisation and political democratisation. If this dimension remains a missing link, explosive situations can arise such as at the time of the Arab Spring in 2011 or within the Eastern Partnership in countries such as Ukraine and Georgia.[13]

That the ENP's limited results have also got through to the offices of the European Commission is apparent from the various policy reviews and two reforms it has initiated. The first reform took place in response to the events in the Middle East and North Africa. The EU was unable to play a significant role in the rapid turn of events from spring to autumn in the Arab world, partly as a result of half-hearted estimates and misjudgements and partly due to a lack of effective decision-making power caused by internal division. In a joint communiqué between the Commission and the High Representative, the need for a fundamentally new approach was repeatedly mentioned, along with the need for the integrated approach launched in the 2009 Treaty of Lisbon to be at the centre of the new ENP. The various instruments within external relations had to be more coordinated: assistance with democratisation and liberalisation had to be integrated with focus areas such as security, mobility, and interregional and intraregional cooperation. Keywords such as sustainable democracy and inclusive growth were emphasised, and a new incentive for the democratisation process was introduced that became known as 'more for more'. This is a form of positive conditionality whereby a country can expect more support if it makes more progress in the field of sustainable democratic development. (NB: Compare this with the 'negative conditionality' in European development policy, where a recipient country could be cut off if it did not meet the conditions of the EU—see previous chapter.) A start was also made to implement a more flexible approach in which various policy instruments could be deployed in a flexible and individual way. This suggested a growing awareness that the neighbours could not be generically supported but that differentiation was necessary. And finally, it was emphasised that the ENP was mainly about partnership and cooperation on the basis of equality. The Commission continued along this line in a subsequent change to the ENP in 2015. Again, the need for a new approach was mentioned, this time mainly inspired by authoritarian tendencies in neighbouring countries, terrorist attacks on European territory, uncontrollable migration flows, the aggressiveness of Russia, and the unpredictability of the so-called Islamic State. One could argue somewhat ironically that the situation on the external borders of the EU between 2011 and 2015 had not improved much. The tone of this communication was less paternalistic, and more emphasis was placed on the reciprocity of the relationship and on the fact that neighbouring countries might have other aspirations than the EU. At the same time, the interests that played a role on the part of the EU were also clearly indicated. Nonetheless, even this change failed to shift opinions about the ENP.

As stated earlier, a large part of the academic literature that deals with the ENP is characterised by a moderately to strongly sceptical tone about the effects of this policy. When talking about the EU as an international actor, as a global player, we must conclude that it is precisely this role that is increasingly coming under pressure, especially in its own geopolitical backyard. There are various reasons for this. To begin with, the EU has never been able to dispel the impression that the main objective of the ENP was to establish the demarcation between member states (and potential candidate countries) and countries whose accession was politically undesirable or geographically impossible, and that it was set up largely out of enlightened self-interest. Combined with the relatively small amount of available financial resources, it can be seen that the stimulus provided by the ENP to implement substantial reforms was limited. Closely linked to this is the disappointment that has been generated in neighbouring countries (and beyond) regarding the many promises made by the EU since the end of the Cold War—promises that have not been kept or only partially kept. A lack of conflict-resolving power—for example with regard to the ongoing tensions in the Middle East but also in the conflicts between Russian and Ukraine or Georgia—is having an impact on the EU and causing it to leave the playing field to other powers or, occasionally, to one (or two) of its member states.

The EU's limited capacity for action is also the result of its own division or lack of foreign policy cohesion. If we take Russia's role as an example, it is clear that for Europe, it is two-fold: as a threat, and as a supplier of essential raw materials.

But different member states have differing views of Russia's role, which are partly motivated by economic interests. For example, the energy dependence on Russian gas is sufficient reason for some member states to opt for a moderate approach. Another example is that for many citizens in the EU (and for some of their leaders), the new neighbouring countries are not only transit countries for gas, oil, and export products but also for unwanted people. Such citizens argue that the external borders must be closed, and if that proves impossible then the EU's internal borders should be closed.

However, the EU's limited capacity to deal with ENP countries is not only related to internal division. The perception of the EU outside of the EU has suffered an enormous blow due to the way in which the Union has tried to solve the recent euro crisis but also the way its citizens have responded to refugees. This demonstrates that turbulence in the international system—and in particular in the EU's close neighbours—have played, and may play, an important role in the domestic politics of most member states but that developments such as populism and Euroscepticism threaten to blemish the European idea at its very core, and thereby the role of the EU as a global player.

5.5.   Conclusion

The end of the Cold War and the concomitant collapse of socialism in Central and Eastern Europe had a wide range of consequences. One important result was the shift in attention within the EU's external relations away from regions and countries that were geographically distant from the Union—whose development prospects had not significantly improved despite decades of aid—and towards democratising and liberalising the 'other Europe'. This was further encouraged by the fact that the typical Cold War fear of a domino effect, i.e. the spread of left-wing revolutionary and anti-Western tendencies in the Third World, was reduced (if not completely dissipated) as a result of the demise of communism. This took away a significant reason for development cooperation. (That the increase in national implosions and the phenomenon of new wars that were also a result of the end of the Cold War created completely new security dilemmas and fears was not fully appreciated everywhere during these first euphoric years after the fall of the Iron Curtain.)

Based on the idea that charity begins at home, the EU developed a comprehensive enlargement strategy in the 1990s of which the final accession of CEE countries in 2004-2007 formed the apotheosis. The Copenhagen criteria were key to this strategy. This chapter has shown that although the generally formulated and strictly formal and nominal criteria are seen as the cornerstones of the EU as a transformative power and are even the most effective part of what the EU can do as a global player, reality is more complicated. The difference between transition and transformation plays a central role in this. Transformation also means <u>real</u> social-political and economic convergence accompanied by a change in mindset among elites and citizens. Recent developments in Central and Eastern Europe have shown that this distinction is relevant. This is one of the four meanings given to the notion of 'beyond conditionality' in this chapter. The successive governments in CEE after 2004-2007—that is, after having met EU conditions for accession—have indeed fulfilled their formal obligations within EU institutions but have also experienced a certain setback in the political transformation process. Corruption is widespread, and some governments are increasingly turning to authoritarian, xenophobic and Eurosceptic practices.

In the EU's relationship with the current candidate countries and with the countries participating in the European Neighbourhood Policy—two other meanings of 'beyond conditionality'—it can be concluded that considerations of its own security have become increasingly important for the EU. In the case of the candidate countries, there is a risk that the EU will repeat its previous mistake regarding the big bang enlargement but this time with potentially more serious consequences due to the continuing instability of the candidates. In the case of the ENP, the EU has increasingly become the victim of the following contradictions in its external relations: forced democratisation imposed from the outside can lead to greater instability in the surrounding countries, and increased instability among neighbours can increase the feeling of insecurity within the EU to such an extent that it ultimately endangers the entire integration process. Migration is an important factor here, but it is certainly not the only source of insecurity and scepticism towards the EU, as will become clear in the next chapter.

Suggestions for further reading

The references to literature in this chapter can serve as a starting point. The authors mentioned are regularly found in the leading journals in the field of European integration (see also the suggestions in chapter 2). Having said that: (Mayhew 1998) is the best overview for the period of the 1990s, the period in which the enlargement strategy as such was established; and (Grabbe 2006) is of course the book that established the notion of transformative power.

As far as I know, there are no recently published overviews available of the EU's enlargement strategy. The recent (Börzel et al. 2018, previously published as a special issue [24(2), 2017] of the *Journal of European Public Policy*) focuses primarily on developments after the big bang enlargement. A book that deals in particular with the consequences of the neoliberal turn for countries in Central and Eastern Europe after the 1989 revolutions is (Ther 2016).

The two books by Richard Youngs (2014, 2017) that were quoted in this chapter offer a good introduction to the two main regions within the ENP—the Arab world and Eastern Europe—and the crises that are occurring there (in the EU's backyard, as it were).

Furthermore, a useful European Commission website is also available on the subjects of enlargement and ENP: https://ec.europa.eu/neighbourhood-enlargement/. Here, for example, all progress reports on current candidate countries can be consulted as well as the relevant documents concerning the ENP strategy of the Union.

6.   Internal-external

Security in a liberal and multipolar world order

'We love the countries of the European Union.
But the European Union was set up to take advantage of the United States,
to attack our piggy bank. And you know what? We can't let that happen.'
– Donald John Trump during a 'Make America Great Again' rally,
Fargo, North Dakota, 28 June 2018

A significant change took place in 1989 in most policy domains related to the EU's external relations; that much has by now become evident. This was due to two closely intertwined developments, or better yet, processes: the policy and ideological shift from Keynesianism to neoliberalism; and the transition from a bipolar confrontation between two models of society and their corresponding spheres of influence towards a multipolar, international state system characterised by an unprecedented, complex interdependency. The era of a compartmentalised—and, in retrospect, relatively stably configured—global politics now belonged definitively to the past.

This new reality, which has been forced upon us in ever-more explicit ways for the past three decades, has not led to a greater insight or sense of urgency across the board about what is often euphemistically referred to as 'new challenges'. In reality, these challenges are old and new *threats* to our security, where the new variants are frequently old threats in a new guise. Moreover, not all dangers are real or acute. Some are difficult to pinpoint—let alone quantify—on the basis of facts, and even in the case of generally accepted threats such as climate change, debates about the causes of such threats often persist.

This chapter looks at the EU's security environment in a changing world. In the discussion I use a broad definition of security that goes beyond the traditional outlook on political-military dangers. Genuine, supposed, and imaginary threats and dangers can be external but also internal; they are political-military but also social, economic, and psychological in nature; and they ultimately boil down to the distribution of power as well as the distribution of welfare. In the previous chapters I analysed the policy instruments of what is called the EU's external action (one part of its broader external relations—see also the foreword for a more detailed definition). We saw that these policy domains to some extent also touch upon security issues: trade as a weapon in power politics, structural underdevelopment as a cause of conflict, and enlargement as a source of instability on Europe's outer borders. In this chapter I will first examine the external dimension of EU's internal policies in a unique way. I posit that the neoliberal shift in EU member states and the relaunch of the integration process—through the completion of the internal market and the establishment of the EMU—were inextricably linked to each other. I also argue that both are at the root of growing socioeconomic inequality as well as rising social discontent. This discontent has since turned against the EU. It would not be an exaggeration to claim that Europe is going through an existential crisis, one that may have been amplified by the euro crisis of 2008-2013 and the migration crisis of 2015 but that essentially has more structural, deeper roots. The sense of insecurity is widespread. This is not the sort of climate in which the EU can make a big leap forwards and assert itself as a global player.

At the same time, there *has* been some activity in the area of the Common Foreign and Security Policy (CFSP) since the 1990s. This is the second theme of this chapter: what exactly did the EU do in the last three decades to enhance its capacity to act in the traditional domains of diplomacy and security? Have these initiatives been effective? And is it necessary to focus on hard power capabilities in a world where security threats are much broader and, in the case of the EU, largely non-military?

These two themes are tied together in this chapter via an examination of the relationship between the US and Europe after the Second World War. The decline of the US as a hegemonic power stands in sharp contrast to its initiating role in what I will refer to as the neoliberal turn. How can we make sense of this, and what were the consequences for the EU? This complicated transatlantic relationship will be the topic of the first section.

Four long-running debates will be the leitmotif implicitly playing in the background in this chapter: 1) the debate between those who see the process of European integration largely as an economic project focused on a free market and a single currency, and those who believe the EU can only be complete once a social dimension is added; 2) the debate between those who favour an Atlantic Europe and those who believe European integration should ultimately lead to a European Europe that is freed from the constraints of the Atlantic alliance; 3) the debate between those who believe the EU should maintain its predominantly intergovernmental constellation and those who see the ultimate aim more in terms of supranational integration; and finally 4) the debate between those who consider Europe's role as a global actor in the military sense to be inconceivable and unnecessary, thus seeing the EU mainly as a small power, and those who advocate a more normative approach and emphasise the role of 'Global Europe' as a community of values.

6.1. European integration and Atlantic security during the Cold War

The postwar integration process in Western Europe took place within an Atlantic context and as part of the economic and military cooperation under the banner of Pax Americana. This 'American peace' was the logical consequence of the decisive role that the US played in the Allied victory over Hitler's Germany, a role that was comparable in terms of impact only to that of the Soviet Union. It gave the US a political and moral leverage over the political leaders and populations of the countries freed by American troops.

In the process of redeploying its war industry to civil production, it was in America's interest to create a new world order based on open borders and stable monetary relations. The Europeans, meanwhile, simply wanted to recover from the plundering, the mass murder, and the ravages of war. The Americans left their mark on the agreements reached in Bretton Woods in 1944 which were to determine the postwar financial-economic and monetary constellation, and as an emerging nuclear superpower the US guaranteed the security of its European allies. Some European countries could for a while still cling to the illusion that they had a say in the decisions taken by the US in economic or military matters (Great Britain in the case of the former, France in the case of the latter)—for example in the solution to the so-called German Problem—or that they could maintain an independent position. However, the Suez Crisis of 1956 crushed all such illusions and left no doubt about the new balance of power within the Western sphere of influence during the Cold War.

American hegemony was initially based on two building blocks—one economic and the other political-military—that were inextricably intertwined in the way they impacted the 'allies' in Western Europe. Many factors can be given for the economic rise of the US—demographic and sociogeographic developments, technological innovation, cheap energy, foreign investment, etc.—but there is no doubt that what determined the true character of the American century was the combination of two innovations that occurred between the two world wars. The first of these innovations was a revolutionary change at the microeconomic level, of which Henry Ford's car factory in Detroit can be seen as the iconic starting point. Inspired by such concepts as the so-called scientific management approach (otherwise known as Taylorism), Ford came up with a method to increase the productivity of his workers. He introduced the assembly line, which meant that his workers stood still while the product that was to be manufactured moved along the conveyor belt. As a result, each individual worker carried out a specific task in the production process instead of manufacturing the entire product—in this case, a car—from beginning to end. The standardisation of the production process meant that the work itself became more monotonous and boring, but this was offset—and this was the ingenious aspect of this new model—by paying the labourers more, namely the Five-Dollar-A-Day wage.[1] The idea was as simple as it was effective: the spectacular increase in productivity made it possible to mass-produce cars at lower costs; this allowed for workers to be better paid and, as a necessary corollary, for mass consumption to be generated. Given that success stories often give rise to imitation, companies in other sectors soon copied Ford's new formula for success. The mass production of consumer goods became a national phenomenon and laid the basis for the emergence of the 'American way of life'.

This brings us to the second innovation that emerged on the eve of the Second World War: Roosevelt's New Deal. In retrospect, we can see this macroeconomic development as a partially successful strategy to provide American free market capitalism with elements of a welfare state. To effectively manage the virtuous cycle of increasing productivity (mass production) and rising real wages (mass consumption), an active government role was essential. The government could provide supplementary services such as education, healthcare, and social security; it could also contribute to the stimulation of domestic demand through an increase in government expenditure (made possible in part by rising tax revenues); and through regulations it could help to bring about the necessary macroeconomic stability. The result was a tacit tripartite pact between employers, employees, and the government—a social-corporatist agreement based on converging interests.

Both innovations, which in combination are sometimes referred to as the Fordist growth model, became part of the international expansion of American capitalism after the Second World War and the establishment of an American sphere of influence in the bipolar reality of the Cold War (even though Ford's new production method had already been introduced in Europe before the war—in Nazi Germany and the Soviet Union, for example). The Bretton Woods system and the European Recovery Program, better known as the Marshall Plan, played an important role in the rise of Atlantic Fordism, alongside the growing interdependence of the American and European industrial and financial sectors. As Benn Steil puts it, the Bretton Woods system laid 'the economic foundations for a durable postwar global peace, one that would allow governments more power over markets, but fewer prerogatives to manipulate them for trade gains' (Steil 2013: 1). This was the idea, at least initially, but the global reach of this vision soon turned out to be unattainable when Stalin showed no interest in going along; besides that, the system did not last for more than three decades. Nonetheless, the period 1946-1973 can be considered the peak in transatlantic relations in terms of political-economic coordination and ideological like-mindedness. Moreover, this Atlantic constellation had broad-based support in society. The prewar New Deal model was implemented in Western Europe from 1946—albeit not in an identical way—initially as part of the postwar reconstruction, and then in the 1960s as part of a period of unparalleled economic growth. Of the many labels for this postwar growth model, the three most salient are: 'Keynes at home, Smith abroad' (a slogan conceived by James Mayall and cited in Gilpin 1987: 355), embedded liberalism (John Ruggie 1982), and the European rescue of the nation-state (Milward 1994). The first two notions essentially refer to the same phenomenon, namely that market integration and free trade among countries (Adam Smith's—and Ruggie's—liberalism) went hand in hand with a greater role for governments at the national, socio-economic level (i.e. John Maynard Keynes' state intervention, as a result of which markets became nationally embedded). The economic growth generated by cross-border trade flowed partly into the state's coffers and partly—via rising wages in the Fordist mode of production—into the wallets of the new middle class. The improvement in purchasing power and the arrangements provided by the welfare state took the sting out of class struggle and brought trade unions to the negotiating table as 'responsible partners'. European integration played a key role in all of this, largely because the first steps towards integration were aimed at the removal of trade barriers. In this sense, the first steps in the process of European economic integration in the 1950s were a direct outcome of the involvement of the US in European reconstruction through the Marshall Plan of 1948. Although the philanthropic intention of this financial support scheme should not be underestimated, particularly in terms of its psychological and ideological (read: anti-communist) importance, its real significance lay largely in the conditionality that the US attached to Marshall aid. Countries that wanted to be eligible for such aid had to unequivocally follow the path of reciprocal trade liberalisation and, moreover, had to open up their markets to American exports according to the age-old principle of quid pro quo.

The effect was felt in multiple domains. Not only were trade unions promoted to the status of active partners in social compromises at the national level ('Keynes at home'), but workers in the Fordist industries also began to form part of the so-called new middle class. In the process, communist parties in various Western European countries found that the wind had been taken out of their sails (if they had not already been thrown out of government coalitions under pressure from the US). The expansion of welfare states further reinforced this development. As mentioned earlier, all of this was made possible by the postwar growth spiral that went hand in hand with the European integration process. Contrary to what was expected or feared, economic openness ('Smith abroad') did not result in an erosion of the nation-state but rather a strengthening of it, an outcome Milward refers to in the above-mentioned title of his book. Government intervention in socio-economic affairs assumed major proportions (the welfare state), and instead of integration leading to the erosion of state power, the member states of the Western European free trade association became stronger than ever.

A year after the launch of the Marshall Plan, the second, political-military pillar under American hegemony was set up: the North Atlantic Treaty Organization (NATO). The cornerstone of this treaty, which in the context of the nascent Cold War was primarily directed against the Soviet Union and its sphere of influence in Central and Eastern Europe, consisted of mutual or collective defence and security. Article 5 of the founding treaty explicitly states that an attack on one of the member states is regarded as an attack on all, with a joint reaction as the logical consequence. As both superpowers became increasingly engaged in an arms race, with the threat of a nuclear war only averted through mutual deterrence, the Western European allies became more dependent on the US, even though Great Britain and later France came to possess their own arsenal of nuclear weapons. In the strategic calculations of the Cold War, the US was the only power that was up to the job of meeting the threat from the East and offering a security guarantee for its European allies.

The protection offered by the US within the framework of NATO and the proclaimed territorial and ideological unity of 'the West' were an important source of inspiration for one of the first European integration theorists. In a study dating from 1957, Karl Deutsch and his team of researchers raised an important question: under what conditions could a lasting or even permanent peace be reached in the North Atlantic area? A central concept in their work was that of a 'security community', which they defined as a political community of states that was established for peaceful change, based on a *sense of community* and *institutions and practices* that were strong and widespread enough to guarantee its population *long-lasting and dependable expectations of peaceful change*. A sense of community and social cohesion played an important role in their analysis. They distinguished two kinds of security communities: a unitary or amalgamated security community, and a pluralistic security community. In the latter variant, two or more countries created a security community without infringing on the national sovereignty and legal independence of the individual governments. The researchers saw the transatlantic integration within Pax Americana as a nascent example of this type of security community. An amalgamated security community, such as the United States after its War of Independence and its Civil War, came about when previously independent political entities became part of a larger whole, in the process subordinating themselves to an overarching federal or unitary authority (Deutsch et al. 1957: 6).

6.2. The trans-Atlantic impasse: EU-US relations after the Cold War

While Deutsch et al. did state in their conclusions that a pluralistic security community was emerging in the North Atlantic area, with NATO and the 1952 European Coal
and Steel Community as international or functional organisations, they also feared
that the underlying sense of community was mainly based on military grounds
and directed against the Soviet Union. With a remarkable degree of foresight, they
argued that a possible collapse of communism could lead to the disappearance of
Atlantic solidarity. In fact, Deutsch and his colleagues gave due weight to a reverse
movement: the disintegration of security communities, including the return of
armed conflict (ibid.: 199ff).

In this chapter I not only define security in broader terms than simply 'the
absence of armed conflict'; as we will see later on, I also have a broader than strictly
military interpretation of postwar Pax Americana and American hegemony. A
comparison with the so-called Hegemonic Stability Theory (HST) within the
discipline of international relations is useful here. Adherents of this theory can
be found within realism and liberalism as well as within neomarxism (for a critical
overview, see for example Strange 1987). Despite considerable ontological and
epistemological differences between these 'isms'—and the lack of consensus within
each of them—virtually all academics argue that the international system can only
achieve a stage or phase of balance and stability if one of the states comes forward as
primus inter pares, i.e. as a hegemonic power that determines and institutionalises
the rules of the game in consultation with the other states. Hegemony is therefore
different from dominance or domination because it is based on persuasiveness
and consensus rather than repression (or the threat of repression). Think back
to our discussion on the concept of power in chapter 3. As a correction to his
original definition of power, Lukes later argued that A's exercise of power over B
did not need to go against B's best interests; B could indeed benefit from the power
of A and therefore also accept this power. An important element in HST is the
phenomenon of public goods, i.e. goods that are accessible to every participant.
In the case of American hegemony after the Second World War, the US primarily
offered public goods in the form of financial support (the Marshall Plan and the
World Bank), participation in an international free trade system (GATT), a system
of stable exchange rates linked to balance-of-payments support (IMF), and military
protection (NATO). This was not an insignificant system of public goods, and it
was reason enough for the member states of these international organisations to
accept American leadership as the best of all possible worlds. Providing guidance
and direction are important raisons d'être for a hegemonic power; this must be
conceived and subsequently presented as something in the general interest, but

agreements must also be adhered to, if necessary with other, more compelling means. The problem of free riding had to be avoided at all times: it is about rights and responsibilities. Unforeseen imbalances between the two could, in the absence of effective and credible action by the hegemonic power, affect the entire hegemonic structure at its base and herald the beginning of the end of a hegemonic cycle. (Seen from this perspective, a recent example is telling. In one of his ukases directed against Europe, Donald Trump blamed Germany for three things that, seen in combination and from a US perspective, did not sound illogical: Germany devoted far too little of its economic welfare to defence, had a huge surplus in its bilateral trade with the US, and, to make matters worse, used part of its saved and earned money to buy Russian gas. The post-war self-evidence of American hegemony and its mirror image in the form of German reticence in external economic, political, and security relations had definitely come to an end.)

6.2.1.   Hegemonic stability under fire

As stated above, most authors argue that a *primus inter pares* within the international state system can provide political-military and/or economic stability, but they disagree about how hegemonic power is established and about which factors are important for explaining (and predicting!) the dynamics of rise and fall within a hegemonic cycle. Some emphasise military capabilities and see a new hegemonic power emerging as a victor from a global war, powerful enough to set the rules for a long period of time (they do not shy away from putting the duration of a hegemonic cycle—i.e. the period between two global wars—at approximately 100 years; see, for example, Modelski 1987). Political-military leadership, essential for stability during the hegemonic phase, will increasingly be challenged in the course of the cycle and slowly erode as a result. Ultimately, the emergence of a political-military challenger will trigger a so-called power transition, after which a new cycle will begin (for the original version of the power transition theory, see Organski 1958). Adherents of this approach leave it unclear whether such a transition necessarily has to be preceded by a global war.

In contrast to this focus on hard power, Immanuel Wallerstein emphasises the primacy of economic processes to explain the rise and fall of hegemonic powers. He defines hegemony as 'a situation wherein the products of a given core state are produced so efficiently that they are by and large competitive even in other core states, and therefore the given core state will be the primary beneficiary of a maximally free world market' (Wallerstein 1980: 38). The technological superiority of the state in question gives it a competitive advantage that then translates into commercial superiority, giving rise to a trade surplus. Subsequently, this results in financial superiority, as there is more money coming in than flowing out. If the

technological, commercial and financial superiority of one state over other core
states coincide, we can speak of hegemony. Wallerstein adds that such a hegemonic
phase is short-lived. The downfall will take place in the same order: first, other
core states will reduce the hegemon's technological lead, for example by copying
the success of the hegemonic power. If subsequently the competitive advantage
is lost, the surplus on the trade balance will also decrease, and ultimately the
financial lead of the hegemonic power will disappear—and possibly turn into a
debt position (ibid.: 38-39).[2]

No matter whether we put the emphasis on political-military or economic supremacy, we can establish that American postwar hegemony is declining and,
in any case, no longer uncontested. From a military point of view, the US is still
the country with the highest defence spending in the international system, but
Americans are increasingly confronted with the reality of emerging powers (China
is particularly prominent in the recent literature on power transition) and the
renewed assertiveness of Russia.

In hindsight we can conclude that the hegemonic phase was relatively short in
the financial-economic sense, from the late 1940s to the early 1970s. There were
different moments at which a relative but definite demise could be discerned.
The emergence of a trade deficit at the end of the 1960s was experienced as a
shock, not least in the US itself. Other shocks came when, under President Nixon,
an important foundation holding up the post-war Bretton Woods system—the
system of fixed exchange rates and the convertibility of international dollars to
American gold—was punctured, and when US troops had to make a shameful
retreat from Vietnam in the early 1970s. The 1980s saw the relaunch of the process
of European integration—single market, single currency—accompanied by a
growing assertiveness and a strengthening of European competitiveness on the
world market. Moreover, the introduction of the euro created an alternative to the
dollar as a means of international payments and as a reserve currency. The 1990s
showcased the globalisation of neoliberal ideas—ostensibly an expression of the
resurgence of Anglo-Saxon capitalism but possibly a final convulsion—as well as the
rise of the so-called emerging economies and the emergence of an interdependent
and multipolar state system. Since the turn of the millennium, we have increasingly
seen that the US no longer has the exclusive right to a world order strategy, that
no state has the power to control all corners of the earth by modelling security
in its own image, and that China in particular is working hard to catch up with
the US on almost all fronts as an economic, political, and ultimately also military
superpower. Finally, we can conclude that the financial crisis that started in the
United States with the bankruptcy of Lehman Brothers in 2008 has set in motion
a chain of populist and nationalist reactions and authoritarian tendencies that are

at odds with the liberal world order proclaimed just after the velvet revolutions in Central and Eastern Europe and the collapse of the Soviet Union. The irony of history is that the 'America first' movement under President Donald Trump is an integral part of this countermovement.

6.2.2.   Towards a post-American Europe?

Despite the overwhelming power of the US, the countries within the American sphere of influence retained their own identity and pursued their national interests as far as possible. The point here is that subordination to the power of a hegemonic state is never merely idealistic or ideological—in the sense of 'the liberator from Nazi tyranny', 'the protector of the free world', or 'the defender of free-market capitalism'—but is always (and perhaps primarily) in need of a material (self-) justification. For some, this justification may have been the existential fear of a military attack by the Soviet Union, and for others the prospect of considerable profit if they followed in the footsteps of American business or banking. At the level of those in power, subordination is never disinterested. Thus if there is no longer any interest being served, the hegemonic constellation will come under pressure. (And vice versa, the American attitude towards European integration was never—and is still not—only idealistic or ideological. This was apparent when the EU attempted to deepen the integration process from the 1980s onwards; the extended relaunch soon laid bare the ambivalence of the United States. The establishment of the EMU and in particular the introduction of the euro were outwardly praised but inwardly seen as a threat to the dollar as an international reserve currency. And initiatives to strengthen European defence cooperation were positively assessed but it was noted that they should not lead to a drifting away from the Atlantic alliance.)

In a publication for the European Council on Foreign Relations, a pan-European think tank, Jeremy Shapiro and Nick Witney took stock of the changing global power relations, the end of the global dominance of the US, and the consequences for what they referred to as a post-American Europe (Shapiro and Witney 2009). European governments and elites, they argued, have not mastered the new reality and still live with the illusion of their special relationship with the US in the context of Pax Americana. They wallow in complacency and idleness and believe that their servile attitude towards the US allows them to keep their privileged junior partnership. Nothing could be further from the truth, according to the authors. The US does not want European respect and submission; what the Americans are looking for is a robust relationship with a Europe that is able to upgrade its own role in the alliance. The robust relationship that exists in the economic field must also be realised in the field of security. The post-America Europe that the authors advocate is not a submissive Europe or an independent Europe but a Europe that caters to the US (a good example of such nudging is Americans' repeated demand for European govern-ments to significantly increase their defence spending). Apparently, the authors are mainly concerned with the unity of 'the West', which, as we have seen, had and still has an economic and political-military component but has come under pressure since the end of the Cold War. Later in this chapter I turn to the political-military aspects, but I will first examine the economic buttress of Western cohesion.

The comparison with economic policy that Shapiro and Witney draw is interest-ing. The transition from Keynesianism to neoliberalism in the 1980s and 1990s was discussed earlier (see foreword), and we can assume that the authors were fully aware of this change at the time of writing. Thus, when they speak of a robust relationship, they must be referring to the convergence of neoliberal policies. We now know that the neoliberal turn started in the US under Ronald Reagan and in Great Britain under Margaret Thatcher. These forerunners of the 'new truth', also referred to as the 'Anglo-Saxon model of capitalism', denounced the achievements of the post-war period: the exorbitant welfare state, the excessive protection of labour, the unacceptably strong position of the trade unions, and so on. There are two factors that explain the advent of an alternative ideology in the 1970s. One part of the literature on the rise of neoliberalism takes the first major economic crisis after the Second World War as evidence that Fordism—as the basis of Keynesian demand management—had run its course. The growth model had been exhausted and simply had to be replaced by a more dynamic and flexible system of production. Another part of the literature points out that the US, faced with declining hegemony, was trying to reverse its downfall. In that sense, the neoliberal revolution can be seen as a headlong rush. By focusing on the supply side of the economy, the US was able to increase the competitiveness of its businesses. By deregulating global capital markets successfully, it succeeded in strengthening the dominant position of Wall Street (and the City of London). In this context, Europe (read: the European business community and European governments and elites) had no choice but to follow the US once again. So it was not an idealistic or ideological motive that prompted Europe to converge; at most, this served as legitimation. Enlightened self-interest was the main motive (see also chapter 3).

In the remainder of this section I will first briefly discuss the main features of neoliberalism, and then indicate how the relaunch of the European integration process in the 1980s and 1990s was instrumental to the neoliberal turn in individual member states. The purpose is to show the difference between the transatlantic convergence of neoliberal policies and the almost organic model of hegemony of Pax Americana during the growth decades after the Second World War. International cooperation and national harmony were replaced by intensified global competition and national social strife, resulting paradoxically in a further erosion of both American hegemony and Western cohesion.

Neoliberalism

For a variety of reasons, neoliberalism is a difficult concept. To begin with, there is considerable theoretical ambiguity and disagreement about what the notion actually means (or should imply) in terms of economic policy. Secondly, the precise application of neoliberal ideas at the national level is very different and heavily dependent on local political, economic, and cultural peculiarities.

Despite this elusiveness, the concept has been given a bad name. (Many politicians and economists even refuse to use the term.) Social scientists have, in fact, linked neoliberalism to a series of negative developments in highly developed societies, such as those of the EU, from the 1980s. For example, the application of neoliberal ideas has been held responsible for having brought about a certain withdrawal of the government from the economy, something referred to as the shift from government to governance. Governments are less involved in the following areas: entrepreneurship (through a process of privatisation), enacting regulations that are to the detriment of entrepreneurs (through deregulation), and erecting obstacles aimed at companies (through liberalisation). Governments are withdrawing from the welfare state; in fact, they are actively engaged in the (partial) dismantling of provisions for the unemployed, the sick, and the needy in general.

Welfare states have begun to converge, but in a downward adjustment, a so-called race to the bottom. The mechanism by which this is achieved is called regime competition. Greater economic openness leads to the rapid movement—and potential relocation—of capital and investment. To keep companies operating within their own economy, governments compete with each other for the favour of companies and providers of capital. They do this by offering a favourable investment climate. If a government takes a step in the 'right' direction, other governments will soon follow and the policy measure will be copied or improved upon, and so on—resulting in a downwards spiral movement. Two prominent policy areas in this context are taxation and labour market policy: capital is taxed less, while labour is taxed more. With regard to labour, governments move away from a levelling tax regime. All this results in widening differences in income and welfare, particularly within countries and between different strata in society. The diagnosis of adherents of neoliberalism is that labour markets are far too rigid and hinder free enterprise. They must therefore be deregulated, and work must become flexible again. All this results in the reduction of various protective constructions (such as protection against dismissal). Finally, Western governments do not limit themselves to their own countries when it comes to the introduction of these measures; they believe that it is right to export neoliberal ideas, as there is no alternative, they argue, especially after the collapse of communism as a 'second world' (alongside the first world of capitalism and the third world of poor, underdeveloped countries). The recipe of free markets and a reduced role for the state is imposed on governments in developing countries, indirectly—via international organisations and private lenders—through the debt financing mechanism (see chapter 4). This leads to greater income and welfare differences in these countries too.

Let us briefly zoom in on the aspect of the changing role of the state, also referred to as the hollowing out of the state. First of all, the privatisation of state functions in the economy has altered the balance between states and markets. In the course of capitalist development, the state directly interfered in the national economy as an entrepreneur and investor in productive activities, or as a banker. This involvement was sometimes born out of necessity, due to the absence of private investors, and sometimes out of the conviction that certain services were best provided by governments. Often this servicing took the form of a state monopoly. When the decision was made to complete the European single market, measures were taken not only to realise the free movement of goods, people, and capital but also to enable the free movement of services—that is, a liberalised services sector. This meant the end of state monopolies and the beginning of full competition. Utilities, postal services, railways, telecommunication and media companies were among the sectors that were privatised and opened up to cross-border competition. At present, there are very few state-owned companies in Europe left (among them the financial institutions that were nationalised as a result of the euro crisis, as part of the so-called socialisation of private losses).

A second interpretation of the notion of 'hollowing out of the state' concerns the shift in decision-making from the national to the sub-national and supranational level. Almost thirty years ago, the American political scientist Philippe C. Schmitter argued that the EU represented a new and unique form of political domination in which the relevance of territoriality and the necessity of sovereignty decreased. He saw the EU as a paradigmatic case of an unfolding post-Hobbesian order, very similar to what I referred to as multi-level governance (MLG) earlier in this book. The EU is more than an international organisation in which decision-making takes place on a strictly intergovernmental basis, but it explicitly does not constitute a supranational state in the making. The result is a hybrid form of governance in which state and non-state actors, in cooperation with European institutions, participate in policy-making at different levels.

Finally, a change has taken place that has not so much led to the hollowing out of the state as to the erosion of democracy and the deterioration of social cohesion. Within the public sector, the importance of certain policy areas has increased, while the importance of other areas has decreased. Here, too, the EU has played an important role. Within the realm of ministries and policy priorities, the financial-monetary sector has grown exponentially. Ministries of finance and central banks are in charge of the EMU. They keep governments 'focused' and bear responsibility for the austerity measures, i.e. cuts in collective spending, which are partially imposed by Europe. A not insignificant additional effect of this shift is the technocratisation of politics—and with that the erosion of democracy. Another effect is the different view on social policy, which has shifted from positive and progressive (a better and more secure life for everyone through the expansion of welfare state provisions) in the decades after the Second World War to negative and regressive under the banner of neoliberal austerity. Social policy is now associated with unemployment, benefits, aging, and unaffordability: in short, with untenability.

Asymmetrical regulation
In what way has the EU played a role in this turnaround in thinking and policy and in the changed (or hollowed out) role of the government? One way has been free and full competition in the single market. The decision to complete this internal market, taken in 1985, came from two considerations (compare this with the US motivation above). First, the crisis of the 1970s and the early 1980s brought to light, also in Europe, the fact that the post-war growth model had been exhausted. Stagnating Fordist sectors, rising unemployment, and increasing government deficits played an important role in this consideration. Secondly, the American policy aimed at improving competitiveness challenged European economic and political elites to copy this policy (a kind of regime competition). The single market became the first major project in the neoliberal turn and heralded the emergence of a predominant discourse of competitiveness. Competition in the single market meant two things: first, the principle of the survival of the fittest inherent in free markets led to the relocation of production and employment in Europe and the subsequent emergence of new winners and losers; and second, national governments were no longer able to intervene actively in the economy (read: to shield the losers from negative effects) via subsidies to ailing companies, non-tariff trade barriers, or productive investments for the general interest.

But the role of the EU in the neoliberal turn was even more radical as a result of the decisions taken in Maastricht regarding the EMU architecture. As I already noted in the first chapters of this book, in some policy areas there is a shared competence between different levels of government, in other areas there is a transfer of sovereignty, and in still other areas there are exclusive national competences. The European Commission has far-reaching powers to enforce the principles of the single market, and the European Central Bank (ECB) has essential instruments of monetary policy under its supranational wing. In the field of social policy, however, member states have retained full control, with a few exceptions. There is no question whatsoever of supranational social regulation or, to put it differently, positive harmonisation of social policy. We could consider this a simple matter of a division of labour or competence, but there is more to the story than that. It is significant that the transfer of powers in the economic and monetary fields has led to constraints on the nation-state's room for manoeuvre in the social domain. That is, the often loudly claimed national self-determination with regard to social issues turns out to be largely based on illusions. I have referred to this mechanism elsewhere as asymmetrical regulation: '(it) not only refers to the discrepancy between European economic and monetary free market regulation, on the one hand, and the lack of social regulation (or harmonisation) at the European level, on the other, but—more importantly—to the adverse impact of economic and monetary integration at the European level on social cohesion at the national level' (Holman 2004: 716).

It has become a truism since the euro crisis of 2008-2013 that the eurozone has been a composition of unequal quantities right from the start—i.e. uneven and unevenly performing member states. From the beginning, monetary *union* actually boiled down to different levels of economic growth, and different rates of inflation and unemployment. What could governments within the EU and the EMU do if their countries were affected by these macroeconomic 'imbalances'? Subsidies to national companies were out of the question due to the single market. The old mechanism of a downward adjustment of interest rates was no longer possible because the ECB decided on the interest rate for the entire eurozone. Stimulating the economy through an increase in government expenditure was also impossible because the so-called Stability and Growth Pact did not allow national governments to increase their budget deficits. And it goes without saying, finally, that national exchange rate policies were no longer possible within the eurozone.

What remained in theory were three mechanisms or policy options: austerity measures, regime competition (for example in the field of taxation), and micro-economic structural adjustments on the supply side. The latter option is better known as 'reform of the labour market', which usually refers to flexibilisation. It is crucial to understand that all of these reforms have had—and still have—direct consequences on social cohesion within member states. Austerity measures are generally regressive because they first and foremost affect those citizens who depend on government support. Regime competition leads to lower taxes on capital that have to be compensated by a rise in the tax burden on labour and/or an increase in indirect taxes (such as the sales tax or the value-added tax). And labour market reforms result in an increase in social insecurity. Here, too, a reduction in labour market protection has an uneven effect on different strata of the population.

The essence of asymmetrical regulation is that national governments' room for manoeuvre to conduct their own social policy is drastically curtailed. The available policy instruments are adapted to the requirements of the supranational market and currency. Indirectly, therefore, national social policy is dictated by Europe, which means that national sovereignty is by and large an illusion. Government budget cuts, improvements in competitiveness, and structural market-oriented reforms are the European guidelines that set the course at the national level.

This would probably not be a problem if the effects of European agreements had a positive effect on everyone, or if it could in any case be presented as such. It is here that the European project runs aground on its own ambitions, for the EU is not seen as a partnership that serves the general public interest; it *is* associated, however, with greater inequality and unequal opportunities and has been a fertile breeding ground for populist and eurosceptic movements (see also chapter 5). The elimination of obstacles to the free movement of goods, capital, services, and people (even before the arrival of non-European refugees, it was the new EU citizens from Central and Eastern Europe who aroused fear and aggression) and the removal of restrictions on competitiveness—in the literature this is referred to as 'negative integration'—reduced the likelihood of positive integration, i.e. the creation of new policies at the European level. The powerless citizen is then thrown back to their equally impotent state, and both are unable to dispel their own insecurity or the perception of this insecurity. In order to understand the consequences of this for the European integration process, we must first turn our attention to the concept of security itself. This may seem like an abrupt break in the chapter's narrative—from the neoliberal turn via asymmetrical regulation to security—but the connection will gradually become clear. A broader view of security will help us come to a better understanding of the deterioration of internal and external social cohesion within the so-called West. What some might call a robust cooperation between the United States and a post-American Europe can perhaps be described better as a slowly but surely eroding Atlantic security community.

6.3.   New security threats and old reflexes

A simple and useful description of security for our purposes is *the absence of threats*. From the perspective of this book, this description has a number of advantages (see Buzan and Hansen 2009: 10-12). First, it gives us the leeway to make an analysis of security that is much broader than the interstate dynamics of action and reaction. Well-known concepts such as national (or international) security take the nation-state as a starting point and see the security of subnational actors as dependent on and subordinate to state security. As already mentioned several times, territorial integrity and sovereignty are important core values in this restrictive view of security. However, if we shift the reference point of threats to people (or groups of people), the security palette becomes more colourful and a reverse cause-and-effect reasoning takes hold: instead of external threats such as armed conflict first affecting the state and only thereafter individual citizens (nation as in *national* security is considered to be indivisible), multifarious threats can pass state borders almost unnoticed and affect people directly. If the threat subsequently gets bigger and more widespread, and starts to have electoral consequences for example, then calls for the state to intervene will become louder and more effective.

Second, and closely linked to this, is the fact that threats do not have to be of a political-military nature. In an open society such as the European one, national and individual security are no longer synonymous with military security. Risks to food security or energy supplies, pandemics, transnational organised crime, and cyberattacks are some of the many non-military security threats that can have an impact on the lives of individual citizens and that could result in bottom-up pressure on governments to solve these using non-military means.

Third, these examples show that a strict separation between internal and external security can no longer be made. States are interconnected—for better or worse, as neorealists like to see it—but their societies and citizens are often just as interconnected. In any case, citizens of different states often have similar preoccupations about their security and any threats to it. Many current threats have a transnational character. As a result, the distinction between internal and external security has become blurred.

Fourth, the widespread belief among people in the East and the West that the nuclear arms race between the US and the Soviet Union would result in mutual destruction (an external threat) is no longer a matter of central concern in our post-Cold-War world. The urgency of a nuclear war, its all-encompassing character, and indeed its potential for destruction have been reduced in recent decades to the fear of proliferation, in particular the fear that nuclear weapons could fall into the wrong hands. The contemporary fear of a terrorist attack evokes memories of the fear of nuclear confrontation at the time of the Cold War, but every right-minded person realises that this comparison is flawed, if only because the probability of becoming the victim of an attack is extremely low.

With nuclear threats moving to the background and with the disciplinary effect of the Cold War spheres-of-influence politics waning, all sorts of smaller security problems are coming to the fore. The research area of security studies has accordingly expanded. The broadening and deepening of international security studies (ISS) is how this changed view of security is commonly described (see part 2 in Collins 2016). This can be illustrated using some key concepts from the new literature. First, the notion of human security must be mentioned. The state-centric perspective is replaced by an emphasis on the individual, for if we talk about security, we are ultimately talking about people (see, for example, Smith 2010: 41-43). An important reason for this shift in the level of analysis is the dramatic increase in what Mark Duffield calls the new wars (Duffield 2001). Conflicts—often with an ethnic or religious background—that laid dormant during the Cold War, and that had been kept in check fairly successfully, virulently surfaced in the 1990s in the form of national implosions. The consequences of violent and bloody civil wars in the former

Yugoslavia and in Rwanda are still firmly etched into the international political memory, as is the constant stream of displaced people who have to build a new life hundreds or thousands of miles away from what is left of their hearth and home.

In addition, the socio-economic position of individuals is a topic that is central to the debates on individual (human) security. Again, this is related to the end of the Cold War, together with the acceleration of globalisation processes. Greater economic openness in the form of trade, investments, and speculative capital has its winners and losers. People in the Western world are losing their economic security and are not always (and everywhere) supported by generous social safety nets. In what is known as the Global South, the challenges are more immediately about combating extreme poverty and guaranteeing a minimum standard of living as well as improving healthcare, providing primary education, and protecting the most basic human rights. Here we find a clear relationship with peace research conducted in the 1960s (as briefly pointed out above, through the work of Johan Galtung—see chapter 3).

This individualisation of security resonates in a certain way with another concept that often appears in the new security studies: the notion of societal security. This was originally defined by the so-called Copenhagen School as 'the ability of a society to persist in its essential character under changing conditions and possible or actual threats' (Waever et al. 1993: 23). This much-quoted definition is rather vague and needs some explanation. The theorists who introduced this concept were initially referring to the effects of changing environmental factors on ethnic-national identities. After the Cold War, old resentments emerged in the new democracies in Central and Eastern Europe that had been skilfully kept under wraps under communism but had not disappeared. The rights of Hungarian minorities in Romania and Slovakia and of Turkish minorities in Bulgaria were a constant source of tension, not to mention the bloody conflicts that erupted between the people of the former Yugoslavia. Societal security became the term for these early forms of identity politics. In subsequent years, the deterioration of social identity and cohesion was given a broader scope in order to encompass the threats associated with globalisation (see, for example, Roe 2016). Local communities are losing their cohesion as a result of open borders and the spread of other ways of life. The situation becomes explosive when large groups of people feel as though they are wedged between two cultures: the culture of alienation, individualism, and (paradoxically) cosmopolitanism on the one hand, and the culture of foreigners on the other.

The experience of security (or insecurity) and the resulting need for protection is extremely subjective. The line between acute danger ('the enemy has gathered its troops on our external border') and potential danger ('our neighbouring country has announced the general mobilisation of its army') is often difficult to identify, as is the difference between real and imagined dangers. If these lines cannot be drawn clearly, there is room for moods to be manipulated and for inflating or even creating security threats. This brings us to another area of ISS, namely the notion of securitisation—and its opposite, de-securitisation. Subject matters that caused no problems for a long time can quickly become security threats. Migration is a clear example of this. Conversely, a security problem can suddenly disappear even though it has determined the geopolitical agenda for centuries. Peaceful cooperation and integration on the European continent and in particular the pacification of the French-German relationship are illustrations of this. To paraphrase the famous quote of the social-constructivist Alexander Wendt (see chapter 1): security (or insecurity) is what states, societies, and individuals make of it!

How does this short summary of some key issues in the ISS literature bring us further in the story about European external relations in general and the CFSP in particular? Is it not the case that with such a broadening of the concept, almost everything can be considered a possible threat? Should we not limit ourselves to the 'good old' political-military threats inherent to relations between sovereign states? These questions touch upon the central debate on the plausibility and desirability of cooperation, and possible integration, of defence policies at the European level. In response to the first question: ISS teaches us that the distinction between internal and external security is disappearing; that individual, societal, and national security are interlocking; and that the difference between objective threat and subjective experience carries important political consequences. Returning to what was written above about the link between globalisation, Europeanisation, and liberalisation as three inseparable and interacting processes, and in particular zooming in on the feelings of insecurity and dissatisfaction that have been unleashed among large sections of the populations, we immediately see the importance of a new view on security (and insecurity). This is important if only for the fact that social dissatisfaction translates into Euroscepticism, and for the fact that a stronger opposition to 'Europe' also has consequences for the decisiveness of the EU in its external relations, i.e. the EU's actorness.

In response to the second and third questions: the broadening of the concept of security is not just an exercise in cleverness but a reflection of concrete developments in our immediate environment. And if this makes evident the multiplicity of contemporary security problems and perceptions, we should prepare ourselves for the answers instead of remaining trapped in the old way of thinking about power political rivalries among sovereign states. It could indeed be the case that times of war on the European continent are over and that the member states of the EU should, jointly, focus on tackling all those other security dilemmas. The question is whether the European elites also think so, or whether they allow themselves, for reasons of their own, to get carried away by the provocations and rearguard actions of the US as a superpower in decline and isolation. This is the question I will be investigating throughout the rest of the chapter. For this, we need to address the third component of the EU's external relations, namely the CFSP, and to focus on the world of real and perceived *external* threats, all in connection with the nascent multipolar world and the changing role of the Americans in that world.

6.4. European security and defence policy

Based on an analysis of old and new external (or global) security threats and the relationship between military and non-military dilemmas, we can map out the capacities and policy means that the EU has at its disposal. Using the broadest definition of security and defence policy, we can identify the following components:

- the military capabilities that the EU has at its disposal to defend its own territory—whether or not via pre-emptive attacks (i.e. in self-defence according to Article 51 of the Charter of the United Nations);
- the military capacity that the EU has at its disposal to carry out military operations outside its own territory in order to bring large-scale violations of human rights to a halt (on the basis of the Responsibility to Protect doctrine) and/or to bring about regime change;
- the military, logistical, and financial means that the EU has at its disposal to carry out military and civilian peacekeeping operations in (former) conflict and war zones outside the territory of its member states;
- the material and immaterial capabilities and policy instruments that the EU has at its disposal to settle current and future, acute and potential conflicts with third countries and/or persons using means other than military force.

As I indicated earlier, EU security policy is part of the CFSP or, more accurately, a spin-off of it. Since the Treaty of Lisbon, this is known as the Common Security and Defence Policy, or CSDP. (Until 2009, this was called the ESDP, where the 'E' stood for European. I will use the most recent acronym in the remainder of this chapter.) Of the four aforementioned components, the last one, namely non-violent means, does not belong to the CSDP, strictly speaking. It concerns the EU's external action that has been dealt with in different variants in previous chapters. In fact, only the third component is currently applicable to the CSDP, and even then, with varying degrees of success.

6.4.1.   A brief history of the CSDP

In this section, I will leave aside earlier attempts at European cooperation in the field of defence and security, i.e. attempts from before the end of the Cold War such as the European Defence Community and the Western European Union, which never materialised and died a quiet death in its sleep, respectively. The Maastricht Treaty represented the first serious step towards better cooperation between member states; the CFSP was introduced as a separate pillar in the new post-Cold-War EU architecture. At this stage it mainly entails better coordination and institutional cooperation between the foreign policy elites of the EU, in which common principles and positions adopted earlier are (or are meant to be) guiding factors in member states' foreign policy behaviour. This is the world of EU diplomacy—the 'foreign' in the Common Foreign Security Policy—which basically boils down to a rather toothless act ('we're warning you for the last time') in the absence of concrete *collective* backing via legal, economic, or military means. However, for tougher and more effective measures—in the light of external action this might involve freezing development funds, hampering trade, or postponing accession—unanimity within the EU is necessary, which means that all member states must actively agree. This step—the move from laudable standpoints and promises to actual action—is not self-evident, as history has shown. And this certainly applies to the use of military means (the 'security' part of CFSP).

This is further complicated by the actions of the larger member states in international organisations. The United Nations Security Council is a case in point. Two EU member states, France and Great Britain, are permanent members of this body and articulate positions that are first and foremost national in nature. Moreover, the recent past has shown that they are also prepared to proceed to military intervention outside the framework of the Security Council. A third, not insignificant EU member state, Germany, is the great absentee in this forum but nonetheless—and paradoxically—remains firm in its belief that the most extreme form of 'concrete action', namely military intervention, should only take place when supported by a Security Council resolution.

Many observers qualify the EU as an economic giant but at the same time note that its political-military capacity for action remains extremely limited, as we saw in chapter 2. Particularly in the area of high politics, and especially in defence policy, member states stubbornly adhere to principles of national sovereignty. As a snapshot of the current situation, this observation is correct and justified. However, if we look at the historical process, especially from the 1990s, we arrive at a different conclusion. Something has happened in the past two to three decades, with the process accelerating in the 2010s. It is admittedly the politics of small steps, and some steps have come to very little, but overall there has clearly been a change.

The Maastricht Treaty explicitly mentioned the possibility of a future common defence, even if the same text emphasised that this should not be in conflict with member states' existing obligations (read: within the framework of the Atlantic Alliance). It was the first time that this ambition was worded in a treaty —it was repeated in the Treaty of Amsterdam in 1997—but it never went further than that during those first years. The war in the former Yugoslavia, and in particular the inability of EU member states to jointly stop the warring parties, was the direct impetus for taking more concrete steps. The aim was to enlarge the EU's own responsibility within NATO, partly to suppress increasing calls in the United States for more balanced burden-sharing. According to the then British prime minister, Tony Blair—speaking at a press conference following an informal European Council meeting in October 1998—the Kosovo crisis had taught Europe that diplomacy doesn't work without a credible threat of force (Rutten 2001: 3). Europe could contribute to the latter by strengthening Europe's identity within NATO (read: greater military autonomy).

In December 1998, France and Great Britain called on the government leaders of the EU to take action on 'the progressive framing of a common defence policy in the framework of CFSP'. Known as the Saint-Malo Declaration, this joint French-British declaration emphasised in particular the need for a credible European defence capacity to be able to respond autonomously to international crisis situations outside the scope of NATO (for the full text see www.cvce.eu). Saint-Malo is for many the actual beginning of the CSDP, even though this acronym was only introduced half a year later at the Cologne European Council, and the policy was further developed in the period up to the 2001 Treaty of Nice. In December 1999, the Helsinki European Council—the same council that, not without significance, gave the green light to the big bang enlargement of the EU (see chapter 5)—decided to formulate the so-called Headline Goal. This involved the establishment, by the member states of the EU, of an intervention force in the form of a rapidly deployable army corps of 50,000 to 60,000 soldiers. Such a force was intended to carry out so-called Petersberg tasks (named after a small town close to Bonn where these tasks were formulated back in 1992): humanitarian missions or rescue operations, peacekeeping, and crisis management (including peacemaking, if necessary by force). This had to be operational by the end of 2003 at the latest. This ambition did not materialise for various political, financial, and logistical reasons, and in 2004 a more modest concept emerged in the form of so-called Battlegroups. Rapidly deployable combat units of about 1,500 men and women had to be operational by 2007. This initiative has to date also amounted to little, as all sorts of problems stood in the way of effective implementation and deployment. Just recently, in 2016, the drafters of the European Union Global Strategy (EUGS, see next section) again spoke of the need to remove 'the procedural, financial and political obstacles which prevent the deployment of the Battlegroups' (EEAS 2016: 47).

It is worth remembering that these are attempts to create a military rapid reaction force that can be deployed quickly under the flag of the EU. This requires common ground on many fronts, and that is exactly what is lacking to this day. However, the fact that these headline goals have not been realised does not mean that EU *member states* are not taking military action or that the EU does not undertake any civilian and military missions. EU member states have fought outside Europe and have done so within the framework of NATO, the UN, or entirely on their own. France and Great Britain intervened together with the United States in Libya in 2011, and two years later France intervened by itself in the civil war in Mali in the absence of support from other EU member states. To date, such military interventions have not taken place within the CSDP framework of the EU. The EU has, however, taken responsibility for around 35 civil and military missions within the framework of the Petersberg tasks.[3] The differences are subtle but important: the EU has the ambition to be able to intervene in conflict areas, with rapidly deployable units and of course the best intentions, but member states cannot reach agreement; some member states have taken up arms but have done so outside the EU framework; all member states are willing to jointly send personnel (military personnel but also police officers and all sorts of non-military advisors) to unstable countries and regions to contribute to peacekeeping there. This is, in short, the state of affairs, and the conclusion must be that there is no common defence policy, let alone a European army. That does not mean, however, that a CSDP with substance and military capacity to act is out of the question or impossible to realise (in the long run). I will return to this later in the chapter.

Thus the first cautious attempts to militarise the European integration process have yielded very little. It cannot be ruled out that the previously quoted Shapiro and Witney are right in their observation that European governments in those early years of CSDP still too easily relied in all confidence on the American security guarantee. Another, to a certain extent complementary, analysis focuses more on the field of broader security to seek an explanation. The start of CSDP has raised a fundamental question about the essence of the role of the EU in the international system. Until then, the EU had been seen mainly as a civilian, normative, or soft power (see also chapter 3), which meant that discussions about the development of a military component—however cautious and insignificant—consequently touched upon the very essence of the EU. The aforementioned military and civilian missions and operations within the framework of peacekeeping and post-conflict stabilisation formed a good compromise: the non-hazardous dispatch of military and civilian personnel to unstable countries and regions explicitly steered clear of combat action. The missions had an unambiguously positive message, namely the maintenance of peace and the protection of human rights in the world.

However, this positive, optimistic—and according to some, somewhat naive and unrealistic—view of the role of the EU as a global player quickly came under pressure under the influence of a number of dramatic events. The terrorist attacks on the Twin Towers in New York in 2001 and the subsequent war in Iraq revealed a politically very painful divide within the EU: some EU member states were only too willing to take part in the US-led coalition of the willing, while other countries (including, significantly, France and Germany) refused to do so. This schism with Atlantic repercussions gave rise to a new discussion in Europe about security that eventually resulted in the first so-called European Security Strategy (ESS) in December 2003. The opening sentence still shows a strongly optimistic slant: 'Europe has never been so prosperous, so secure nor so free. The violence of the first half of the 20th century has given way to a period of peace and stability unprecedented in European history' (European Council 2003: 1). But, the document continues, there are new challenges and threats that Europe cannot and must not ignore. Recent developments in the Balkans have shown that war on the European continent is not yet a thing of the past; moreover, Europe is facing threats such as international terrorism and the proliferation of weapons of mass destruction. In addition to identifying the key threats, the ESS emphasised the importance of security and stability in the areas immediately adjacent to the EU (such as the Mediterranean and the Western Balkans) as well as cooperation within international organisations. The latter, referred to in the ESS as effective multilateralism, should focus on the connection between different global security challenges, in particular on the relationship between security and development issues. The EU could not ensure a 'better world' on its own, but it did intend to achieve a better coordination of (and coherence between) its own policy instruments, such as trade, development policy, and CFSP. In the ESS, we see a view of security that corresponds with our broad definition in the previous section (and with a broad view of the EU's external relations), anticipating the later comprehensive approach of the Treaty of Lisbon.[4]

6.4.2. The *Global Strategy* of the European Union and the CSDP

In his book on EU security and defence policy, Jolyon Howorth states four reasons for the launch of the CSDP in 1998. In his opinion, it was not so much internal actors as external factors and developments that explain it (Howorth 2007: 52-57). The first factor he mentions is the end of the Cold War and the corresponding change in the American attitude towards Europe. From the perspective of the US, the strategic importance of Europe noticeably declined after 1989. The EU was thus forced to think about its own security. Second, he mentions the change in opinion about the desirability of military interventions in the domestic affairs of a sovereign state. During the Cold War, there was a tacit agreement between the two superpowers that interventions in each other's spheres of influence had to be avoided. Good and evil were strictly separated on both sides of the Iron Curtain. In the so-called new world order, the possibility of intervention was open to discussion—partly under the influence of the new wars discussed earlier—in order to protect human rights and/or to prevent genocide. A normative dimension was introduced, and with it also the subjective interpretation of humanitarian necessity. Third, as we have seen, the war in the former Yugoslavia—and the inability of EU member states to effectively engage in crisis management—played an important role in the establishment of the Franco-British declaration of 1998. Only as a fourth reason does Howorth mention an internal factor. After the extended relaunch of the single market and monetary union, he argues, the EU wanted not only to be a single market and currency but also to play a role as a political actor. We could call this a form of functional spillover (see chapter 2). Indeed, it cannot be ruled out that many policymakers in Europe had dreams of such a leap to high politics in the first years that the CSDP was being developed—and on the waves of euphoria regarding the introduction of the euro on 1 January 2002 (and perhaps inspired by the academics discussed in chapter 3 who, around the same time, predicted the future role of the EU as a superpower). The same applies to the European Commission which, of all the European institutions, had the most to gain from a strengthening of the political role of the EU. In this respect it is interesting to note that Howorth mentions a fifth, albeit indirect, reason for the establishment of the CSDP. It concerns the role of the European arms industry which, for a number of reasons, had and still has a vested interest in the CSDP. I will come back to this later, in connection with the role of the European Commission.

Thus, the first steps in the area of the CFSP and CSDP in the course of the 1990s were, according to this analysis, not a reaction to the decline of American hegemony but rather the result of a change in the American attitude towards Europe. The idea was that the EU member states might have to rely on their own strength for their future security, and it would be best for them to prepare for this as soon as possible. This was not stated openly, but this new insight did explain the remarkable convergence between France and Great Britain in the run-up to the Saint-Malo declaration. Until then, Great Britain in particular had been a fierce opponent of a European pillar within NATO; it feared that this would push the US in the direction of isolationism. France, by contrast, had always expressed the view that a strengthening of the European defence effort within NATO would be positively received in Washington. The new reality of the first decade after the Cold War brought both countries closer together in their ambition to strengthen the European identity within NATO (ibidem: 36-37). Europeanisation within Atlantic frameworks was not only new and unique in itself—partly due to the unexpected alliance between France and Great Britain that formed the basis for it—but it also raised the discussion about the so-called *finalité politique* (the end goal of *ever closer union* from the preamble of the Treaty of Rome) to another, if not higher, plane. This may very well in time become one of the most important consequences (and, in line with the theory of historical institutionalism discussed in chapter 1, mainly unintended consequence) of the development that was set in motion in Saint-Malo: acceptance of the CSDP, which was intended as a reinforcement of the Atlantic alliance, has unintentionally shifted the balance in the discussion towards a more independent Europe.

But it is again necessary to emphasise that we are dealing here with a long-term process whose outcome is uncertain. We can say with certainty that US military supremacy is a given in the short and medium term. According to the Stockholm International Peace Research Institute (SIPRI), the US accounted for approximately 35 per cent of total global defence spending in 2017, which amounts to $610 billion (out of a world total of $1,739 billion), an amount that is higher than the total defence spending of the next seven big-spending countries. The SIPRI researchers also note the following (SUPRI 2018; the list is limited to the most relevant data for this chapter):

- the total military expenditure of the 29 NATO members amounted to $900 billion, an equivalent of 52 per cent of total global spending;
- France, Great Britain, Germany, and Italy were—after the US—the countries with the highest expenditures within NATO: respectively $57.8, $47.2, $44.3, and $29.2 billion in 2017 (but together not even 30 per cent of total US military expenditure);
- in Western Europe, and in Central and Eastern Europe, expenditure rose by 1.7 and 12 per cent, respectively, compared to 2016. In both regions, expenditure fell in the period 2009-14 as a result of the euro crisis. This was followed by an upward movement, partly as a result of agreements on this matter within NATO;
- Russian expenditure amounted to $66.3 billion in 2017, a decrease of no less than 20 per cent compared to the previous year. SIPRI attributes this decline to the country's economic and financial problems since 2014 (as a result of Western economic sanctions and declining revenues from oil exports);
- the estimated value of Chinese expenditure amounted to $228 billion. The percentage share of China in global military spending rose from 5.8 to 13 per cent in the 2008-2017 period;
- total global defence expenditure amounted to 2.2 per cent of total global gross domestic product (GDP). This amounts to $230 per capita.

These figures put things into perspective. The expenditure of the EU member states is far behind that of the US, and Russia's expenditure is far behind that of NATO and behind that of the EU member states put together. The four EU member states with the largest defence budgets spend more than three times as much as Russia. I should add that these are the figures for 2017. In the initial euphoria of the end of the Cold War, EU member states reduced their military expenditure as a percentage of total government spending and as a percentage of GDP; despite the non-binding agreement made during the NATO summit in Prague in 2002 to spend at least 2 per cent of GDP on defence, the percentages declined further, in some cases to well below 2 per cent in 2014. Rising government deficits as a result of the euro crisis and the subsequent budget cuts obviously did not have a positive effect on attempts to fulfil the agreements made, to the frustration of successive US presidents (Barack Obama used different words than Donald Trump, but the bottom line was the same). The SIPRI figures for 2017 show an overwhelming difference in expenditure within NATO, between NATO and Russia, and between the EU and Russia, in the latter case despite the decline in EU spending throughout most of the period since 1989 (while Russian expenditure as a percentage of GDP over the same period, though fluctuating, averaged about 4 per cent—see the SIPRI database at https://www.sipri.org).

This short exercise gives the quantitative background against which a new phase in the CSDP started in 2013, culminating in the 2016 Global Strategy of the EU and the establishment of the European Defence Fund in 2017. In hindsight we can say that it was remarkable how a large number of announcements, initiatives, and decisions came together in a short period, comparable to the first phase between 1999 and 2003. A communication from the European Commission in July 2013 with the overblown title *A New Deal for European Defence* sketched a worrying situation. Under the influence of years of budget cuts, research on new weapons technologies threatened to stagnate and the European arms industry risked ending up in difficult straits due to competition from outside Europe and declining government demand within Europe. The gap with the US in the field of research and technological development (RTD) was steadily growing, while at the same time the US was shifting its strategic balance towards Asia (this was Obama's famous pivot to Asia). In addition, emerging countries such as China, India, Brazil, and Russia were spending twice as much on RTD as the EU. This development threatened to undermine not only the competitiveness of the European arms industry but also the capacity of European armies to act. Action was needed (European Commission 2013).

What is interesting is the link made in the European Commission's communication between geopolitical shifts, the consequent need for the EU to ensure its own security, the importance of research into new weapons technologies, and the strengthening of the European arms industry through coordinated public-private action at the European level, within the framework of the CSDP. The completion of the internal market for public procurement in the field of defence played an important role in this. A year later, the Commission published a roadmap, which included the establishment of an advisory body consisting of decision-makers and so-called experts. This advisory body was established in 2015 under the name Group of Personalities and published its final report a year later, in February. A few months later, this was followed up by the European Commission's presentation of a European Defence Action Plan, which ultimately resulted in the establishment of the European Defence Fund in 2017. Through co-financing, this fund contributes to collaborative projects between member states in the field of research on the one hand and joint development and acquisition of defence technology and equipment on the other. The fund provides financial support within the current multiannual budget and after 2020 will have a budget of €500 million (for research) and €1 billion (for development and acquisition) per year.

European Commission President Jean-Claude Juncker had already announced this defence fund in his State of the Union speech of September 2016, in which he elaborated on the policy guidelines he had presented when he took office and in which internal and external security were prioritised. The main thrust of his message was that the EU could no longer rely on its soft power. Cooperation in the field of defence was essential if Europe wanted to remain a powerful global player. After all, the world was getting bigger and Europe was becoming smaller: in 2050, Europeans would make up only 5 per cent of the world's population. Moreover, Juncker proclaimed, 'our enemies (sic) would like us to fragment... our [economic] competitors would benefit from our division'. Action was therefore required, and in this context Juncker announced both the aforementioned defence fund and the bundling of defence capabilities through a so-called permanent structured cooperation (see below). One notable detail was an example that Juncker mentioned in support of his plea for a deepening of cooperation in the field of defence. 'Europe can no longer afford to piggy-back on the military might of others', he said, 'or let France alone defend *its honour in Mali*. We have to take responsibility for protecting *our interests* and the *European way of life*' (italics added, Juncker 2016: 18-19). Joint hard power is thus necessary to defend European honour in remote areas as well as Europe's interests and way of life. The latter—the European Way of Life—and the first part of the quote clearly refer to a Europe that is breaking away from American military protection and the American way of life.

The bold print in the written version of the speech, as though the EU had found itself in an environment that was increasingly dangerous, gives an impression of urgency that also dominates the European Union Global Strategy (EUGS) published the same year under the direction of Federica Mogherini. Thirteen years after the first European Security Strategy, the opening sentence is significantly more apocalyptic: 'We live in times of existential crisis, within and beyond the European Union. Our Union is under threat. Our European project, which had brought unprecedented peace, prosperity and democracy, is being questioned' (EEAS 2016: 7). Gone is the

earlier positive and optimistic attitude of the text written under the direction of
Javier Solana. The new security strategy is permeated with the idea that the world has
become less safe and that the EU is no longer an island of stability in an otherwise
turbulent environment. Europe cannot evade contemporary security threats and
is in fact an integral part of them, and thus must jointly address them. Keukeleire
and Delreux write in an update to their handbook on European foreign policy that
the new security strategy has been received much more positively by CSDP experts
than the 2003 version, and they attribute this positive reception to the fact that
the EUGS is more realistic.[5] The 'principled pragmatism' referred to in the EUGS
indicates a less idealistic and normative approach. If we look at the text of the EUGS,
it is striking that the EU's own security is mentioned as the first priority. The EU
must take greater responsibility for the protection of its citizens and territory, it says,
and not shy away from a political-military approach to security. Such pragmatism
is also reflected in the second priority: building 'state and societal resilience to our
East and South'. The key word here is resilience. States and societies in the EU's
neighbouring regions must be resilient enough to deal with internal and external
crises. It has rightly been pointed out that with this extremely vague formulation,
the more fundamental and idealistic promotion of democracy, human rights, and
the rule of law is no longer the primary objective, and anyway the impression
is given that in some cases state and society benefit from a less liberal political
approach (Wagner and Anholt 2016). The third priority of the EUGS is to apply the
same principle already mobilised in the Lisbon Treaty, namely the promotion of
an integrated approach—the comprehensive approach—of conflicts and crises.
All available policy tools of the EU should be used in a coherent way, implying that
the CSDP must also play a significant role. The last two priorities reflect the older
ambitions and positions of the EU, namely greater regional cooperation between
states in other parts of the world (with the European integration process as a shining
example, I might cynically add) and an emphasis on strengthening the structures
of global governance, in particular the multilateral rule-based order within the
framework of the United Nations and the WTO (EEAS 2016: *passim*).

It is not enough to conclude that the 2016 strategy has a more realistic tone than
its predecessor from 2003. We subsequently have to ask ourselves what exactly this
realism or pragmatism means. Is this a growing awareness that Europe indeed does
not live on an island and that it is surrounded by all kinds of threats—also within
its own borders? Is it, in short, a strategy of collective self-defence at the EU level?
Or is it a strategy with more offensive intentions to defend the EU's vital interests
elsewhere, if necessary with the use of force, especially now that the US can no
longer assume the role of the leader of the West? Is it a strategy of pre-emptive
intervention to pacify trouble spots outside Europe, largely out of enlightened
self-interest? Or is it—as a third option and closer to home—an attempt to draw

attention to the new threat from the East, to the alleged reality of a resurgence of Russian assertiveness and territorial expansionism in combination with the sinister attempts of the Putin regime to disrupt our democratic systems and open societies? Is it a tougher stance on, and reaction to, the Russian bear who can only think in terms of power politics and in zero-sum scenarios?

It is fair to say that the EUGS—and the promotion films on the corresponding website of the EEAS—also contain many statements that have the best for human-kind in mind from a more idealistic-normative perspective. Closer cooperation in multilateral frameworks, better cooperation between states in regional integra-tion associations, a strengthening of the resilience of people and societies in less developed and stable countries (particularly neighbouring countries)—these are all aspects that the average do-gooder can hardly object to. The comments made in the EUGS about the relationship between development and security in developing countries are also worth mentioning. The authors not only tried to involve as many actors as possible in the EUGS using a thorough catch-all approach, but they also took the adjective 'global' seriously. This was, interestingly enough, not primarily a synonym for 'worldwide', but for 'integral' and 'comprehensive' (as the third priority already indicated). In the words of Nathalie Tocci: 'Federica Mogherini wanted a "global" rather than just a "security" strategy. And the most important interpretation of what "global" meant was thematic rather than geographic' (Tocci 2016: 464).

However, the question is whether, despite all good intentions, we are not left with a great gap between principles, intentions, and resolutions on the one hand and concrete policy implementation and actual actions on the other, and whether, in this light, the challenges have lost out against the threats. In chapters 3, 4, and 5, I concluded that the end of the Cold War and the changes in economic policy in the fields of international trade, development policy, and enlargement strategy were accompanied by a stronger emphasis on unadulterated self-interest or, more euphemistically, a 'more realistic attitude' in the EU's external relations. It is the necessary preliminary conclusion of this book's author that such a development, albeit with a certain delay, is also occurring in the field of EU's security policy, within the CSDP. If this observation is correct, we can indeed expect, in the longer term, a strengthening of cooperation in the area of defence among the EU member states. We are, however, still a long way from this; there are still too many factors and actors that are hindering a more driven integration.

6.4.3. Factors and actors

A snapshot of 2018 could be described as follows: European politicians have spoken and written lofty words in recent years, but little has been done in terms of deeds. The EU's common security policy is still in its infancy, and there is certainly no 'militarisation of the European integration process'. The Common Security and Defence Policy had—and still has—little to say about defence, and it is difficult to see anything 'common' in it (Keukeleire and Delreux 2014: 173-74). This was also the impression that emerged in almost all the interviews that my colleague Marijn Hoijtink and I conducted with a series of stakeholders in European decision-making bodies, think tanks in the area of foreign and security policy, and the defence industry (at the time of writing, the results of this research remain unpublished). Without exception, scepticism was exhibited with regard to the chance of actual Europeanisation of defence policy and capabilities. Using the previously introduced conceptualisation of Karl Deutsch et al., we can indeed conclude that the EU falls far short of a so-called *amalgamated* (i.e. unitary) security community and not even close to the pluralistic variant either. I would add two things to this. First, Deutsch and his team attached great importance to a sense of community as the foundation of a security community. If we apply this to the EU in the present, this sense of community could be referred to as a common European identity and pan-European solidarity based on a certain degree of social cohesion within the EU and its member states. If anything is clear from an earlier part of this chapter, it is that such a condition is absolutely not present in the current EU. If it ever existed, we can safely say that, due to the neoliberal turn and the rise of populist counterforces, a pan-European sense of community and solidarity is virtually non-existent. Deutsch also expressed his concern about the primacy of military security interests (directed against the Soviet Union in the context of the Cold War) in the North Atlantic security community (read: NATO). One might call this an early warning against an all-too-limited view of security. If the foundation of such a community was limited to this (i.e. military security), he believed, the downfall of communism would eliminate a common external threat and thereby also the rationale for further integration. This was a prescient view, because the prediction appears to have come true (unless the conflict between the US and the Soviet Union was in hindsight not primarily an ideological conflict but purely a political power confrontation). If the underlying reasoning is correct, then this also applies to a possible bundling of European forces: this too should have a broader foundation than just a common external threat of a military nature.

Secondly, and as a hypothetical alternative to a disintegrating NATO, it is also difficult (if not inconceivable) to imagine a pluralistic security community identical to the current EU28, as the differences between the member states are simply too great. Just think of the different national security cultures in Europe, the completely different perceptions of security threats and their related solutions and defensive mechanisms. There is no commonly observed external military threat, real or imagined, and there is no common sense of urgency. No matter what a minister from Portugal may declare, he or she will not really believe that Russia is a real military threat to his/her country. Compare this with a minister from one of the Baltic states, and any further explanation is superfluous. Incidentally, this does not mean that the Baltic minister is right per se or that his/her conviction is based on an objective reality, but the subjective perception is already politically relevant enough. There is less difference between Germany on the one hand and France and Great Britain on the other, but the difference is still life-size with regard to the use of military resources in international politics. Think of the smaller member states that have completely subordinated their security interests to NATO, which for these countries is tantamount to the United States. And to complete the picture, there are also what are labelled the neutral member states of the EU that take a stand against any form of Europeanisation in the area of security (in the narrow sense) and defence. The Permanent Structured Cooperation (PESCO), launched in December 2017, will probably not alter the situation significantly. This PESCO offers the possibility for those member states 'who are able and willing' to cooperate at a deeper level in the field of defence. This implies the concept of a core group and a Europe of multiple speeds. But even such a core group will have to cope with irrevocably occurring differences of opinion and conflicting interests.

And yet, things are changing. There is activity at the front line of security. As mentioned above, European institutions (in particular the European Commission and the EEAS) launched a series of initiatives from 2013. I already compared this with the period of increased activity between 1998 and 2003. Analogous to the four reasons that Howorth put forward to explain this first phase, let us mention four reasons that together provide a possible explanation for the post-2013 activity. First, the changing relationship with the US plays an important role here too. And, again, the analysis of the declining hegemony, if it is being made at all, seems less important than the observation that the United States is moving away from Europe in general and the EU in particular. This is not President Trump's doing, for this observation dates from earlier times (as I have indicated above). The presidency of Trump is, in that sense, the continuation of a trend. Second, a different view of the use of military means has emerged within Europe. If threats get violent—militarised, as it were—the EU must be able to use so-called military capabilities, out of self-defence or in order to protect its vital interests. This is what some call the more 'realistic view' in the EUGS. Third, the period of increased activity coincides with the end of the dramatic euro crisis of 2008-2013. This crisis further strengthened processes that had started earlier: the speculative destruction and aggressive greed that had preceded the crisis, the massive buy-out 'by taxpayers' in the period thereafter, the socio-economic consequences of the austerity policies, and finally the ultimate return to business as usual. These caused significant damage to confidence in national and European politics, and to confidence in political and economic elites.

In the case of the EU, this was compounded by the migration crisis. All in all, there was enough reason for large parts of the national electorates to punish traditional parties and to support populist, xenophobic, and anti-European movements. In this Europe of ethnic nationalism, the EU does not stand a chance, unless a new raison d'être can be found. We could once again call this a functional spillover, only with a different meaning than the original theorists intended. One step in the integration process creates new questions and challenges and then requires the implementation of follow-up steps. This is what the politics of small steps is all about: a positive process towards an ever-closer union.

In the present case, we are dealing with the disastrous consequences of a major step in the economic integration process that has placed the EU in an existential crisis. The EU's raison d'être has disappeared, unless new life can be revived in another area—and that area is security and defence policy. 'But how do we sell such a step in the integration process, in the field of high politics of all things, in times of Euroscepticism?' 'By emphasising the need for such a policy; by emphasising the unsafe world around us; by identifying the threats.' 'Yes, but what if there are no acute threats?' 'Then we create them!'

Let us consider by means of a fourth reason whether this hypothetical dialogue holds water.

Fourth, the revival of activities mentioned above is not only a question of factors but also of actors. Howorth also mentioned the role of the European Commission in connection with the role of the defence industry. Both actors also play a key role in the recent surge in activity. The domain of CSDP operates is above all an intergovernmental domain in which the European Commission has no say and cannot play an initiating role, at least not directly. However, the European Commission does have considerable powers in the area of the single market and plays an important role in determining the EU's multiannual budget. Since the end of the Cold War, the European defence industry must not only deal with fierce competition from American giants such as Lockheed and Boeing, but is also faced with declining European defence budgets since the 1990s. This has led on the one hand to a process of cross-border mergers between European companies and on the other to a greater emphasis on dual-use technology and production. Dual use means that companies produce for both the civilian and military markets and that investments in RTD have a dual application. Above, we saw that the European Defence Fund came about at the initiative of the European Commission and also on the advice of the Group of Personalities. The latter group consisted of a number of what were labelled independent experts, a few politicians, and a large number of executives from the defence industry. (In a recent judgment, the European Ombudsman pointed out the dubious construction that CEOs from the arms industry contributed to an influential recommendation that ultimately resulted in financial support for the very same companies they led—see *EUobserver* of 28 September 2018). Without exaggeration, we can say that both actors—the Commission and the defence industry—have joined forces on the basis of complementary interests. For the defence industry there is money involved, and for the Commission there is prestige and influence. By means of a market-oriented approach, the Commission gets a foot in the door in a policy realm where sovereignty and national interest still prevail. Incidentally, the European Commission had already built itself another bridge with the CSDP via the Treaty of Lisbon: the High Representative of the EU for Foreign Affairs and Security Policy leads the secretariat of the intergovernmental Council but is also vice president of the European Commission.

There is more. Why would the EU channel money to the arms industry? The reason is twofold: the industry is in danger of losing competitiveness against its main competitors and of falling behind, especially in the development of a new generation of high-tech weaponry. In itself, the sector is economically relevant enough because of the employment that it generates directly and indirectly. The second reason has to do with European security. More and more dangers are emerging in the vicinity of the EU, and old and new (potential) enemies are threatening to take an ever-increasing lead in the technological field and thereby ultimately in terms of capabilities. Action is needed. The simultaneous plea to adjust national defence budgets upwards again plays an important role here. The knife cuts both ways: the defence industry benefits from market expansion and can sell its new products on the European growth market, and European governments can improve and increase their defence capabilities and thus their resilience against ubiquitous dangers.

6.5.   Towards a multipolar world? Changing power relations in the international system

The question then is where those ubiquitous dangers come from and how we should interpret the *existential crisis beyond the European Union* and 'the fact' that the EU is *under threat* (as the EUGS would have us believe). In other words: against whom or what should we arm ourselves? Let's look at the possible candidates. Bear in mind that we are talking about dangers that make it necessary for EU member states to arm themselves again, to pump more money into the development of new weapons technologies, and to strengthen cooperation within the framework of the CSDP—all this in order to increase the EU's military capabilities and military capacity to act.

First of all, the US is not a threat to the physical security and territorial integrity of the member states of the EU, and has never been one—on the contrary, one could add. There is, however, an indirect danger in the most recent US attitude towards Europe: if the US gradually withdraws from the Atlantic security community and thereby weakens its security guarantee towards EU member states, the member states must reconsider their security policy and a strengthening of cooperation may then be necessary and/or desirable. But then the question still has to be asked: against whom or what should this cooperation be initiated, i.e. against whom or what must the member states arm themselves if necessary? The changing relationship between the US and the EU explains the question but does not answer it. It even remains to be seen whether a possible continuation of the trans-Atlantic security relationship will not indirectly subject the EU to a much greater danger. We only need to refer to the above-mentioned statistics on defence spending and to the notion of the security dilemma. The increase in defence budgets of the EU member states of NATO—propagated if not demanded by the US—can very well be regarded by Russia as a threat and thereby provoke counter-reactions. In this way, the member states of the EU create their own existential threat.

The same observation—namely that a country does not pose a threat to the physical security and territorial integrity of EU member states—also applies to China for obvious reasons. What does not exist can still happen, of course, but this emerging superpower is not a threat in the short or medium term. The great threat to world peace in the case of China is the explosive nature of the geopolitical tensions in the region of the South China Sea on the one hand and the issue of power transition on the other (see earlier in this chapter). The confrontation with the United States has its risks, but it is difficult to understand how a greater European capacity to act can contribute to a substantial pacification. A completely different subject matter is the increasing assertiveness of China in non-military areas. China is developing a genuine global strategy with focus areas in every corner of the world. A specific example is China's involvement in Africa. Chinese companies are at the heart of what is called the new scramble for Africa, sometimes to the detriment of European companies. China also spearheads the group of countries that offer development aid outside the established frameworks of the West (including the Development Assistance Committee of the OECD—see chapter 4 and Dreher et al. 2013). In the case of tied aid, this also works to the detriment of European businesses. And finally, China is increasingly involved with Europe and with some EU member states in particular, notably through direct investments. Chinese interference in the recent debt crisis in Greece is a good example of this, while the recent contacts China has developed with the new EU member states in Central and Eastern Europe are less known but are potentially of great significance. It suggests that China has started a well-considered strategy of 'divide and conquer' towards the EU. This is all true—or seems to be true or to become true—but none of the developments mentioned is a reason for EU member states to increase military security. It concerns elements from our broader definition of security that cannot be combated with military means.

The threat also does not come from the core countries of the so-called multipolar world. Over the past twenty years, various acronyms have been circulating to encapsulate the emergence of new powers. The more recent TIMBI is less known than the older and notorious BRICs, but in fact it does not matter very much which abbreviation we use. It is clear to everyone that regional leaders emerge that gradually fill the vacuum created after the end of sphere-of-influence politics. Whether this concerns South Africa or Brazil, whether we zoom in on the new assertiveness of Turkey, look at the silent power of India, or examine the position of an old power like Japan, the picture of multipolarity is irrevocably self-evident. But is this a military threat against which the EU must arm itself? To begin with, the suggestion of cohesion emanating from indications such as BRIC is misplaced. The countries in question do not form a security community, do not share each other's values and norms (if they are even familiar with them), and have no ambition to do so either. The common interest they share seems to consist mainly of their attempt to break the dominance of 'the West' (for example through the establishment of alternative international organisations such as the New Development Bank, or the Asian Infrastructure Investment Bank set up by China). Second, most countries that are part of the 'emerging economies' category are plagued by major internal economic and political problems. Persistent corruption and poverty in countries such as Brazil or South Africa; authoritarian tendencies in Turkey, India, and Indonesia; and drug-related crime in Mexico are all indications that 'emerging' does not indicate a straight path upwards. And here too, while the above-mentioned problems may have consequences for the EU, its member states, citizens, and businesses in one way or another, they do not constitute an immediate cause for militarisation.

The question that remains is Russia. It is always useful to assess matters realistically, also from a historical perspective. In modern times, the major powers in Western Europe have been a greater threat to Russia than vice versa. Twice, French and German troops have penetrated deep into Russian territory, only to be defeated in their struggle against the Russian winter. The history of Central and Eastern Europe and the Balkans is a different story. This region has for centuries been a plaything of various great powers, not just Russia. Germany, Austria-Hungary, and the Ottoman Empire have likewise played a role. The most recent piece of history lingers on the longest, of course, which explains why most citizens in Central and Eastern Europe harbour less resentment towards Germans than towards Russians. And in Russia's case, appearances work against it. The war with Georgia in 2008 and the annexation of the Crimea in 2014 are serious indications. But does anyone wonder why precisely these two countries (Ukraine in the case of the Crimea annexation) were victims of an otherwise limited intervention? Doesn't the explanation lie in the fact that the two countries are post-Soviet states and that both are repeatedly associated with NATO expansion (and in the case of Ukraine with EU enlargement)?

And could it be that Russian leaders have felt that enough is enough after yet another provocation from the Western side? Because let's face it, the disintegrating Soviet Union was once given the promise that NATO—its archenemy during 40 years of Cold War—would not expand to the countries in Central and Eastern Europe. This promise was broken in the second half of the 1990s by President Clinton; within a short time period the NATO expansion towards the East had become a fact (for an impressive analysis of the connection between the episode of NATO expansion and the crisis in Ukraine, see Sakwa 2015). And thus NATO became its own security threat, for the security dilemma never sleeps. Finally, looking at the figures that SIPRI presented regarding arms expenditure, we can once again put the extent of the Russian danger into perspective, this time in a quantitative sense. All in all, this seems too fragile a base on which to predicate a total package of new military and security initiatives.

6.6.   Conclusion

The statement by Donald Trump quoted at the beginning of this chapter is significant in several respects. He expressed his love for *the countries* of the EU and explicitly not for the EU itself, which he said was set up to take advantage of the US and to plunder the American piggy bank. In attempting to make the US great again, a harder approach to that accursed EU is fitting. Trump verbalised his 'chronicle of a trade war foretold' by saying that Americans should no longer put up with their market being flooded with Mercedes or BMW cars. Incidentally, and for those who have seen the eponymous film by the Coen brothers, the fact that the speech was held in Fargo is more than a random coincidence.

This chapter has shown that the period of 'hegemonic stability' has run its course, not least because of the changes in US foreign policy. The US has partly turned away from Europe or, rather, is focused on other partnerships. This chapter has again shown that the end of the Cold War was a development of unprecedented significance. With a certain delay, EU member states and EU institutions started to reflect on the consequences of this change. The result of this reflection is the CSDP. This policy domain provides the framework within which the EU can eventually develop its own defence and security policy. But reality is complicated. The EU has shot itself in the foot by subjecting itself to the dictates of the US too ideologically, and for too long. This is evident in the deliberate choice to go along with the neoliberal turn initiated by the US. And it is even apparent in Europe's most recent attempts to give the EU a military identity. The increase in defence spending, implemented partly at the instigation of the Americans, is something that, given the neoliberal principle of austerity, irrevocably leads to a shift in budgetary priorities.

A greater emphasis on defence at the expense of other policy areas must, of course, be legitimised.

As of now, it is too early to speak of a militarisation of the European integration process, but in conclusion we can say that there is undeniably a movement towards enhanced cooperation in the field of defence. In addition to the debates that are taking place around this theme—between Atlanticists and Europeanists, and between intergovernmentalists and supranationalists—perhaps the most relevant debate is about what type of military power the EU should develop: a proactive intervention force that can also be used to discipline or deter opponents (which according to the security dilemma would quickly amount to provocation) or a structure that takes the accompanying acronym seriously, namely a policy-oriented and institutional architecture based on communality and defence (or self-defence). It is ultimately a debate about the role of Europe as a global player. A European security strategy that unequivocally nestles between offensive realism and power politics on the one hand, and naive idealism on the other, allows for a broader understanding of the concept of security, including the socio-economic security of its own citizens. Such a shift almost irrevocably implies a gradual socio-economic and political-military emancipation from Europe's former ally on the other side of the Atlantic Ocean. The question, however, is whether such a strategy is realistic and feasible within the current multi-level balance of power, both within and outside the EU.

Suggestions for further reading

In the general studies and textbooks mentioned at the end of chapter 1, one or more chapters are often devoted to the EU's foreign and security policy (see, for example, McCormick 2017 and Wallace et al. 2015, but also of course Keukeleire and Delreux 2014, Jørgensen et al. 2015, and Hill et al. 2017). However, the CSDP is one of the most dynamic policy areas within the EU, with changes or announcements following each other in rapid succession. It is often unclear whether developments are new or simply repetitions of previous, unrealised initiatives. This requires precise and detailed empirical research that, to my knowledge, is not available in any of the voluminous tomes out there. The best strategy is to start with reading one of the general, more or less introductory works written by an authority in the field of European defence policy. Candidates include (Smith 2017) or my personal favourite (Howorth 2007). The latter may seem somewhat dated but offers valid explanations and expresses the central debates that are still relevant today. The most recent developments can then best be followed via the website of the EEAS, https://eeas.europa.eu. This is also where one can gain insight into the institutional structure of the CSDP. The academic world generally reacts with a certain delay to current events, but quick reactions and interpretations can be found in the world of think tanks. The EU's official think tank, the European Union Institute for Security Studies (EUISS), offers a wide range of publications (see https://www.iss.europa. eu). This institute claims to be autonomous, but its positions and analyses should be nevertheless adopted with some caution.

The field of international security studies is richly studded with textbooks. My preference goes to (Buzan and Hansen 2009) and (Collins 2016). The latter is an edited collection that gives a fairly complete overview of the many themes in this area. An alternative is (Smith 2010).

The relationship between the EU and the US has also been the subject of many studies. A recent overview is given by (Peterson 2019). (McGuire and Smith 2008) is somewhat older but very informative. A classic that offers much insight, especially into the first decades after the Second World War, is (Grosser 1978). I myself have been influenced by the academic work of Kees van der Pijl (see, for example, Van der Pijl 2006 and 2014) and by the cooperation in the field of international political economy within what is known as the Amsterdam School (see Jessop and Overbeek 2018). Finally, we cannot neglect to mention two studies that emphasise the historical (Berend 2016) and political-economic (Ryner and Cafruny 2017) influence of the US on the origin and development of the EU.

Epilogue

In these concluding pages, I will cover a number of topical issues that do not necessarily belong to the domain of external relations per se but that do have important areas of overlap. In any case, it is my belief that these issues will partly determine the context within which the EU manages (or fails) to manifest itself as a global player in the coming years.

Throughout this book, I have only occasionally paid attention to the issue of climate change. The theme is of such a magnitude from a social point of view, and technically so complex, that it would not be appropriate to rank it alongside the aspects of the EU's external relations discussed here. Global warming is a problem that far exceeds the importance of European integration. It hangs like the mythical sword of Damocles above our heads. All the major policy areas and challenges addressed in this book—regarding economic growth, socio-economic inequality, development, world trade, security, enlargement and neighbourliness—shrink into insignificance compared to this overriding and overarching threat. Fortunately, environmental awareness is spreading rapidly across the Earth—if only because larger and larger groups of people are experiencing the physical and economic impacts of climate change in their daily lives. The question, however, is whether things are going fast enough and whether we humans will leave the party in time, as Damocles once wisely decided.

Nonetheless, the fight against human-induced global warming is continuously present in this book's examination of the EU and its external relations, albeit indirectly. European policy in the context of climate change is typical of the overall problem of the EU's capacity to act as an international actor. This has an external and an internal dimension. In the decades preceding the Copenhagen climate summit in 2009, the EU appeared to be playing a leading role in international fora, but it became painfully clear that the EU was not taken seriously by the US and a number of emerging countries. There are famous photos in which the political leaders of the BRICS and President Barack Obama consult each other, while the EU and its member states are conspicuous by their absence. The Paris climate summit of December 2015 seemed to give the EU momentum in international climate negotiations, but it was the concrete agreements that were made there that subsequently accentuated the division between EU member states. As soon as something must be implemented, member states fall back on their short-term self-interest. Part of the explanation for the lack of internal cohesion is the emergence of populist movements that, if they do not deny that humans are impacting climate change, are very much opposed to binding European agreements on concrete measures.

The small member state of the Netherlands is certainly no exception in this regard. Climate sceptics on the right of the political spectrum rightly claim that a Dutch reduction of CO_2 emissions can only make a very small contribution to the slowdown in global warming. But this same small country will experience a disproportionately large effect from, for example, the rise in sea levels. In other words, a joint European approach can carry far more weight and perhaps save the Netherlands from even worse consequences. The Netherlands therefore also has an interest in a joint approach. It should be noted that cooperation between member states on a voluntary basis and on the basis of a shared sense of urgency is not sufficient. Only binding agreements at the European level, if necessary enforced by European institutions, can offer the necessary guarantee. Sustainable cooperation without an institutional framework is an illusion.

But the interface between this book and the issue of climate change goes further than that. In the foreword to this book, I mentioned three developments within which the EU's action as a (potential) global player should be understood. First, the world has become smaller, a process that is referred to as globalisation. Our products are supplied over long distances, and the mobility and movement of people have taken on unprecedented forms. Climate change is in any case one of the most radical manifestations of globalisation, in particular with regard to the (anticipated) effects. Second, the world has become multipolar. This has clear consequences for power politics, as became clear during the Copenhagen climate summit, but the underlying process is of a socio-economic nature. The multipolar world owes its name to a series of emerging countries; these countries are undergoing rapid economic development, which often boils down to industrialisation and is accompanied by strong CO_2 emissions; the new middle classes in these countries are adjusting their consumption patterns, with Western preferences and practices often being copied; and so on. Third, the world has become more liberal but at the same time more unequal and less democratic. The increase in authoritarian leaders does not bode well for a multilateral approach to environmental problems. In addition, most studies on the effects of climate change assume strong North-South differences. The so-called Global South not only has to endure more as a result of climate change, but it also does not have the means to protect itself. In the EU member states too, citizens are gradually becoming aware of the effects of what is known as the energy transition, particularly in a financial sense. Without policies to offset this burden, the measures that will need to be taken in the context of this energy transition will further increase existing inequalities. And this book has made it clear that since the 1980s the neoliberal turn has weakened the institutional and policy safeguards that are needed to guide the less-well-off citizens through this transition, i.e. without great social unrest and instability.

We had a taste of such social discontent and protests in France in the autumn of 2018. The yellow vests movement, initially a spontaneous social reaction to an announced increase in the fuel tax, soon became a massive protest against the socio-economic policy of the French government. We might criminalise these protesters and fight them with violence, as the French government did; or we can cynically conclude that this movement will see its strength dwindling in due course, just as happened with the anti-globalists and alterglobalists around the turn of the century and with the Occupy movement in the 2010s. But if we do so, we forget an important phenomenon in our European political systems: elections. Once every few years, politicians are held accountable for the consequences of the measures they introduce. And the current era has taught us that electoral responses have taken on a new form that blurs the traditional distinction between left and right. The new keywords are nationalism and patriotism, which have caught on like wildfire in recent years and spread rapidly. It is mainly extreme right-wing populists who have been able to appeal to the patriotism of citizens, and with remarkable success.

The socio-economic inequality and the feeling of social and political exclusion among large sections of the population are an important breeding ground for this new patriotism. Moreover, the resulting discontent increasingly translates into an aversion to the ultimate scapegoat: the EU in the form of the unspecified European political elite. The role of scapegoat is given a second dimension due to the influence of another breeding ground of patriotism, namely cross-border migration. Socio-economic inequality and mass migration form an explosive combination, and it is the patriotic-populist movements that have understood this the most.

In short, the spectre of patriotism haunts Europe. We can either be afraid of this or accept that the history of Europe has been a history of (often violent) unification and fragmentation since time immemorial. At the same time, we must realise that the post-war (peaceful) integration of previously hostile peoples has been a unique experiment that is unparalleled in history. In addition, the most urgent security threats require us to work together like never before. As mentioned, this cooperation can only be sustainable, effective, and successful if it takes the form of institutional and policy integration—i.e. if we move beyond non-commitment. This irrevocably pushes Europe towards political union: the ever closer union mentioned in the preamble to the Treaty of Rome. We need to hurry, and there is no time for short-sighted, short-term playing with fire by patriotic populists with an apocalyptic desire for drama.

But reality is more complicated than that. The prospect of further and deeper political integration at the European level seems further away than ever before. A possible explanation for this is the fact that, faced with a large number of dilemmas, we no longer precisely realise what a dilemma is. The dictionary definition of a dilemma is a situation in which a choice must be made between two paths, both of which present major objections. We can reformulate this choice between two less attractive options as a rational assessment of the costs and benefits, with an emphasis on a long-term perspective. It may very well be the case then that, in time, the benefits of the current policy—based both internally and externally on neoliberal ideological principles—do not outweigh the material and immaterial costs.

The chapters in this book have identified some of the most pressing dilemmas. To begin with, the tension between national sovereignty and identity on the one hand and supranational integration on the other is a recurring theme. Even in the most communitarian domain of the broader external relations—the EU's trade policy—there is a turf war being fought between different layers of government and various national and sectoral interests. The policy of commercial internationalism that came into existence in the course of the 1980s has served many people in the EU well, but at the same time it has to be said that a lot of human capital has been lost under the name of greater competitiveness.

Secondly, and closely related to this, the transfer of powers to supranational institutions was perceived in some areas as non-problematic by national decision-makers but encountered insurmountable objections in other areas. This form of asymmetrical regulation was then partly the cause of the increasing resistance among national populations against further European integration or even against the EU itself (as exemplified by the hard Euroscepticism expressed in the Brexit referendum).

Thirdly, the EU's external relations with the least developed countries in the international system gradually came to be less inspired by postcolonial guilt and more by enlightened self-interest. Development policy has been reduced to poverty alleviation in exchange for security, that is, security for the EU itself. After all, development in the form of industrialisation is not in Europe's interest (due to climate change), but it is certainly in Europe's interest to discourage people from travelling to Europe. At the same time, EU member states protect their agricultural sectors against cheaper products from the Global South, but they do contribute to the continuation of violent conflict through sustained and unbridled European arms exports to unstable regions and regimes. Probably, the inventors of the catchy slogan 'everything but arms' had a different policy outcome in mind.

Fourthly, the EU's enlargement policy has reached a crossroads. Should the EU maintain the strict demands of democratic transformation before it even starts negotiating the other criteria—i.e. taking the, in retrospect, incomplete democratisation of the new CEE member states into account—or should it anticipate further attempts by the new powers in the multipolar world by trying to accelerate the process of pulling the candidate countries in the Balkans into the Western sphere of influence? A similar dilemma arises in the relationship between the EU and its new neighbours to the south and east. Here too, a trade-off between normative considerations in external relations and geopolitical and geo-economic interests plays a major role.

In both cases, security issues are key. It is not always sufficiently appreciated how the protection of one's own security can provoke counterreactions elsewhere. In line with my broad definition of security explained in chapter 6, the so-called security dilemma has a much more comprehensive meaning than just power politics. The issue of migration is one example of this; the approach to climate change is another. Yet the political-military significance of the concept of the security dilemma also applies to present-day Europe and to the position of the EU within it. Does it make sense in the longer term to put further pressure on Russia, either through the Atlantic Alliance or through a militarisation of the European integration process, taking into account that this will irrevocably provoke a reaction in Russia and encourage a further Eurasian rapprochement between China and Russia? Do EU member states stand to gain from a role as plaything in the impending power transition in the multipolar world system? And could they possibly spend their money better than on shelling out an arbitrary two per cent of GDP on purchasing American weapons? This last point touches on the relationship between the EU and the US at its heart—a relationship that itself can increasingly be reformulated as a dilemma.

These are, as said, some of the most pressing issues facing the EU. In this and many other areas, the member states and European institutions are at a crossroads together. And in all its simplicity, the choice is between further—that is, deeper—integration or fragmentation and disintegration. An in-between way of muddling through, and compromising between centripetal and centrifugal forces, can only be a temporary solution. It is to be hoped that the choices will be made carefully; that is, in a rational manner. We have seen at the beginning of this book that such rational choices always serve a specific, particularistic interest and purpose. In other words, such soft rational choices always reflect existing power configurations. And these power configurations include not only state but also non-state actors. It is important to realise once again that the current struggle at the proverbial crossroads seems to be one between patriotic-populist drama and neoliberal profit and speculative destruction. The outcome of this struggle has irrevocable consequences for the course of external relations and for the future of 'Global Europe'.

The big question is how the forces in society, the member states, and the institutions of the EU can reverse the 'Europe of centrifugal forces'. Or, to put it in the terms used above, how can we change the substance of the many dilemmas and alter the direction of the choices? Tailor-made answers to this question cannot be provided, but the most likely scenario is that the course of history will be determined by a combination of ad hoc crisis measures and coincidence. However, two points can be helpful when considering this issue.

The first point relates to the countermovements in Europe—and in particular the patriotic-populist and Eurosceptic counterforces. It makes little sense to combat this as a symptom. The source of social discontent must be addressed. If the above analysis is correct that the breeding ground of populism is twofold, namely a decline in perceived prosperity and welfare, and cross-border migration, then the route is not difficult to determine. On the one hand, the asymmetry in European economic and monetary regulation will have to be removed. The principle of free competition and the architecture of the EMU correspond with the transfer of powers to the European Commission and the European Central Bank, which means that national leeway is drastically reduced, particularly in the field of social policy. There is no 'single labour market' or one social system in Europe but several labour markets and systems that also compete with each other for the prize of the most attractive investment climate. There are two potential solutions: either we withdraw behind national, well-guarded borders, or we try to give substance to a long-held but never-realised European social dimension. A consistent and coherent migration policy at the European level must be achieved whereby measures against an uncontrolled influx of migrants should be combined with an external policy aimed at 'positive peace' (Galtung). The abandonment of the compulsory distribution of refugees and migrants across the EU area seems like a good decision, as it was difficult enough to bring the reluctant member states in CEE to the water, let alone making them drink. At the same time, we must realise that the so-called refugee crisis has now become a political crisis in the EU. Muddling through is not a solution here either, and European decision-making seems to be the only acceptable path to a more structural solution.

The second point refers to the Brexit issue as the context within which the EU's external relations will develop in the coming years. The definitive decision-making in Great Britain about the exit treaty has been postponed to beyond the final completion of this manuscript. At the time of writing (the end of December 2018), the situation could go in any direction: a new British referendum, this time resulting in a remain majority; a Brexit in name only, a so-called soft Brexit; or a hard exit without an agreement. Even without knowing the outcome, we can establish that the Brexit question will not be without consequences. We should not underestimate the precedent-setting nature of the fact that there has been withdrawal instead of entrance for the first time in the history of the EU. It is no longer only theoretically possible (since the Treaty of Lisbon) to leave the union, and this brings to a close in one fell swoop the illusion of a joint commitment to a common end goal. It is also possible that the difficult and painful scenes of divorce will provide a source of inspiration for other (national and subnational) separatist movements, under the motto that the 'will of the people' will ultimately prevail despite everything.

This so-called 'will of the people' is, on closer inspection, only the will of a small majority (who would perhaps turn into a large minority after a small change in the electoral system). And this is an observation that, independent of the final Brexit decision, has important repercussions. The situation in Great Britain confronts us with a social divide that has developed in other EU member states too—but not (at least not yet) in a similarly virulent way everywhere. It concerns a divide of a socio-economic nature, and between highly educated people and people with low levels of education, between young and old, and between city dwellers and people living in rural areas. In some cases it would not be an exaggeration to speak of a 'cold civil war' between several, mutually exclusive social layers that hardly communicate. Paradoxically, this conclusion can also be given a positive twist. If Brexit (soft or hard) is eventually implemented, which seems the most likely scenario, then a fervent proponent of a policy aimed at privatisation, liberalisation, and deregulation (that is, Great Britain) will have disappeared from the Brussels circuit of decision-making. In theory, this could shift the balance to the social and political forces that favour a more social and equal (and, indeed, a more regulated) Europe.

Whether it will come to that is, of course, the big question. Much will depend on the precise shift in the balance of power within the EU following Brexit (and even if an exit is abandoned, it will take a long time for Great Britain to regain some of its lost prestige and confidence). As so often in the history of the European integration process, the power of the Franco-German locomotive will be decisive in terms of both the course of internal policy integration and the further development and direction of the EU's external relations. The internal and external dimensions are inextricably linked, but the way in which this coherence is given substance will determine whether the EU can attain a position as a global player of significant proportions. Here we should not focus our attention on the political-military consequences of a possible Brexit. There has already been ample anticipation of this within and outside NATO. The joint statement by the French President Macron and German Chancellor Merkel about the desirability of a European army should therefore not be taken too seriously for several reasons, aside from the finite political expiration date of both politicians. It is the hope that, but also the question whether, their successors can lead the EU sensibly through the many dilemmas it faces.

Notes

1. Introduction

1. The chairman and chief executive officer (CEO) of the Blackstone Group, Stephen A. Schwarzman, was at the time chairman of the *Strategic and Policy Forum*, a group of CEOs who advised the president on economic matters. ExxonMobil was the company of which Rex Tillerson was the CEO before becoming the first Secretary of State under Trump (see *The Washington Post*, 20 May 2017). The Forum was disbanded in August 2017, and Tillerson was replaced in March 2018.

2. A genuine neorealist would probably conclude that cooperation within the Pax Americana would not have been possible without the existence of the all-encompassing Soviet threat. For fear of being annihilated, sovereign states made the rational decision to work together under the nuclear umbrella of the US.

3. The euro crisis of the last ten years has amply demonstrated the importance of discussing asymmetry when talking about complex interdependence. As the crisis dragged on, the differences between the southern members of the euro group and the northern members increasingly came to be referred to as a centre-periphery relationship which implicitly assumed that the countries in economic surplus such as Germany and the Netherlands were partly responsible for the deplorable situation in economic-deficit countries such as Greece, Spain, and Portugal (see also chapter 6).

4. A good example is the European summit in Maastricht in December 1991. As mentioned earlier, it was decided at this summit that a further step in the direction of an Economic and Monetary Union would be taken. This was the explicit desire of France and Germany. However, treaty amendments—and therefore also this decision—require unanimity, and the less developed member states under the leadership of the then Spanish prime minister Felipe González were only willing to sign the agreement if net contributor Germany put up extra financial funds. At the last minute, Chancellor Helmut Kohl gave in and accepted the establishment of a so-called cohesion fund (Dyson and Featherstone 1999).

5. In the literature that has been published over the years under the heading of neo-functionalism, various forms of spillover have been introduced. Here I limit myself to three: functional, political, and geographic spillovers.

6. As reader in international relations, I taught for years at the Netherlands Defence College (Instituut Defensie Leergangen) in Rijswijk. In my contacts with officers from the highest ranks of the Dutch army, it was made clear to me time and again that cross-border cooperation *within the EU* between units of what were previously strictly nationally operating armies—for example via international peace-keeping operations—contributed significantly to the realisation of a commonly experienced purpose and task and to the formation of a common identity based on shared norms and values.

2.   **Foreign policy theories and the external relations of the European Union: factors and actors**

1.   Hill could not have imagined back in 1993 that the EU would come awfully close to the second option in the last ten years. The euro crisis and the tensions this has generated within the EU, the way the EU has dealt with the refugee crisis, and more generally, the rise of Eurosceptic and xenophobic populism have had a negative impact on the image of the EU as an island of stability and a beacon of freedom and solidarity. In addition, expectations in Africa have not so much been tempered as they have shifted, away from the so-called Western powers and towards the emerging powers such as China and—albeit so far to a lesser extent—India, Brazil, and South Africa. I will return to this in later chapters.

2.   A simple hypothetical example can demonstrate the importance of this. A third country can, in view of the development of the EU as a would-be superpower, adjust its expectations regarding the EU's actorness in two different ways. First, it can anticipate a spillover from economic integration to political-military integration and therefore count on EU military intervention in times of conflict. Second, the EU can be seen as an economic superpower that uses part of its prosperity to combat inequality in the international system and fulfill humanitarian needs around the world, thereby reducing the likelihood of future conflicts. Both expectations are still utopian, but for some reason the first scenario is currently considered the most realistic.

3.   I would add here that the art of *non*-decision-making can equally be seen as decision-making and, moreover, is very effective in some cases. I will return to this in later chapters.

4.   This socio-economic explanation for a particular element or a particular priority in the foreign policy of the Netherlands does not in this case have to be the sole or even main reason and can also change over time. First, the well-known saying that 'it takes two to tango' applies here; a political change in the US or Brexit could have immediate repercussions for the Dutch economy and consequently result in a change or adjustment to Dutch foreign policy strategy. Second, the mechanism of Europeanisation of national policies applies here. The Netherlands is no longer solely dependent on its own response (in the sense of a strategic adjustment) but will also notice the consequences of a shifting EU stance on Atlantic relations. And finally, the possibility cannot be excluded that, ultimately, Dutch bilateral economic relations with the US will have to be subordinated to the security interests of the EU.

5.   Most of the actors mentioned in the table need no further explanation and will be given their place in the following chapters. A short word, however, is needed on the category of 'parties'. National parties play an important role, not only in the formulation of national foreign policy, but also directly or indirectly in the EU's external relations. One example of this is the succession of government parties in Poland after 2004 (the year it joined the EU) and the way Europhile and Eurosceptic positions have alternated. The table also refers to the role of parties at the transnational level, which pertain to the so-called political families in the European Parliament

that function as transnational alliances. These families play a demonstrable role in the shaping and development of the EU's external relations (see Raunio and Wagner 2017).

6.   Here, the distinction I made earlier between the CFSP on the one hand and the EU's external action on the other (plus the external consequences of internal policy areas) is key. As European institutions increasingly acquire supranational or exclusive competences, it becomes more relevant for non-state actors to move their activities to Brussels. Most intergovernmental elements in the EU's external relations, and in particular within the CFSP, were until recently much less sensitive to this political spillover. However, we will see in chapter 6 that a turnaround can also be observed in the sensitive field of defence cooperation.

3.   The trade policy of the European Union

1.   In the preface to Leonard's original English edition, written a month after the French referendum, he refers to the 'Non' vote. And in the preface to the Dutch edition, which was written after the Dutch referendum and which appeared in September 2005, both rejections are reformulated to support his network power argument. With their no vote, French and Dutch voters had, after all, shown that decisions could no longer be taken from above and imposed on the population. The idea of a federal Europe would from this point on stumble over the obstacle of network democracy. In 'European Promise', published in 2010, Hill explicitly mentioned the credit crisis, but here too the events were presented in such a way—namely that it was mainly due to the perverse excesses of American casino capitalism—that they seamlessly fit into his prevailing approach.

2.   This emphasis on the unique, hybrid character of the EU is in line with Bretherton and Volger's 1999 analysis (an analysis that they developed further in the second edition published in 2006). They consider the EU to be a global actor *sui generis*, meaning that, based on its specific institutional structure, the EU cannot be assessed in the usual neo-realist, state-centric way. To some extent, the EU is 'one of a kind' and, as such, cannot be compared to more conventional actors (Bretherton and Vogler 1999). This does, however, cause a logical problem in connection to NPE. Accepting that the unique hybrid structure of the EU leads to the development of norms, it does not necessarily follow that these norms, via diffusion, will be applied by actors (such as conventional states) that do not possess such unique structures. This is possibly the most important contradiction in Manners' argument.

3.   We have already noted the striking simultaneous publication of a number of studies about the EU as a superpower at the turn of the millennium (and above we indicated that this was to a large extent due to the external political and internal integrational context). The simultaneous publication of Duchêne and Galtung's analyses is also no coincidence. The EU was on the eve of an enlargement that would include Great Britain, Ireland, and Denmark—the entry of the first of these countries in particular was to furnish the EU with a new international image (see also the next chapter); the EU had just started working on the EPC, the predecessor of the CFSP,

and had furthermore just presented its plans to set up a monetary union (originally planned to be launched in 1980); and the international context—declining American hegemony, which became apparent at the time of the US withdrawal from Vietnam and the appearance of the first contours of an approaching international economic crisis—led to fewer calls for military action and an increase in calls for economic cooperation. It is not surprising that, in the light of these developments, all eyes were on the EU (see Orbie 2008: 7).

4.   François Duchêne also spoke about Europe as a civilian power in predominantly positive tones at the time. This close collaborator of Jean Monnet in the 1950s could not, in any case, be accused of overly critical views.

5.   See ec.europa.eu/trade/policy/eu-position-in-world-trade. Incidentally, it is striking that this general information page was last updated on 2 October 2014.

6.   It may be useful at this point to devote some time to discussing where the relevant statistics on the EU's external relations can be found. In general, the EU's own statistical office, Eurostat (http://ec.europa.eu/eurostat), is a trustworthy source of information on just about all internal economic indicators and on most external data such as trade and investment streams (see, for example http://ec.europa.eu/ eurostat – data – browse statistics by theme – economic globalisation). Global and comparative trade statistics can also be found in the WTO's annual World Trade Report (for 2017: https://www.wto.org/english/res_e/publications_e/wtr17_e.htm). Data on global investments are compiled annually in UNCTAD's World Investment Report (the 2017 edition can be downloaded via http://unctad.org/en/pages/Publi- cationWebflyer.aspx?publicationid=1782). Data on global migration flows are publis- hed periodically in the *World Migration Report* by the International Organization for Migration (https://www.iom.int) and in UNHCR's annual Global Report (http:// www.unhcr.org). Figures on development cooperation are available via the OECD and its annual *Development Co-operation Report* (http://www.oecd-ilibrary.org/ development). And finally, the International Labour Organization (ILO) publishes various sets of statistical data—which are formally not a part of the EU's external relations—on global employment and social conditions, wages, comparisons of gender equality, education, and so on (see http://www.ilo.org).

7.   The consequences of this development—a kind of administrative spillover—were also felt by the British government with respect to the Brexit negotiations. According to a top British civil servant, Great Britain did not have the administrative capacity to provide the same level of expertise as the European Commission. Compared with Britain's paltry 20 civil servants, Brussels had 600 civil servants who were armed to the teeth and ready to enter into the negotiations battle (see Wintour 2016).

8.   Section 3.2. is a shortened and edited version of the aforementioned publication (Holman 2015). Large parts of it have been left out, the order has been changed, much of the wording has been adapted, and some phrases were added.

9.   Meunier even argues that a playing field for NGOs is emerging in the European arena on which civil society organisations in the fields of, for example, consumer interests or the environment, are beginning to prevail over business interests. In her

opinion, this latter category is 'relatively entrenched in domestic politics' (Meunier 2005: 197). This assertion cannot be fully reconciled with the fact that most of what are referred to as NGOs do not have the resources—or, in the case of European umbrella trade unions, have few shared interests—with which to effectively mobilise their lobbying at the European level. For that reason alone, the aforementioned political spillover is asymmetric.

10. Moreover, we cannot rule out the contingency of successive events and decisions—in other words, coincidence. History can only be described as a conspiracy after the fact—and even then, only partly. Chaos theory and conspiracy theory are the extremes; in reality, it is the shades of grey that stick out.

11. And, strangely enough, also one of the least known alliances. The ERT is only infrequently mentioned in handbooks on European integration, and even then only in a list with other lobby groups. This is all the more strange because neither side has made a secret of their cooperation or success. In the past, several European Commissioners (including, significantly, former Commission President Jacques Delors) have spoken of the importance of the ERT. And on its website (which is incidentally very clear and informative), even the ERT itself admits that it played a leading role in the relaunch of the integration process (see https://www.ert.eu).

12. For a comprehensive analysis of the ERT's working methods, priorities, and influence on the European decision-making process, see Cowles (1994) and Van Apeldoorn (2002). This influence reached a peak in the two decades between 1985 and 2005. That the ERT currently has a less prominent role to play is due to a number of factors. To begin with, the ERT has already achieved many of its policy priorities and aims. Secondly, the constitutional crisis and the euro crisis after 2005 meant that decision-makers in Europe had to take into account other interests and interest groups: these were sometimes in conflict with the ERT and its interests. And lastly, there is a link between the greater interest in both internal and external security issues in the European integration process and the rise of new strategic sectors. Good examples are the industrial sectors concerned with safety and defence, and energy companies. In contrast to the ERT, which pushed for an economic and monetary union, these sectors are at the basis of recent efforts to create a European energy union and defence union.

13. I use the term managed multilateralism here in two ways. Firstly, the term refers to the multilateral trade deals at the time of Pax Americana with built-in independent arbitration. An example here would be the WTO. Secondly, the term refers to the practice, followed by the US, the EU, and others, to propagate free trade in the areas in which their economies have a competitive advantage on the one hand, and on the other to bolster protectionist measures, for example in trade in agricultural products, as we shall see later. Open bilateralism refers to a strategy that, in the face of a stagnating multilateral framework, looks for a solution in bilateral trade deals with the possibility of including these in multilateral deals at a later stage.

14. Cited in a press release from the Office of the United States Trade Representative dated 13 June 1997, see https://ustr.gov/archive/assets/World_Regions/Europe_Mid-

dle_East/Europe/1998_US-EU_Mutual_Recognition_Agreement/asset_upload_
file360_7132.pdf.

15.   This is also an interesting example for another reason. Here EU trade policy directly
       affects two other policy areas. The first is European environmental policy, which
       aims to seriously deal with sustainable energy. That is why the EU is such an at-
       tractive growth market for both European and non-European solar panel producers.
       Secondly, and of course closely linked to the first point, solar power is an impor-
       tant element of European energy policy (and the pursuit of a so-called European
       Energy Union). This connection once again shows that the stated aim of the Lisbon
       Treaty—namely to arrive at an external relations policy in which the various
       components and actors communicate with each other and, where possible, form an
       integrated whole—is easier said than done.

16.   There is an apocryphal story related to this—'the scandal of the ears'—dating from
       the second part of the 1980s. Set in a less developed region of Italy, the story goes
       that the reduction in milk production through the introduction of milk quotas was
       considered technically impracticable. An alternative system was devised whereby
       the farmers would take a certain number of their dairy cattle to the slaughterhouse.
       By providing evidence that they had done so, they became eligible for a subsidy. The
       evidence required was one of the slaughtered animal's ears. When an astute Italian
       civil servant was walking through the rolling hills of the region in question one day,
       he noticed something strange about the languidly grazing cows—they were all
       missing an ear (some were even missing two). Dairy production was more often por-
       trayed in the news in a negative light due to its susceptibility to fraud.

17.   In the discussion about the CAP, this is called the multifunctionality of agricul-
       ture. It refers to the non-commercial interests that must also be served, such as
       food safety, environmental protection, or animal welfare. It also includes rural
       development—a theme that has gained a central place in the CAP over the past two
       decades.

4.   Decolonisation and enlargement: the development policy of the European Union

1.   The quotes are from the original treaty and the Dutch government's official com-
       ments on the treaty. Both can be found here: https://www.europa-nu.nl/id/vhi7omf-
       vtjyr/artikel_131_doelstellingen_beginselen.

2.   The group of non-aligned countries was originally labelled as Third World, in a po-
       sitive sense, as a way of indicating that these countries tried to find a kind of third
       way between the capitalist First World and the socialist Second World. This had
       both a socio-economic significance, as an option between free-market economy
       and command economy, and a geopolitical significance, as an alternative to the two
       spheres of influence during the period of Cold War bipolarity.

3.   Towards the end of the 1970s and beginning of the 1980s, the NIEO movement's
       rather radical agenda was weakened and remoulded in the image of Europe by the
       Brandt Commission, named after the former West German Chancellor Willy Brandt.

Although the commission comprised a broad cross-section of representatives of differing political persuasions and from various parts of the world, it was mainly the European social democrats such as Brandt himself, the Dutchman Jan Pronk, and the Swede Olaf Palme who left their mark on the final recommendations. Similar to the NIEO declaration, the commission's report called for an internationally coordinated approach to the differences in development in the international system. In addition to proposing reform of the international monetary system and a more equitable and proportional distribution of power within international organisations, the report's authors argued that the removal of protectionism in the international trade system—global free trade, in other words—would be to the advantage of both developing countries and developed countries. Trade liberalisation should, however, be combined with a progressive system of international taxation and a drastic increase in development aid (see Brandt 1980). The combination of trade and taxes was strongly reminiscent of the postwar class compromise within the West European welfare states—sometimes referred to by the apt slogan 'Keynes at home, Smith abroad'—which combined domestically generated economic growth (via income redistribution and government expenditure) with externally generated growth via trade liberalisation. Most of the Brandt Commission's proposals came to nothing. While its proposal to establish a minimum of 0.7% of GNP for rich countries' development aid was adopted by the United Nations, this minimum has been put into practice by only a few countries, as we shall see later.

4. The example that Ricardo himself used was the trade relationship between England and Portugal, where England exported textile products and Portugal exported wine. He wrote this at the beginning of the nineteenth century with the 1703 Treaty of Methuen apparently in mind. This treaty institutionalised the trade relationship and the aforementioned division of labour between England and Portugal (Watson 2017: 261ff). It reflected England's international position of power and at any rate resulted in Portugal's rudimentary textile industry being nipped in the bud (see also Sideri 1970). It was only at the beginning of the twentieth century that Portugal took the first steps in an industrialisation process that would definitively modernise its national economy.

5. As a self-declared development economist with a keen interest in developments in Southeast Asia, Rostow played an important role in the United States' growing involvement in the fight against communism in South Vietnam. What came to be known as the Rostow thesis stipulated that the US had to prevent the fall of South Vietnam from triggering a domino effect in the region. The dramatic retreat of the US in 1973 and the end of the Vietnam War soon after did nothing to change his mind. According to Rostow, the war had given Vietnam's neighbouring countries time to modernise and thus to resist the temptation of communism. Rostow was by this time no longer an advisor; this message about development was instead taught to a new generation of students. This career switch—from the academic world to politics and back again—is something that occurs frequently in the world of American politics (and economics). One of the many examples of this is another former adherent of modernisation theory, Samuel P. Huntington. The Italian communist and

Marxist Antonio Gramsci came up with an apt expression for this at the beginning of the twentieth century: the organic intellectuals. This refers to people who make their intellectual abilities available to a historically determined power constellation and/or provide the ideological building blocks for an organic system that ultimately translates into a specific foreign policy and prioritisation of external relations (see the first sections in Gramsci 1971).

6.   Despite good intentions, these general goals and the underlying targets were not all met by 2015. Nonetheless, on its own website the UN does call the efforts a success, and it has to be said that without the goals the situation would probably have been worse. The UN did, however, see the need to formulate a new package of goals, the 2030 Agenda for Sustainable Development (see http://www.un.org/en/sections/what-we-do/promote-sustainable-development/index.html). Incidentally, it is not entirely correct to associate the basic needs strategy with a relatively nihilistic view on the possibilities for industrial development. The first formulations of such a strategy date from the 1970s and were drafted at the offices of the International Labour Organization (ILO). The original ideas were in fact embedded in a broader macroeconomic strategy (see unpublished paper: Emmerij 2010).

7.   It is interesting to compare this with the recent discussion within NATO about the percentage that member states of this collective security organisation should spend on defence. The so-called NATO norm was previously fixed at 2 per cent of GNP. On the one hand, it is interesting to compare the two percentages, as it says something about the respective importance of security and development in the external relations of prosperous Western countries. On the other hand, the arguments against both percentages are interesting, partly because politically they represent each other's mirror image. The argument often used against the 0.7 percentage is that it leads to compulsive spending, with donors feeling obliged to spend the amount earmarked even though an approach driven by demand would be better and more efficient. Opponents of the NATO norm argue that, first, it is a simple way for the US to offload its overproduction of weaponry, and second, the combined military power of NATO countries is much greater than that of Russia, even without attaining the 2 per cent norm, so there is no serious threat or need to reach the norm (see also chapter 6).

8.   To a certain extent, this is a purely theoretical exercise. What we saw earlier for the ACP group as a whole—namely that the EU's trade with this group has become less and less important both in terms of imports and exports—holds even more so for the least developed countries. They are hardly relevant as export markets for European businesses. The import penetration of these countries into the European market is also declining as a percentage of total EU imports. This is due to the fact that initiatives such as the Everything But Arms (EBA) scheme are implemented concomitantly to broader free trade agreements concluded within the framework of the WTO and, moreover, are not a viable option for many producers in the poorest countries. According to the currently functioning EBA, the 49 least developed countries have full duty-free and quota-free access to the European single market for all products except for weapons and ammunition (see http://ec.europa.eu/trade/po-

licy/policy-making/). But this presumes that producers in these countries have the financial, infrastructural and logistical means to make use of the opportunities offered, which is not always the case, to put it mildly. This kind of discussion also crops up in the case of the gradual dismantling of protectionist measures in agriculture, as mentioned earlier. Large and efficient producers from exporting countries will be the first to benefit from the opening of the European agricultural market; small and small-scale farmers in the poorest countries will necessarily lose out.

9. The introduction of political conditionality in the Cotonou Agreement appears at first to be a logical consequence of the goals of the EU's external policy as articulated in the treaties. But the non-execution clause also shows that a coherent, consistent and integrated vision with regard to development has yet to be formulated. Can economic development and modernisation be made conditional on political democratisation, or are economic development and modernisation actually the foundation on which political and institutional changes can take place?

10. The securitisation of migration is thus becoming a reality that is playing an increasingly prominent role in the EU's development policy and in financial support for less developed countries. Chapter 6 shows that the EU's security strategy as it has been given shape since 2003 sees security and stability (construed first and foremost as the absence of armed conflict) as a precondition for sustainable development. This primacy of security considerations and concerns is apparent in the EU's focus on the non-proliferation of weapons of mass destruction and anti-terrorism provisions in bilateral agreements between the EU and other countries.

11. Other research shows that an overwhelming majority of European respondents answered positively to the question of whether development aid should have a political conditionality, as discussed earlier (see Bodenstein and Faust 2017).

12. This invites comparisons with the situation at the time of the Rostow thesis (see endnote v). It would appear that in its relations with countries such as Ukraine and Georgia, but also with candidate member states such as Serbia, the EU is trying 'everything' in its power to prevent these countries from falling into the clutches of the Russian Federation. Although there is, of course, no longer a communist threat, tension between the EU and Russia that would result from this would rightly qualify as a kind of new Cold War.

5.   The end of the Cold War, the enlargement strategy and the neighbourhood policy of the European Union

1. It was the then Spanish Prime Minister Felipe González who aptly expressed this in an interview with the *Financial Times*. It was well-known that the Spanish government and the Spanish business community viewed developments in Central and Eastern Europe with suspicion. A successful transformation there would entail the risk that investments (read: German investments) and European structural funds would shift from southern Europe to eastern Europe. Asked whether it was not unfair to be reluctant to enlarge the EU to include the new democracies while Spain had also benefited from European support in its transition to democracy back in 1975, González replied that he could not accept such a comparison. 'Spain went

through a very deep economic crisis between 1975 and 1985. We got a great deal of moral support, but we never received a single peseta in assistance.' He then stated that Lech Walesa, the then prime minister of Poland, should not expect Western Europe to pay the bill for forty years of communism. 'Just like it didn't pay for 40 years of Franquismo. No one feels obliged to pay this bill' (*Financial Times*, 9 May 1991). It worked out differently in the end as a result of the new enlargement strategy.

2. In the previous chapter, specific attention was paid to the introduction of the so-called political conditionality in the EU's development policy. This was introduced at the end of the 1990s in the Lomé IV Convention and later further accentuated in the Cotonou Agreement. Development aid has since been linked to achievements in the areas of human rights, the rule of law, and democratic governance. It is no coincidence that this political conditionality was introduced after a similar system became a key part of the EU's enlargement policy via the so-called Copenhagen criteria (1993). In a more general sense, both 'introductions' are part of a broader post-Cold War phenomenon: in the wake of the popularisation of the concept of governance in the 1990s (see Kohler-Koch and Rittberger 2006), the term good governance was also given political significance. Henceforth, the EU's external relations could no longer be formulated without at least paying lip service to the normative substance of public administration practices.

3. To be perfectly clear, the big bang enlargement will henceforth refer to the largest inclusion of new member states in the history of the EU. On 1 May 2004, Poland, the Czech Republic, Slovakia, Hungary, Slovenia, Lithuania, Latvia, and Estonia did not hang red flags to celebrate Labour Day but instead uncorked champagne bottles due to their festive accession to the EU. The fact that Malta and Cyprus joined at the same time was silently added to the annals. With a certain delay, Bulgaria and Romania joined in 2007.

4. He repeated this veto in 1967. De Gaulle had three reasons for vetoing British accession, and the distribution of weight among these reasons is heavily debated in the literature. For some, including Andrew Moravcsik, De Gaulle was mainly driven by the interests of the French agricultural sector. In contrast to France, Great Britain did not have a significant agricultural sector and therefore had no interest in the continuation, let alone expansion, of the Common Agricultural Policy. The CAP, however, had been one of France's most important objectives in the creation of the EU. De Gaulle was afraid that British membership would shift the balance in the European Economic Community to the detriment of French interests. Secondly, De Gaulle feared that the accession of the United Kingdom would in fact amount to a greater influence of the US in the integration process. This fear has come to be known as De Gaulle's 'Trojan Horse' syndrome. A third reason often mentioned is of a predominantly geopolitical nature. De Gaulle did not want the accession of a third major power and second military superpower to disrupt the fragile balance between West Germany and France (the so-called Bonn-Paris axis) as the engine of European integration or to bring an end to French primacy (as a military power and nuclear power in the making).

5. According to more liberal views on the blessings of the free movement of capital and goods, such a move should not matter. Shareholders and managers of a bank or industrial company have primarily the interest of the company in mind—from a cynical perspective conceived as the increase in share prices and bonuses—and are thereby sufficiently removed from territorial or national loyalties. In a way, the Netherlands is a good illustration of this. This small country on the North Sea was one of the largest investors in CEE from 1989, and Dutch companies were active participants in the privatisation process there. This was mainly due to the fact that the Netherlands is the seat of so-called holding companies that are largely in foreign hands. These are mostly multinational companies of extra-European origin that used the Netherlands as a springboard towards CEE (European Commission 2006: 69, n48). In a global and interdependent world, companies are footloose in the sense that origin, if at all traceable, is of little importance. On the other hand, recent protectionist structures from EU governments against so-called hostile (Chinese or American) takeovers of important national companies show that here too, political practice is more complicated than economic liberalism would have us believe.

6. A comparison with the problems of many developing countries is fitting here (see previous chapter). In particular, countries that have a one-sided export orientation based on raw materials and that are dependent on foreign companies (including for extraction) are often confronted with zero value capture (the addition of *zero* is mine) (see also Draper and Freytag 2015).

7. *Ceteris paribus* is Latin for 'all else being equal' or 'all other factors remaining constant'. It is an assumption that is often used by more quantitatively oriented research strategies that makes it possible—according to its proponents—to reveal the interrelation between an explanatory variable and a variable still to be explained (the correlation between two series of observations, phenomena, or developments). However, a basic problem with this scientific approach is that difficulties arise as soon as one attempts to establish a causal relationship, simply because 'circumstances' and 'factors' are not constant. For example, if we want to establish the link between political transition and political transformation (or between democratic transition and consolidation), we cannot abstract these from other factors such as economic developments and/or socio-economic cohesion.

8. The approach taken by Börzel and Risse in particular gives a prominent place to the diffusion of norms and values. Focusing on these ideas is very much in line with the assumptions in the literature on Normative Power Europe as explored in chapter 3. The critical comments on the NPE literature in that chapter are also largely relevant to the constructivist interpretation of the idea of transformative power.

9. His speech, given on 12 May 2000, became known as the Humboldt Speech, named after the eponymous university in Berlin, and with hindsight can be seen as the last great speech by an influential ex-politician who dared to talk about prospects in the form of a European federation. For the full text of the lecture, see https://www.europa.clio-online.de/quelle/id/artikel-3231.

10. This is in fact a finding from the academic literature on integration. Until then, an explanation was always sought—whether or not based on normative considerati-

ons—for *ever closer union*, for an advancing integration process. This process was therefore the dependent variable, i.e. the phenomenon that had to be explained. After the French and Dutch referenda in particular, it was increasingly concluded that 'Europe was completed', that further deepening would be difficult to achieve and was moreover undesirable. The integration process, which had essentially come to a halt, could now serve as an explanation for other phenomena. The EU had therefore become an independent, explanatory variable.

11. The European Commission publishes annual progress reports on each candidate country. These consistently show that the political dimension has started to play a more prominent role (see the most recent reports at https://ec.europa.eu/neigh-bourhood-enlargement/countries/package_en). The most prominent candidate country is Turkey. In addition to Turkey, there are four candidate countries in the Balkans (Serbia, Montenegro, Macedonia, and Albania) and two countries in the somewhat absurd category of potential candidate countries (Bosnia-Herzegovina and Kosovo). Together, these six Balkan countries are part of the EU's Stabilisation and Association Process with respect to the Western Balkans. The commissioner charged with the expansion portfolio, Johannes Hahn, stated in 2017 that it was up to the Balkan countries themselves to "make the first move". Referring to what he expected from the countries, he emphasised that "(we) would like to see reassurance, guarantees and behaviour … indicating that they have inhaled European values" (cited in the *Financial Times*, 13 July 2017, page 6).

This book does not look specifically and individually at the bilateral relations between the EU and individual countries, unless the country in question has had a key role in the formulation or reformulation of one of the main policy areas within the EU's broad external relations (such as the United States, which will be dealt with in the next chapter). This is therefore not the place to look closely at the difficult relationship between the EU and Turkey, one of the five current candidate countries. This relationship has visibly deteriorated over the past decade as a result of the political developments in Turkey itself, although we cannot rule out that these political developments are at least partly the result of the negative attitude of the EU towards the accession of this immense and strongly divided country. Be that as it may, in its most recent progress report on Turkey, the European Commission noted a level of political regression in the country, thus implicitly suggesting that membership will not take place in the foreseeable future (European Commission 2018a). Likewise, a month before the publication of this progress report, the independent European Court of Auditors stated that the billions of pre-accession aid that the EU had given Turkey had not had the desired effect in terms of political reforms (European Court of Auditors 2018). Incidentally, the sixty pages of this report give a good overview of the difficult relationship between the EU and Turkey.

12. It should be added that Belarus, Libya and Syria only partially participate in the ENP. In the case of Syria, financial support was stopped after the outbreak of the civil war in 2011. Libya and Belarus only have limited access due to their domestic political situations, although there is some movement in the relationship between the EU and Libya due to the EU's interest in controlling migration flows from this

country. The asterisk beside Palestine refers to a standard formulation of the EU (which is also used in the case of Kosovo): that participation of this area in the ENP should in no way be construed as recognition of the Palestinian state.

13.   The British political scientist Richard Youngs has written two critical books: one on the EU's external relations with its neighbours in the Eastern Partnership (Youngs 2017), and one about the EU's response to the Arab Spring (Youngs 2014). In his most recent book, he argues that the EU has learned in particular from the crisis between Russia and Ukraine and subsequently started to pursue a more realistic geopolitical strategy in which the idealism/liberalism of the preceding period has somewhat faded into the background. My argument in this chapter is largely in line with his analysis but also deviates from it in the sense that, in my view, idealism has never been dominant in external relations and has always been subordinate to—or served as a cover for—enlightened self-interest. Another point is that this self-interest was rarely unitary and therefore a plaything of various geopolitical priorities of member states (or groups of member states). As long as security threats and/or economic challenges are not perceived in the same way by all member states, EU external policy will not become more effective and decisive, and the promotion of values and norms will at most serve the higher purpose of concealing this lack of unity and decisiveness.

6.   Internal-external

1.   The principle of the assembly line was not new; a comparable system was already in use in the meat-processing industry in Chicago. What was new was the idea that the increase in productivity—on balance, many more cars (the Model T Ford) were produced per worker—made it possible to pay out higher wages, as a result of which workers obtained more purchasing power and could be the consumers of the product they themselves had manufactured. On the internet there are many photos and movie recordings from the early period of industrial mass production (tip: search using the words *assembly line*). The fact that such assembly lines did not always run smoothly is shown in the 1936 tragicomic film *Modern Times* by Charlie Chaplin. The film can be seen as an indictment of the desensitising character of the Fordist production process. It also brilliantly illustrates the difference between absolute and relative methods of changing the ratio of production costs to profits in favour of the latter. An absolute method was to prolong the working hours and/or to lower wages, while a relative method was to increase labour productivity through mechanisation and rationalisation, often in agreement with stakeholders and in exchange for material compensation. Ford's website reports that the revolutionary introduction of the assembly line brought the production time of an automobile down from 12 hours to 90 minutes. From 1913 to 1927, as many as 15 million Model Ts were brought onto the market. And these, of course, had to be sold! The price of an automobile was gradually lowered and the pay of 5 dollars per working day 'is credited with giving rise to a new middle class of consumers unencumbered by geography, free to travel the open roads, to live where they please and chase the

American dream' (see http://corporate.ford.com/innovation/100-years-moving-assembly-line.html). I would add that the rise in wages paved the way for a new phenomenon: consumer credit. The indebtedness of households thus became an integral part of the American way of life.

2. It is tempting to jump to the present and zoom in on the so-called twin deficits of the US: the fiscal deficit of the federal government and the trade deficit. Both can be seen as indicators of waning or even vanished hegemony. I will not go into the rather complicated twin deficit hypothesis, which states that both deficits can have a mutually reinforcing effect. It is bad enough if both deficits and their increase can be determined empirically (and separately), as in the case of the US. A part of the deficits is financed with foreign money—in the case of the United States, for example, from China, which makes the American economy more vulnerable due to its increased dependency. This eventually even affects national security. What is important here is the link with US defence spending and the tension between persistent deficits on the one hand and global security ambitions on the other.

3. For a complete overview, see https://eeas.europa.eu/topics/military-and-civilian-missions-and-operations_en.

4. The institutional structure of CSDP was also largely realised during the first years of the new millennium. This applies inter alia to the High Representative of the Union for Foreign Affairs and Security Policy, a position that was first held by the former Spanish politician and Secretary General of NATO Javier Solana (from 1999); the Political and Security Committee (PSC), which received formal status in 2000-2001; the European Union Military Committee (EUMC) from 2000; and the European Defence Agency (EDA) from 2004. For an overview of the institutional structure, see the website of the EEAS: https://eeas.europa.eu/headquarters/headquarters-home-page/5392/csdp-structure-instruments-and-agencies_en.

5. The update (from April 2017) can be downloaded via the website of the publisher: https://www.macmillanihe.com. The authors cite some of the participants in a forum about the EUGS in the academic journal *Contemporary Security Studies* (2016, no. 3), which, remarkably enough, was placed online just a few months after the strategy appeared. One of the participants was Nathalie Tocci, who played an important role in the realisation of the EUGS.

Bibliography

Acemoglu, Daron and James A. Robinson (2012), *Why Nations Fail. The Origins of Power, Prosperity, and Poverty* (New York: Random House).

Agh, Attila (1998) *The Politics of Central Europe* (London: Sage).

Alden, Chris and Amnon Aran (2017, 2nd edition), *Foreign Policy Analysis. New Approaches* (London: Routledge).

Allison, Graham (1971), *The Essence of Decision-making: Explaining the Cuban Missile Crisis* (Boston: Little Brown).

Atlantische Commissie (1995), *Stabiliteit en Integratie. De Veiligheidspolitieke Betrekkingen met Midden- en Oost-Europa* (Den Haag: Atlantische Commissie).

Aydin-Düzgit, Senem (2015), 'Social-Constructivist and Discursive Approaches to European Foreign Policy', in: K.E. Jørgensen, et al. (eds.), *The Sage Handbook of European Foreign Policy, Volume 1* (London: Sage), pp. 137-51.

Aydin-Düzgit, Senem (2018), 'Legitimizing Europe in Contested Settings: Europe as a Normative Power in Turkey?' *Journal of Common Market Studies* 56(3): 612-27.

Barraclough, Geoffrey (1967), *An Introduction to Contemporary History* (Harmondsworth: Penguin Books).

Bauhr, Monika, Nicholas Charron and Naghmeh Nasiritousi (2013), 'Does Corruption Cause Aid Fatigue? Public Opinion and the Aid-Corruption Paradox', *International Studies Quarterly* 57(3): 568-79.

Berend, Ivan I. (2016), *The History of European Integration. A New Perspective* (London: Routledge).

Bergmann, Julian and Arne Niemann (2018), 'From Neo-Functional Peace to a Logic of Spillover in EU External Policy: A Response to Visoka and Doyle', *Journal of Common Market Studies*, 56(2): 420-38.

Blomström, Magnus and Björn Hettne (1984), *Development Theory in Transition: The Dependency Debate and Beyond – Third World Responses* (London: Zed Books).

Blyth, Mark (2013), *Austerity. The History of a Dangerous Idea* (Oxford: Oxford University Press).

Bodenstein, Thilo and Jörg Faust (2017), 'Who cares? European Public Opinion on Foreign Aid and Political Conditionality', *Journal of Common Market Studies* 55(5): 955-73.

Börzel, Tanja (2010), 'The Transformative Power of Europe Reloaded. The Limits of External Europeanization', *KFG Working Paper Series*, No. 11.

Börzel, Tanja and Thomas Risse (2009), 'The Transformative Power of Europe. The European Union and the Diffusion of Ideas', *KFG Working Paper*, No. 1.

Börzel, Tanja, Antoaneta Dimitrova and Frank Schimmelfennig (2018) (eds.), *European Union Enlargement and Integration Capacity* (London: Routledge).

Brandt, Willy (1980), *North-South: A Programme for Survival – The Report of the Independent Commission on International Development Issues* (London: Pan).

Bretherton, Charlotte and John Vogler (2006 (1999)) *The European Union as Global Actor* (London: Routledge).

Brittan, Leon (1994), *Europe. The Europe we need* (London: Hamish Hamilton).

Burchill, Scott and Andrew Linklater (2013, 5th edition) (eds.), *Theories of International Relations* (Basingstoke: Palgrave).

Buzan, Barry and Lene Hansen (2009), *The Evolution of International Security Studies* (Cambridge: Cambridge University Press).

Buzan, Barry and Lene Hansen (2010), 'Defining-Redefining Security', in: Robert A. Denemark (ed.), *The International Studies Encyclopedia* (Oxford: Wiley Blackwell / ISA), DOI: 10.1111/b.9781444336597.2010.x.

Buzan, Buzan and George Lawson (2015), *The Global Transformation. History, Modernity and the Making of International Relations* (Cambridge: Cambridge University Press).

Cameron, Fraser (2012, 2nd edition), *An Introduction to European Foreign Policy* (London and New York: Routledge).

Carbone, Maurizio (2011), 'The EU and the Developing World: Partnership, Poverty, Politicization', in: C. Hill en M. Smith (eds.), *International Relations and the European Union* (Oxford: Oxford University Press, 2nd edition), pp. 324-48.

Carbone, Maurizio and Jan Orbie (2015) (eds.), *The Trade-Development Nexus in the European Union. Differentiation, Coherence and Norms* (London: Routledge).

Carbone, Maurizio and Jan Orbie (2015) (eds.), *The Europeanisation of Development Policy* (London: Routledge).

Chang, Ha-Joon (2003), *Kicking away the Ladder. Development Strategy in Historical Perspective* (London: Anthem Press).

Collard-Wexler, Simon (2006), 'Integration Under Anarchy: Neorealism and the European Union', *European Journal of International Relations* 12(3): 397-432.

Collins, Alan (ed.) (2016, 4th edition), *Contemporary Security Studies* (Oxford: Oxford University Press).

Conceição-Heldt, Eugénia da (2010), 'Who Controls Whom? Dynamics of Power Delegation and Agency Losses in EU Trade Politics', *Journal of Common Market Studies* 48(4): 1107-26.

Conceição-Heldt, Eugénia da (2011a), *Negotiating Trade Liberalization at the WTO: Domestic Politics and Bargaining Dynamics* (Basingstoke: Palgrave).

Conceição-Heldt, Eugénia da (2011b), 'Variation in EU Member States' Preferences and the Commission's Discretion in the Doha Round', *Journal of European Public Policy* 18(3): 402-18.

Conceição-Heldt, Eugénia da (2013), 'Do Agents "Run Amok"? Agency Slack in the EU and US Trade Policy in the Doha Round', *Journal of Comparative Policy Analysis* 15(1): 21-36.

Cowles, Maria Green (1994), 'The Politics of Big Business in the European Community: Setting the Agenda for a New Europe', PhD dissertation, The American University, Washington.

Cowles Maria Green (2001) 'The Transatlantic Business Dialogue and Domestic Business-Government Relations', in M. Green Cowles, J. Caporaso and T. Risse (eds.), *Transforming Europe*. Ithaca: Cornell University Press. pp. 159-79.

Cox, Robert (1981) 'Social Forces, States and World Orders: Beyond International Relations Theory', *Millennium*, 10(2): 126–155.

Damro, Chad (2012) 'Market Power Europe', *Journal of European Public Policy*, 19 (5): 682-99.

Delreux, Tom (2015), 'Bureaucratic Politics, New Institutionalism and Principal-Agent Models', in: K.E. Jørgensen, et al. (eds.), *The Sage Handbook of European Foreign Policy, Volume I* (London: Sage), pp. 152-65.

Dent, Christopher M. (1997), *The European Economy: the Global Context* (London: Routledge).

Deutsch, Karl et al. (1957), *Political Community and the North Atlantic Area: International Organization in the Light of Historical Experience* (Princeton: Princeton University Press).

De Ville, Ferdi and Gabriel Siles-Brügge (2016), *TTIP. The Truth about the Transatlantic Trade and Investment Partnership* (Cambridge: Polity).

Dijkstra, Hylke (2009), 'Commission versus Council Secretariat: An Analysis of Bureaucratic Rivalry in European Foreign Policy', *European Foreign Affairs Review* 14(3):431-50.

Dinan, Desmond (2010, 4th edition), *Ever Closer Union. An Introduction to European Integration* (Basingstoke: Palgrave).

Draper, Peter and Andreas Freytag (2015), 'Who captures the value in global value chains? A perspective from developing countries', *Great insights Magazine* 4(6): 11-13.

Dreher, Axel, Andreas Fuchs and Peter Nunnenkamp (2013), 'New Donors', *International Interactions: Empirical and Theoretical Research in International Relations* 39(3): 402–415.

Duchêne, François (1972), 'Europe's Role in World Peace', in: Richard Mayne (ed.), *Europe Tomorrow: Sixteen European Look Ahead* (London: Fontana/HarperCollins), pp. 32-47.

Duffield, Mark (2001), *Global Governance and the New Wars. The Merging of Development and Security* (London: Zed Books).

Dür, Andreas (2008) 'Bringing economic interests back into the study of EU trade policy making', *British Journal of Politics and International Relations* 10(1): 27-45.

Dür, Andreas (2012) 'Why interest groups dominate the EU's foreign economic policies', in H. Zimmermann and A. Dür (eds.), *Key Controversies in European Integration* (Basingstoke: Palgrave), pp.178-83.

Dür, Andreas and Dirk de Bièvre (2007) 'Inclusion without Influence? NGOs in European Trade Policy', *Journal of Public Policy* 27(1): 79-101.

Dür, Andreas and Manfred Elsig (2011) 'Principals, agents, and the European Union's foreign economic policies', *Journal of European Public Policy* 18 (3): 323-38.

Dyson, Kenneth and Kevin Featherstone (1999), *The Road to Maastricht. Negotiating Economic and Monetary Union* (Oxford: Oxford University Press).

EEAS (2016), *Shared Vision, Common Action: A Stronger Europe. A Global Strategy for the European Union's Foreign and Security Policy* (available at http://europa.eu/globalstrategy/en).

Ehrlich, Sean D. (2009), 'How common is the Common External Tariff. Domestic influences on European Union trade policy', *European Union Politics* 10(1): 115-41.

Emmerij, Louis (2010), *The Basic Needs Development Strategy* (UN: unpublished background paper for the World Economic and Social Survey).

Epstein, Rachel and Ulrich Sedelmeier (2008), 'Beyond Conditionality: International Institutions in Postcommunist Europe after Enlargement', *Journal of European Public Policy* 15(6): 795-805.

ERT (1994) *European Competitiveness. The Way to Growth and Jobs.* Brussels: ERT.

European Commission (2006), 'Enlargement two years after: an economic evaluation', *European Economy. Occasional Papers*, No. 24, May.

European Commission (2013), *A New Deal for European Defence. Towards a more Competitive and Effective Defence and Security Sector* (Brussels: European Commission).

European Commission (2015), *Trade for All. Towards a more responsible trade and investment policy* (Brussels: European Commission).

European Commission (2017), *Special Eurobarometer 455. EU Citizens' Views on Development, Cooperation and Aid* (Brussels: European Commission).

European Commission (2018a), *Commission Staff Working Document: Turkey 2018 Report*, Strasbourg, SWD (2018) 153 final.

European Commission (2018b), *A credible enlargement perspective for and enhanced EU engagement with the Western Balkans*, Strasbourg, COM (2018) 65 final.

European Council (2003), *A Secure Europe in a Better World. European Security Strategy* (Brussels: European Council), 12 December.

Europese Rekenkamer (2018), *Pretoetredingssteun van de EU aan Turkije: tot dusver slechts beperkte resultaten.* Speciaal verslag, Nr. 07 (Luxemburg: Europese Rekenkamer).

Europese Unie (2010), *Geconsolideerde Verdragen. Handvest van de Grondrechten* (Luxemburg: Bureau voor publicaties van de Europese Unie).

Eurostat (2017), *Globalisation Patterns in EU Trade and Investment* (Luxembourg: Publications Office of the European Union).

Eyal, Gil, Iván Szelényi and Eleanor Townsley (1997) 'The Theory of post-Communist Managerialism', *New Left Review* 222: 60-92.

FAO (2009), *How to feed the world in 2050* (Rome: Food and Agricultural Organization).

Fiott, Daniel (2015), 'The European Commission and the European Defence Agency: A Case of Rivalry?' *Journal of Common Market Studies* 53(3): 542-57.

Furness, Mark and Stefan Gänzle (2017), 'The Security-Development Nexus in European Union Foreign Relations after Lisbon: Policy Coherence at Last?', *Development Policy Review* 35(4): 475-92.

Galtung, Johan (1969), 'Violence, Peace and Peace Research', *Journal of Peace Research* 6(3): 167-91.

Galtung, Johan (1973), *The European Community: A Superpower in the Making* (London: George Allen & Unwin).

Giddens, Athony (1981), *A Contemporary Critique of Historical Materialism* (London: Macmillan).

Gilpin, Robert (1987), *The Political Economy of International Relations* (Princeton: Princeton University Press).

Glyn, Andrew (2006), *Capitalism Unleashed. Finance, Globalization, and Welfare* (Oxford: Oxford University Press).

Grabbe, Heather (2006), *The EU's Transformative Power. Europeanization through Conditionality in Central and Eastern Europe* (Basingstoke: Palgrave).

Grabbe, Heather (2014) 'Six Lessons of Enlargement Ten Years On: The EU's Transformative Power in Retrospect and Prospect', *Journal of Common Market Studies* 52 (Annual Review): 40-56.

Gramsci, Antonio (1971), *Selections from the Prison Notebooks* (London: Lawrence & Wishart).

Grosser, Alfred (1978), *The Western Alliance. European-American Relations since 1945* (Basingstoke: Macmillan).

Haas, Ernst (2004 (1958)), *The Uniting of Europe. Political, Social, and Economic Forces, 1950-1957* (Notre Dame: University of Notre Dame Press).

Haas, Ernst (2004), 'Introduction: Institutionalism or Constructivism?' New Introduction to the reprint of *The Uniting of Europe*, op. cit., pp. xiii-lvi.

Hadfield, Amelia, Ian Manners and Richard G. Whitman (eds.) (2017), *Foreign Policies of EU Member States. Continuity and Europeanisation* (London: Routledge).

Hall, Peter A. en Rosemary C.R. Taylor (1996), 'Political Science and the Three New Institutionalisms', *Political Studies* XLIV: 936-57.

Heinrich, Tobias, Yoshiharu Kobayashi and Kristin A. Bryant (2016), 'Public Opinion and Foreign Aid Cuts in Economic Crises', *World Development* 77: 66-79.

Heywood, Andrew (2014, 2nd edition), *Global Politics* (Basingstoke: Palgrave).

Hill, Christopher (1993), 'The Capability-Expectations Gap, or Conceptualizing Europe's International Role', *Journal of Common Market Studies* 31(3): 305-28.

Hill, Christopher, Michael Smith and Sophie Vanhoonacker (2017, 3rd edition) (eds.), *International Relations and the European Union* (Oxford: Oxford University Press).

Hill, Steven (2010), *Europe's Promise. Why the European Way is the Best Hope in an Insecure Age* (Berkeley: University of California Press).

Holland, Martin and Mathew Doidge (2012) *Development Policy of the European Union* (Basingstoke: Palgrave MacMillan).

Holman, Otto (1996), 'Bedrijfsleven en Europese eenwording: de rol van de European Round Table of Industrialists', *Internationale Spectator* 50(6): 338-43.

Holman, Otto (1999) 'De toekomst van het Europese structuurbeleid', in Carla Aarsen (ed), *Sociaal Europa* (Amsterdam: Instituut voor Publiek en Politiek), pp. 74-97.

Holman, Otto (2004), 'Asymmetrical Regulation and Multidimensional Governance in the European Union', *Review of International Political Economy* 11(4): 714-35.

Holman, Otto (2015), 'Commerial Internationalism', in: K.E. Jørgensen, et al. (eds.), *The Sage Handbook of European Foreign Policy, Volume 2* (London: Sage), pp. 516-29.

Hooghe, Liesbet and Gary Marks (2007), 'Sources of Euroscepticism', *Acta Politica* 42(2/3): 119-27.

Hooghe, Liesbet and Gary Marks (2009), 'A Postfunctionalist Theory of European Integration: from Permissive Consensus to Constraining Dissensus', *British Journal of Political Science* 39(1): 1-23.

Howorth, Jolyon (2007), *Security and Defence Policy in the European Union* (Basingstoke: Palgrave).

Jackson, Robert and Georg Sørensen (2016, 6th edition), *Introduction to International Relations. Theories and Approaches* (Oxford: Oxford University Press).

Janis, Irving L. (1982), *Groupthink: Psychological Studies of Policy Decisions and Fiascos* (Boston: Houghton Mifflin, 2nd edition).

JCMS (2014), 'Eastern Enlargement Ten Years On', *Special issue of the Journal of Common Market Studies* 52(1).

Jessop, Bob and Henk Overbeek (2019) (eds.), *Transnational Capital and Class Fractions. The Amsterdam School Perspective Reconsidered* (London: Routledge).

Jørgensen, Knud Erik, Åsne Kalland Aarstad, Edith Drieskens, Katie Laatikainen and Ben Tonra (2015) (eds.), *The Sage Handbook of European Foreign Policy, Volume I + II* (London: Sage).

Judt, Tony (2005), *Postwar. A History of Europe Since 1945* (London: Penguin Books).

Juncker, Jean-Claude (2016), *Staat van de Unie. 2016* (ec.europa.eu/soteu).

Kay, Geoffrey (1975), *Development and Underdevelopment: A Marxist Analysis* (Basingstoke: Palgrave MacMillan).

Kershaw, Ian (2018), *Roller-Coaster: Europe, 1950-2017* (London: Penguin Random House).

Keukeleire, Stephan and Tom Delreux (2014, 2nd edition), *The Foreign Policy of the European Union* (Basingstoke: Palgrave).

Khorana, Sangeeta and Maria García (2018) (eds.), *Handbook on the EU and International Trade* (Cheltenham: Edward Elgar).

Kissinger, Henry (1994), *Diplomacy* (New York: Simon & Schuster).

Kohler-Koch, Beate and Berthold Rittberger (2006), 'Review Article: The 'Governance Turn' in EU studies', *Journal of Common Market Studies* 44(Annual Review): 27-49.

Kuijper, Pieter Jan, Jan Wouters, Frank Hoffmeister, Geert de Baere, Thomas Ramopoulos, *The Law of EU External Relations: Cases, Materials, and Commentary on the EU as an International Legal Actor* (Oxford: Oxford University Press, 2nd edition, 2015).

Lavenex, Sandra (2017), 'On the fringes of the European peace project: The neighbourhood policy's functionalist hubris and political myopia', *British Journal of Politics and International Relations* 19(1): 63-76.

Leonard, Mark (2005), *Why Europe will run the 21st Century* (New York: Public Affairs).

Leconte, Cécile (2010), *Understanding Euroscepticism* (Basingstoke: Palgrave).

Lukes, Steven (2005(1974)), *Power. A Radical View* (Basingstoke: Palgrave).

Mayhew, Alan (1998), *Recreating Europe. The European Union's Policy towards Central and Eastern Europe* (Cambridge: Cambridge University Press).

Manners, Ian (2002), 'Normative Power Europe: A Contradiction in Terms?', *Journal of Common Market Studies* 40(2): 235-58.

Massot, Albert (2017), 'De Doha-ronde en de landbouw', Infopagina's over de Europese Unie, Europees Parlement, http://www.europarl.europa.eu/atyourservice/nl/displayFtu.html?ftuId=FTU_5.2.8.html.

Mayes, David (1995), 'Introduction. Conflict and Cohesion in the Single European Market: a reflection', in: Ash Amin and John Tomaney (eds.), *Behind the Myth of European Union. Prospects for Cohesion* (London: Routledge), pp. 1-9.

McCormick, John (2007), *The European Superpower* (Basingstoke: Palgrave).

McCormick, John (2017, 7th edition), *Understanding the European Union. A Concise Introduction* (London: Palgrave).

McGuire, Steven and Michael Smith (2008), *The European Union and the United States. Competition and Convergence in the Global Arena* (Basingstoke: Palgrave).

Merritt, Giles (1986) 'Knights of the Roundtable: Can They Move Europe Forward Fast Enough?', *International Management*, 26 July, pp. 22-26.

Meunier, Sophie (2005), *Trading Voices. The European Union in International Commercial Negotiations* (Princeton: Princeton University Press).

Meunier, Sophie and Kalypso Nicolaïdes (2011), 'The European Union as a Trade Power', in: C. Hill en M. Smith (eds.), *International Relations and the European Union* (Oxford: Oxford University Press, 2nd edition), pp. 275-98.

Meunier, Sophie and Kalypso Nicolaïdis (2006), 'The European Union as a conflicted trade power', *Journal of European Public Policy* 13(6): 906-25.

Meunier, Sophie and Kalypso Nicolaïdis (1999), 'Who Speaks for Europe? The Delegation of Trade Authority in the EU', *Journal of Common Market Studies* 37(3): 477-501.

Milanovic, Branko (2014), 'The Return of "Patrimonial Capitalism". A Review of Thomas Piketty's *Capital in the Twenty-First Century'*, *Journal of Economic Literature* 52(2): 519-34.

Milanovic, Branko (2016), *Global Inequality: A New Approach for the Age of Globalization* (Cambridge, Massachusetts: Harvard University Press).

Milward, Alan (1994), *The European Rescue of the Nation-State* (London: Routledge).

Modelski, George (1987), *Long Cycles in World Politics* (Seattle: University of Washington Press).

Moravscik, Andrew (1993), 'Preferences and Power in the European Community: A Liberal Intergovernmentalist Approach', *Journal of Common Market Studies* 31(4): 473-524.

Moravscik, Andrew (1998), *The Choice for Europe. Social Purpose and State Power from Messina to Maastricht* (Ithaca: Cornell University Press).

Moravcsik, Andrew (2003), 'Striking a New Transatlantic Bargain', *Foreign Affairs*, July/August, pp. 74-89.

Niemann, Arne and Charlotte Bretherton (2013), 'EU external policy at the crossroads: The challenge of actorness and effectiveness', *International Relations*, 27(3): 261-75.

OECD (2017), 'Development Aid rises again in 2016', Paris: OECD/DAC, 11 April.

Offe, Claus (1991), 'Capitalism by Democratic Design? Democratic theory facing the triple transition in East Central Europe', *Social Research* 58(4): 865-92.

Olsen, Gorm Rye (2001), 'European public opinion and aid to Africa: is there a link?', *Journal of Modern African Studies* 39(4): 645-74.

Orbie, Jan (2008), 'A Civilian Power in the World?', in: J. Orbie (ed.), *Europe's Global Role. External Policies of the European Union* (Farnham: Ashgate), pp. 1-33.

Orbie, Jan en Maurizio Carbone (2015), 'The Europeanisation of development policy', *European Politics and Society* 17(1): 1-11.

Orbie, Jan and Simon Lightfoot (2017), 'Development: Shallow Europeanisation?', in: A. Hadfield, I. Manners and R.G. Whitman (eds.), *Foreign Policies of EU Member States. Continuity and Europeanisation* (London: Routledge), pp. 201-17.

Organski, Abramo F.K. (1958), *World Politics* (New York: Alfred A. Knopf).

Palmer, R.R., Joel Colton and Lloyd Kramer (2014, 11th edition), *A History of Europe in the Modern World* (New York: McGraw-Hill Education).

Peterson, John (2019), *Europe and America. Partners and Rivals in International Relations* (Lanham, Maryland: Rowman & Littlefield).

Pierson, Paul (1998), 'The Path to European Integration: A Historical-Institutionalist Analysis', in: Wayne Sandholtz and Alec Stone Sweet (eds.), *European Integration and Supranational Governance* (Oxford: Oxford University Press), pp. 27-58.

Pollack, Mark A. (2001), 'International Relations Theory and European Integration', *Journal of Common Market Studies* 39(2): 221-44.

Prebisch, Raul (1950), *The Economic Development of Latin America and its Principal Problems* (New York: United Nations Department of Economic Affairs).

Putnam, Robert D. (1988), 'Diplomacy and domestic politics: the logic of two-level games', *International Organization* 42(3): 427-60.

Radaelli, Claudio M., Claire A. Dunlop and Oliver Fritsch (2013), 'Narrating Impact Assessment in the European Union', *European Political Science* 12(4): 500-21.

Raunio, Tapio and Wolfgang Wagner (2017), 'Ideology or national interest? External relations votes in the European Parliament', *SSRN Research Paper 2017/01* (Amsterdam: ACCESS Europe).

Ravenhill, John (1985), *Collective Clientelism. The Lomé Conventions and North-South Relations* (New York: Columbia University Press).

Rifkin, Jeremy (2004), *The European Dream. How Europe's Vision of the Future is Quietly Eclipsing the American Dream* (New York: Tarcher/Penguin).

Rist Gilbert (2014, 4th edition),*The History of Development. From Western Origins to Global Faith* (London: Zed Books).

Roe, Paul (2016), 'Societal Security', in: A. Collins (ed.), *Contemporary Security Studies* (Oxford: Oxford University Press), pp. 215-28.

Rosamond, Ben (2000), *Theories of European Integration* (Basingstoke: Palgrave).

Rosecrance, Richard (1986) *The Rise of the Trading State*. New York: Basic Books.

Rostow, Walt W. (1960), *The Stages of Economic Growth. A Non-Communist Manifesto* (Cambridge: Cambridge University Press).

Ruggie, John (1982) 'International regimes, transactions, and change: embedded liberalism in the postwar economic order', *International Organization*, 36(2): 379-415.

Rutten, Maartje (2001), *From St-Malo to Nice. European Defence: Core Documents* (Paris: Institute for Security Studies, Chaillot Paper 47).

Ryner, Magnus (2012) 'Financial Crisis, Orthodoxy and Heterodoxy in the Production of Knowledge about the EU', *Millennium*, 40(3): 647-73.

Ryner, Magnus and Alan Cafruny (2017), *The European Union and Global Capitalism. Origins, Development, Crisis* (Basingstoke: Palgrave MacMillan).

Sakwa, Richard (2015), *Frontline Ukraine. Crisis in the Borderlands* (London: I.B. Tauris).

Scharpf, Fritz (2002), 'The European Social Model: Coping with the Challenges of Diversity', *Journal of Common Market Studies* 40(4): 645-70.

Schmidt, Vivien and Mark Thatcher (2013) (eds.), *Resilient Liberalism in Europe's Political Economy* (Cambridge: Cambridge University Press).

Sedelmeier, Ulrich (2012), 'Is Europeanization through Conditionality Sustainable? Lock-in of Institutional Change after EU Accession', in *West European Politics* 35(1), 2012, pp. 20-38.

Shapiro, Jeremy and Nick Witney (2009), *Towards a Post-American Europe: A Power Audit of EU-US Relations* (London: European Council on Foreign Relations).

Sideri, Sandro (1970), *Trade and Power; Informal Colonialism in Anglo-Portuguese Relations* (Rotterdam: Rotterdam University Press).

Simón, Luis (2017), 'France and Germany. The European Union's 'central' Member States', in: A. Hadfield, I. Manners and R. G. Whitman (eds.), *Foreign Policies of EU Member States. Continuity and Europeanisation* (London: Routledge), pp. 66-82.

SIPRI (2018), 'Trends in World Military Expenditure, 2017', *SIPRI Fact Sheet*, May.

Slater, Martin (1982), 'Political Elites, Popular Indifference and Community Building', *Journal of Common Market Studies* 21(1, 2): 69-87.

Smith, Michael E. (2010), *International Security. Politics, Policy, Prospects* (Basingstoke : Palgrave Macmillan).

Smith, Michael E. (2017), *Europe's Common Security and Defence Policy. Capacity-Building, Experiential Learning, and Institutional Change* (Cambridge: Cambridge University Press).

Smith, Steve, Amelia Hadfield and Tim Dunne (2016, 3rd edition) (eds.), *Foreign Policy. Theories, Actors, Cases* (Oxford: Oxford University Press).

Steil, Benn (2013), *The Battle of Bretton Woods. John Maynard Keynes, Harry Dexter White and the Making of a New World Order* (Princeton: Princeton University Press).

Strange, Susan (1987) 'The Persistent Myth of Lost Hegemony', *International Organization*, 41(4): 551-74.

Szent-Iványi, Balázs (ed.) (2017), *Foreign Direct Investment in Central and Eastern Europe. Post-crisis Perspectives* (Basingstoke: Palgrave MacMillan).

Taggart, Paul and Aleks Sczerbiak (2002), 'The Party Politics of Euroscepticism in EU member and Candidate States', *Sussex European Institute, Working Paper* No. 51.

Ther, Philipp (2016), *Europe since 1989. A History* (Princeton: Princeton University Press).

Tocci, Nathalie (2016), 'The Making of the EU Global Strategy', *Contemporary Security Strategy* 37(3): 461-72.

United Nations (1974), *Declaration on the Establishment of a New International Economic Order*, Resolution adopted by the General Assembly, 3201 (S-VI), 1 May.

Van Apeldoorn, Bastiaan (2002) *Transnational Capitalism and the Struggle over European Integration* (London: Routledge).

Van der Pijl, Kees (2006), *Global Rivalries from to Cold War to Iraq* (London: Pluto Press).

Van der Pijl, Kees (2014), *The Discipline of Western Supremacy. Modes of Foreign Relations and Political Economy, Volume III* (London: Pluto Press).

Van Schendelen, Rinus (2013, revised edition), *The Art of Lobbying the EU. More Machiavelli in Brussels* (Amsterdam: Amsterdam University Press).

Waever, Ole (1995), 'Identity, Integration and Security: Solving the Sovereignty Puzzle in EU Studies', *Journal of International Affairs* 48(2): 389-431.

Waever, Ole, Barry Buzan, Morten Kelstrup and Pierre Lemaitre (1993), *Identity, Migration and the New Security Agenda in Europe* (Basingstoke: Palgrave).

Wagner, Wolfgang (2017), 'Liberal Power Europe', *Journal of Common Market Studies* 55(6): 1398-1414.

Wagner, Wolfgang and Rosanne Anholt (2016), 'Resilience as the EU Global Strategy's new leitmotif: pragmatic, problematic or promising?' *Contemporary Security Policy* 37(3): 414-30.

Wallace, Helen, Mark A. Pollack and Alasdair R. Young (2015, 7th edition) (eds.), *Policy-Making in the European Union* (Oxford: Oxford University Press).

Wallerstein, Immanuel (1980), *The Modern World-System II. Mercantilism and the Consolidation of the European World-Economy, 1600-1750* (New York: Academic Press).

Watson, Matthew (2017), 'Historicising Ricardo's comparative advantage theory, challenging the normative foundations of liberal International Political Economy', *New Political Economy* 22(3): 257-72.

Wendt, Alexander (1992), 'Anarchy is what States Make of it: the Social Construction of Power Politics', *International Organization* 46(2): 391-425.

Wendt Alexander (1995), 'Constructing International Politics', *International Security* 20(1): 71-81.

Wiener, Antje and Thomas Diez (eds.) (2009, 2nd edition), *European Integration Theory* (Oxford: Oxford University Press).

Wintour, Patrick (2016), 'UK lacks expertise for trade talks with Europe, says top civil servant', *The Guardian*, 28 June 2016.

Woll, Cornelia (2008) *Firm Interests: How Governments Shape Business Lobbying on Global Trade*. Ithaca, N.Y.: Cornell University Press.

Woll, Cornelia (2009) 'Who Captures Whom? Trade Policy Lobbying in the European Union', in: D. Coen and J. Richardson (eds.), *Lobbying in the European Union: Institutions, Actors and Issues*. Oxford: Oxford University Press. pp. 268-88.

Woll, Cornelia (2012) 'EU Foreign Economic Policies: the autonomy of EU institutions', in: H. Zimmermann and A. Dür (eds.), *Key Controversies in European Integration*. Basingstoke: Palgrave. pp. 184-9.

Wong, Reuben and Christopher Hill (eds.) (2011), *National and European Foreign Policies. Towards Europeanization* (London: Routledge).

World Bank (1996): *From Plan to Market. World Development Report 1996* (Oxford/Washington: Oxford University Press).

Young Alasdair R. and John Peterson (2013), '"We care about you, but ...": the politics of EU trade policy and development', *Cambridge Review of International Affairs* 26(3): 497-518.

Young Alasdair R. and John Peterson (2014), *Parochial Global Europe 21st Century Trade Politics* (Oxford: Oxford University Press).

Youngs, Richard (2014), *Europe in the New Middle East. Opportunity or Exclusion?* (Oxford: Oxford University Press).

Youngs, Richard (2017), *Europe's Eastern Crisis. The Geopolitics of Asymmetry* (Cambridge: Cambridge University Press).

Zimmermann, Hubert and Andreas Dür (2012) (eds.), *Key Controversies in European Integration* (Basingstoke: Palgrave).

Index